Create FrontPage™ Web Pages in a Weekend

How To Order:

For information on quantity discounts, contact the publisher: Prima Publishing, P.O. Box 1260BK, Rocklin, CA 95677-1260; (916) 632-4400. On your letterhead include information concerning the intended use of the books and the number of books you wish to purchase. For individual orders, turn to the back of this book for more information.

Create FrontPage™ Web Pages in a Weekend

David Karlins

PRIMA PUBLISHING

Publisher: Don Roche, Jr.

Acquisitions Manager: Alan Harris

Managing Editor: Tad Ringo

Product Marketing Specialist: Julie Barton

Acquisitions Editor: Jenny Watson

Assistant Acquisitions Editor: Jill Byus

Development Editor: Barb Terry

Project Editor: Kelli Crump

Copy Editors: Judy Ohm, Kevin Harreld

Technical Reviewer: Tony Schafer

Cover Design: Mike Tanamachi

Indexer: Emily Glossbrenner

ISBN: 0-7615-0743-4

Library of Congress Catalog Card Number: 96-70881

Printed in the United States of America

97 98 99 BB 10 9 8 7 6 5 4 3 2 1

To the memory of Mark Salzer

Acknowledgments

It took calm, understanding, and patient people to make this book happen and I wasn't always one of them. Thanks to all of the folks at Prima for their hard work on this book, including Jenny Watson and Alan Harris who signed me.

Special thanks go to all of the content editors. Barb Terry encouraged me to stray from the beaten path to keep this book useful and entertaining. Judy Ohm made sure every paragraph made sense. Tony Schafer checked the facts. Kelli Crump made the whole book come together. Extra special thanks go to Jill Byus for helping me organize the project and for making sure that I got paid!

I constantly bugged my friends, colleagues, family, and strangers on the street for advice—subjecting them to endless "how does this sound?" queries. Thanks for listening!

I received ongoing technical help from computer guru/horseman/musician Gordon Schaad and Web designer/windsurfer Margaret Trumbull. William Murphy at Infomatique gave me a Web site to test all of the cool FrontPage features explored in this book and responded to hundreds of e-mails from me with informed technical information. Author and education expert Ellen Geist shared important writing insights, especially the suggestion that readers keep a large pile of chocolate chip cookies handy. Rhoda and Sheldon Karlins provided encouragement and went over my contract with a fine tooth comb. Finally, thanks to Sasha Karlins for insight and perspective that only a teenager can provide.

Contents at a Glance

Contents

Chapter 2
Saturday Morning: Making Your Site Look Good 47

Chapter 3
Saturday Afternoon: Designing Graphics with Image Composer   85

Chapter 4
Saturday Night: Live and Hyperlinked   135

Chapter 5
Sunday Morning: Letting Visitors Plug In with Forms

169

Chapter 6
Sunday Afternoon: Activating FrontPage's
Handy RoBots   219

Chapter 7
Sunday Evening: Publishing Your Site
on the World Wide Web   259

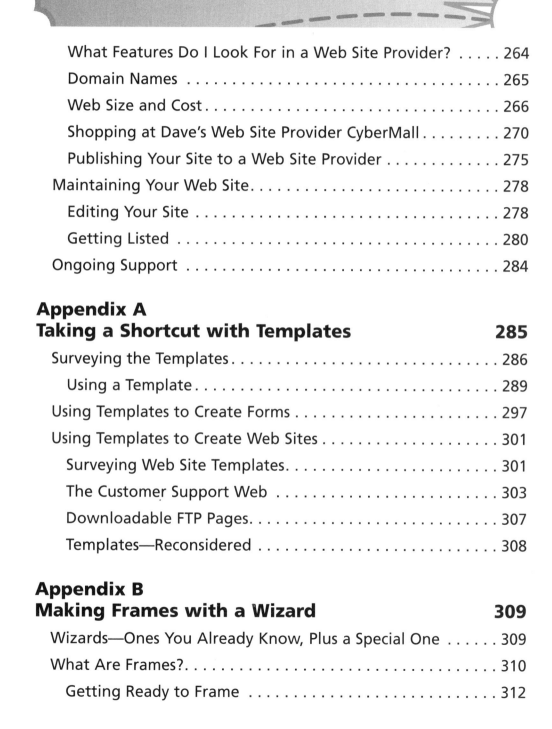

Appendix A
Taking a Shortcut with Templates 285

Appendix B
Making Frames with a Wizard 309

Introduction:

Getting Ready for a Wild Weekend

elcome to the brave new world of creating your own Web site using Microsoft FrontPage 97. You don't need for me to hype the Internet here, it's probably a little overhyped as it is, and you didn't pick up this book if you were unaware of the role an Internet Web site can play in letting you interact with the world.

Will you really be able to create a Web site in a weekend? Yes, you will, but it helps if you are prepared. A bottle of your favorite extra-strength headache reliever shouldn't be necessary, but a supply of chocolate chip cookies and a comfortable, quiet place to create might help. This introduction ends with a checklist of things you want to have in place before you start work on Friday evening. The most important preparation, though, is for you to think about the message you want your Web site to project, and what you want to learn from those who visit your site.

This book walks you through the process of creating a Web site. By the end of the weekend, you'll be able to create a professional, attractive, and useful Web site. You will find that FrontPage 97 lets you incorporate just about any feature you wish to include in your Web site—colored backgrounds, sounds, video, images, and attractive fonts. I've thrown all these features on a page in my own site, which is shown in Figure I.1.

Who Is This Book For?

This book is for "the rest of us"—those of us who:

❖ Want or *need* a presence on the World Wide Web

❖ Have a statement to make that the world—or at least the part of it that's online—needs to see

❖ Haven't had the resources, until now, to create that Web site

Figure I.1

A FrontPage Web site with video, frames, colors, and fonts.

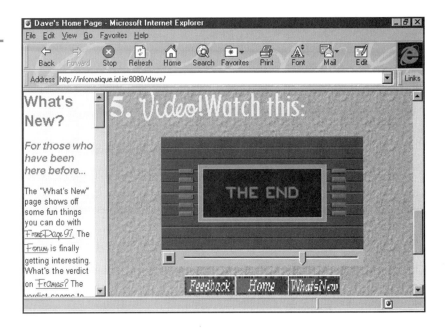

In order to create a site for the Internet that can be viewed by folks surfing around with their World Wide Web browsers, the site must be created in Hypertext Markup Language, or HTML. Until recently, if you wanted to create your own Web site, you were required to become experts at using HTML. To create anything but a primitive, one-page site, you also needed to be a guru of Web site interaction and a student of cryptic coded programming modules called Common Gateway Interface (CGI) scripts. Pocket protectors were optional.

Microsoft FrontPage allows people without those particular skills to create polished, attractive, smoothly meshed Web sites. Even if you have done some HTML coding or picked up a few pre-fab CGI scripts off the Net, Microsoft FrontPage gives you a whole new level of freedom to create sophisticated Web sites. Web sites, especially the really useful and fun ones, are much more than HTML Web pages. What may appear to a visitor as a single Web page is likely to be a collection of objects—objects that let the visitor see pictures, find out when your site was last updated, and search through the site for just what they're looking for. With the inclusion of input forms, you can let your visitors interact with your Web site, leave you information, and even contribute to the Web site.

What Does This Book Cover?

This book covers the entire process of creating a Web site—everything you need to know to create your Web site and place it on the World Wide Web. You'll explore ways to make your site easy to navigate and attractive to visit. This book explores adding graphic images and text, editing, spell-checking, and formatting pages. It also covers exciting features built into FrontPage, such as the ability to get input through forms and other ways to interact with your visitors. You'll even explore FrontPage 97's ability to add video and sound to your site. An appendix explores the Image Composer graphics program that is bundled with the FrontPage 97 Bonus Pack.

What Do I Need to Know to Use This Book?

This book includes plenty of pictures and easy-to-follow steps. This isn't a book that requires you to buy another book to look up everything you read here. Familiarity with Microsoft Windows 95 is a big help. If you're brand new to your PC, I suggest that you postpone this weekend for a week while you get some basic training in Windows 95.

What Hardware and Software Do I Need to Use This Book?

You need a PC with Microsoft Windows 95, and you need to install Microsoft FrontPage 97. The FrontPage packaging itemizes the system requirements needed to install the program. I review those criteria and add my two cents worth here:

❖ A PC with a 486 processor or higher (I think you'll be happier with something like a 100MZ Pentium or faster.)

❖ Windows 95 or Windows NT version 3.51 or later (FrontPage does not run under Windows 3.1.)

❖ Microsoft Office for Windows (While the packaging says this software is required, I think you can get along without it if you don't have it installed.)

❖ 8MB of memory (You'll really want 16MB using either Windows 95 or Windows NT.)

❖ 20MB of available hard disk space . . . you'll fill that up in a hurry! FrontPage Web pages aren't petite. If you don't have a few 100MB free, you might want to expand your hard drive capacity before embarking on this weekend experience.

❖ CD-ROM drive—this drive is necessary to install FrontPage, unless you're purchasing the downloaded version from Microsoft's Web site.

❖ VGA or higher resolution video adapter (SVGA 256-color recommended)

❖ Microsoft Mouse or compatible pointing device

You also need to have access to the Internet via an Internet Service Provider, and an Internet browser that allows you to visit World Wide Web sites. Microsoft Internet Explorer is bundled with the FrontPage 97 Bonus Pack, and it works fine. The installation procedure for Internet Explorer assists you in finding and signing up with an Internet Service Provider. If you are using Netscape Navigator 3.0 or higher, that browser also works well with FrontPage sites. Although FrontPage places videos on Web sites in a way that is more easily viewed using Internet Explorer.

How Can I Prepare for the Weekend?

This book walks you, step by step, through the process of creating a Web site. But what will go on that site? How will it look? How far you get in creating a Web site in a weekend depends on how clear an idea you have of what you want on your site. It may be helpful to use the basic example I used in this book—a homeowner's association Web site.

If you've seen a lot of sites, done a lot of doodling, maybe even attempted a Web site on your own but ran into roadblocks you couldn't break through, you can emerge from your weekend with a FrontPage that is ready to upload or put on your server.

Whether you're a hard-core Net surfer or you've never seen a Web site, one thing that is helpful in preparing to create your site is to spend some time surfing the Net. Log on with your Internet access provider, use your favorite browser, and search for sites that might be similar to yours, and those that aren't. It's all part of expanding your vision of the possibilities.

Elements To Look For

Look for some of these features on Web sites: cool graphics, attractive page layouts, helpful links, nice color schemes, and headers and footers that give a Web site continuity. Things that are missing or annoying can be put on your "Don't do this!" list.

You will not be able to incorporate every feature you see on Web sites. It all depends on the constraints in space and features provided by your Net site provider. For example, dozens of large images do not fit in a Web site limited to 10MB of space, but you'll be impressed that many of the features you want can be created in FrontPage, without any knowledge of HTML.

Most Web browsers have a print capability, so you can print and keep pages you like. Before you can be a creator, it helps to be a visitor. After you've cruised the Net, sit down with a piece of paper and outline what you'd like to present on your page.

As you work your way through this book, you'll find other features and approaches. You will be most productive if you begin the process with an idea of what you want.

How Do I Get FrontPage Up and Running?

In order to avoid frustration and have a productive weekend, I recommend installing and making sure FrontPage runs during the week. That way, you'll be prepared to get down to business on Friday evening.

Follow the instructions to install Microsoft FrontPage 97. The new installation program that comes with FrontPage 97 has simplified the process. The following section provides some background, advice, and step-by-step help.

The Microsoft FrontPage 97 Bonus Pack is a suite of five programs: FrontPage 97 itself, Microsoft Image Composer, the Microsoft Personal Web Server, Internet Explorer, and the WebPublishing Wizard (see Figure I.2).

Figure I.2

Installing the FrontPage Bonus Pack

Which of these programs should you elect to install?

❖ FrontPage 97 is a must. This is the program that lets you create a Web site.

❖ I recommend installing Microsoft Image Composer. It's optional, but it's a powerful graphics package that lets you design all kinds of images that enhance your Web site.

❖ You should install the Personal Web Server. This allows you to test your Web site on your own computer before you contract with a site provider to place your site on the World Wide Web. Even after you post your site on the Web, the Personal Server comes in handy for editing your site offline on a server. Although theoretically the Personal Web Server can enable your own computer to function as a World Wide Web site on the Internet, its most practical use is to enable you to test your Web site on your own computer before you copy or upload it to a site provider.

❖ If you don't have Internet Explorer, I recommend installing it. Even if you have Netscape Navigator 3.0 or higher installed, Internet Explorer has some features that come in handy for testing your site.

❖ I don't recommend installing the WebPublishing Wizard. This program lets you publish your Web site on a server that doesn't really support the features that FrontPage 97 allows you to use. With the approach I take in this book, you won't need the WebPublishing Wizard. At the end of this book, I provide you with a long list of site providers that *do* support all of FrontPage's features.

Most of the time you spend creating a Web site, you will be working with FrontPage 97. You will most likely rely on the Personal Web Server as well. Those components are essential. Internet Explorer and Image Composer are both recommended. To install and start Microsoft FrontPage:

1. Take the Al Green's Greatest Hits CD out of your computer's CD player first—you'll need the FrontPage 97 CD to install FrontPage, unless you downloaded it from Microsoft's Web site.

2. Place the FrontPage 97 CD in your CD drive.

3. Select Start, Run from the Windows 95 taskbar, and choose the drive with your CD player from the Look in list, and double-click on the Setup icon in the Browse window, as shown in Figure I.3.

4. Click to select FrontPage 97 installation and select Image Composer, the Personal Web Server, and Internet Explorer from the Bonus Pack options. If you already have any of these components installed, a message (**Already Installed**) appears next to the buttons (see Figure I.4).

5. Microsoft prompts you to enter little personal details about yourself, such as your name. Humor them, and tell them what they want to know. In return, you'll get FrontPage 97 installed for you (see Figure I.5).

6. The Typical Installation option works fine (see Figure I.6).

Figure 1.3

Launching setup from
the FrontPage CD

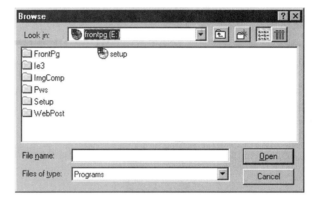

Figure 1.4

Starting to install
FrontPage 97

 TIP You can elect to wait to install Image Composer. If you decide to install it later, use the same routine—just don't lose the FrontPage 97 CD.

7. When the installation process is finished, click OK on the dialog box, and you're ready to start FrontPage.

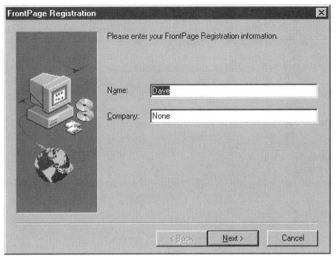

Figure I.5

Getting personal with FrontPage

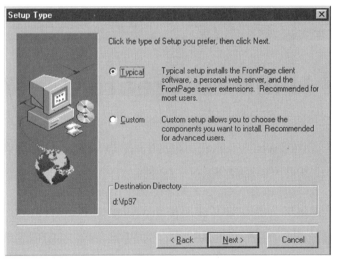

Figure I.6

Choosing a typical installation

8. You start FrontPage like you start any other Windows 95 application—by clicking Start on the taskbar and selecting FrontPage from the Program drop-down menu (see Figure I.7). Your Program menu will be different than mine, but find FrontPage 97 and click.

Figure I.7

Launching FrontPage 97

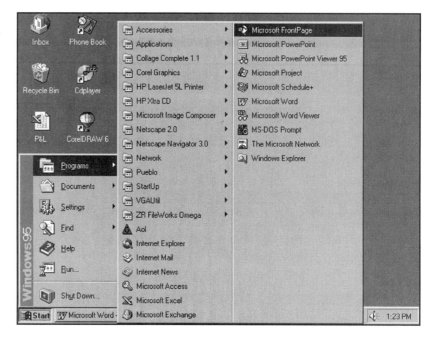

What Else Do I Need to Create a Web Site?

The FrontPage 97 Bonus Pack comes with everything you need to create a Web site. You get a browser, Internet Explorer, to test your site to see what it looks like when folks come to visit. If you want to add graphics, get Microsoft Image Composer. The only thing not included with FrontPage 97 is a Web site provider who rents you space to put your site on the World Wide Web. They're easy to find, and I cover that in Chapter 7 of this book.

Using the Latest and Greatest Browsers

In order to test your Web site before you post it, you need a Web browser. Microsoft gave you a copy of Internet Explorer with your FrontPage 97 Bonus Pack. However, the hard-working folks at Microsoft are constantly tweaking and upgrading their browser, so you might want to periodically check-in and download the latest version. Netscape Navigator is the other most popular browser. It, too, is constantly being refined.

If you want to get, or make sure you have, the latest version of these browsers, you can download them from their respective Net sites. You can purchase Netscape Navigator by going to

```
http://www.netscape.com
```

That page shows you how to download the latest version of Netscape, as shown in Figure I.8.

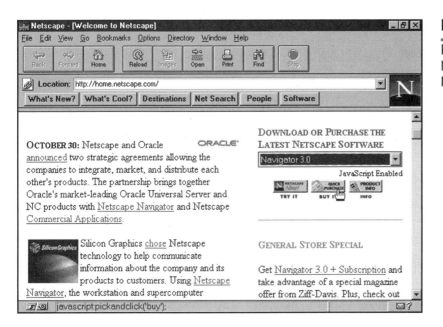

Figure I.8

Purchasing Netscape Navigator from the Netscape Web site

Microsoft's Internet Explorer can be downloaded from

```
http://www.microsoft.com/ie/ie.htm
```

The site changes frequently, but it's always easy to find the button that lets you download the latest version of Internet Explorer (see Figure I.9). If you're aiming your site for access by other browsers, you can use both Navigator and Internet Explorer to test your site.

Figure I.9

Downloading the latest version of Internet Explorer

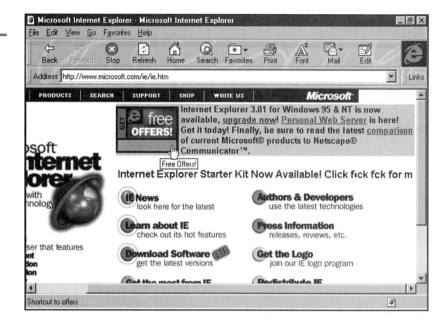

Publishing Your Site on the World Wide Web

You can create and test a Web site on your stand-alone PC, but in order to actually publish your site on the World Wide Web, you'll need to find a Web site provider who provides you with space on their server. If you're designing a Web site for your company and already have a server site available, you should find out from your network administrator where to copy your site, to move it onto the server, and make it accessible.

If you need to shop for a provider, the options are many and the field is becoming competitive. Microsoft provides a list of server providers who promise to support all of the goodies you put on your pages using FrontPage. You can get the list from Microsoft's Web site at

```
http://www.microsoft.com/frontpage/ispinfo/isplist.htm
```

The site providers listed there gives you price lists that usually vary, depending on how many files you'll be posting and how large. I cover this process in detail in Chapter 7 of this book.

If your vision of a Web site is more modest, many connectivity providers (such as America Online and CompuServe) provide small Web sites at no additional charge as part of your monthly logon fee. The drawbacks with these free sites is that they don't allow you much space—only room for one or two small graphic images. They also don't support all the cool stuff FrontPage lets you put on a site, such as video, sound, or interactive forms that allow visitors to talk to you when they visit.

Creating Graphic Images

FrontPage comes with the built-in graphics program, Microsoft Image Composer. You'll spend Saturday night creating some fun graphic images using this program. If you want to add graphic images to your Web site from other sources, FrontPage makes it easy to convert pictures in any format to the two formats that are supported by the World Wide Web and its popular browsers. If you can open a file in Windows 95, you can place it on your Web site. Therefore, if you'll be creating and editing pictures, you need software to do that.

Getting Ready for the Weekend

FrontPage is installed and running. When you start the FrontPage Explorer from the taskbar, your screen should look like Figure I.10.

Here is the checklist for the weekend:

- ☑ An Internet browser such as Microsoft Internet Explorer or Netscape Navigator is installed.

- ☑ You have some ideas about graphic images you might want on your Web site.

☑ You've done some Net surfing, and you've got some ideas for your page, but you can always learn as you go.

☑ The fridge is well-stocked, the kids have a date for the movies, and you're ready to have some fun.

If everything's in place, see you Friday night when you start to create your Web site.

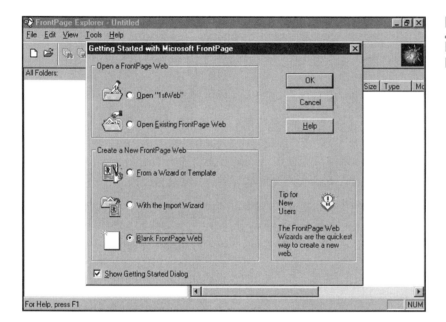

Figure I.10

Ready to create a new FrontPage Web site

CHAPTER 1

Friday Evening:

Creating a Web Site in One Night!

This is going to be fun! You've already installed FrontPage and played around with it just enough to get excited. You've got some ideas for a Web site, but you want to see all the possibilities. If you're like most folks diving into this process, the whole thing is a little mind boggling. The Editor? The Explorer? When do you get to create a Web site? How about right now? Start off by creating and testing a real life Web site. Tonight.

Getting the TCP/IP Test Out of the Way

For the most part, the TCP/IP Test, the Personal Web Server, and the Server Administrator function in the background while you create your Web site with FrontPage Explorer and FrontPage Editor. TCP/IP (or TCP IP) stands for Transmission Control Protocol/Internet Protocol. Internet Protocol is the set of rules that programmers follow so that your computer can exchange data with others. Transmission Control Protocol is an additional layer of rules that programmers use to specifically ensure that data gets transported correctly. TCP/IP enables all kinds of computers to speak to each other over the Net —Macintoshes, Windows 95 systems, and so on.

One of the handy things about Microsoft FrontPage is that it checks and, if necessary, installs TCP/IP connectivity. Passing the test doesn't mean that your system is directly connected to the Internet, but only that connective capability exists. If you are working on a stand-alone system or on a network but planning to copy your Web site to a server, the TCP/IP protocol on your system simulates connecting with the Internet and lets you work as if you were on the Net. To run the TCP/IP Test:

1. Select Start, Run from the Windows 95 taskbar.

2. Navigate to the folder with your FrontPage 97 program and double-click the tcptest icon (see Figure 1.1). Click OK in the Run dialog box. This file is in the bin folder.

Figure 1.1

Locating the TCP/IP test

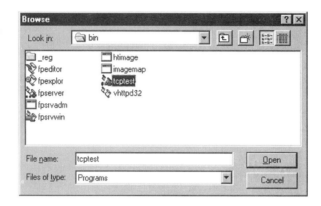

3. In the FrontPage TCP/IP Test dialog box, click the Start Test button, as shown in Figure 1.2.

Figure 1.2

Starting the TCP/IP test

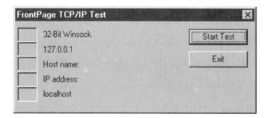

4. When the test acknowledges that your machine is compatible with the TCP/IP, the results look something like Figure 1.3.

5. To make certain that you are able to work with Web sites on your system, click the Explain Results button in the FrontPage TCP/IP Test dialog box. You'll see an explanation like the one in Figure 1.4.

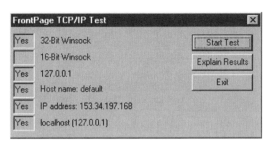

Figure 1.3

TCP/IP results:
You passed!

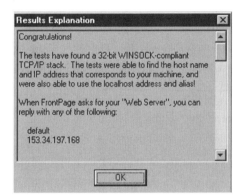

Figure 1.4

Results of TCP/IP
test explained

If your system passes the TCP/IP test, I'll leave it up to you if you want to read the detailed explanation. Isn't reading a lot of details what you're trying to avoid by using Windows 95 (or Windows NT) and FrontPage?

If your system is not TCP/IP enabled, don't panic. If your computer does not yet have TCP/IP capability, here's the routine:

1. You'll be prompted to install TCP/IP using the Network tool in the Control Panel. You need to install new files from your Windows 95 CD-ROM during this process, so have your Windows 95 CD-ROM handy. The Internet Install Window looks like Figure 1.5.

2. When Windows presents you with the Network dialog box, you should select TCP/IP from the Configuration tab, and then click OK on the Network dialog box to install TCP/IP on your system.

You can now start to have fun creating your Web site.

Figure 1.5

Installing TCP/IP

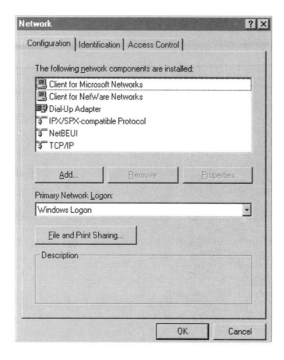

Starting a New Site with FrontPage Explorer

The FrontPage Explorer is what makes FrontPage the powerful program that it is. By the time this weekend is over, you'll have generated Web sites with dozens of files that are linked together like a spider's Web. (Get it, "Web?") Click a picture, and zoom, you're off to a section of text. Click another hotspot and you're off to another Web site. FrontPage Explorer keeps all these connections straight. When it comes time to upload the Web site to a site provider, it makes sure all your files get to their final location safely. FrontPage Explorer is more than all that, but here's how it works. To use FrontPage Explorer to create a new Web site:

1. Select Start, Microsoft FrontPage from the Windows 95 taskbar.

2. Click the Blank FrontPage Web radio button in the Getting Started with Microsoft FrontPage dialog box, and click OK on the dialog box, as shown in Figure 1.6.

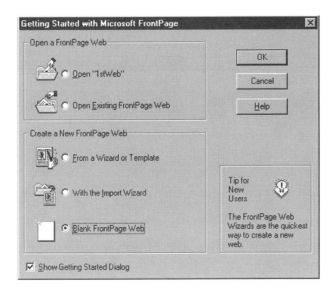

Figure 1.6

Starting a new
FrontPage Web

Leave the Web Server name as Default and enter a name for your Web site,
as shown in Figure 1.7.

Figure 1.7

Name your new
FrontPage Web, mine
is called "SVA."

4. Even though a filename can be 256 characters long under Windows 95, you
may be working with programs that transfer these files to other systems. It's
best, therefore, to keep all filenames to eight characters and follow the old-
fashioned DOS file naming rules—no spaces, periods, or commas.

5. Enter your name and password, and click OK on the Name and Password
Required dialog box.

NOTE FrontPage has many sophisticated, pre-made templates to choose from. You'll explore some of them later. For now, you'll start with a sample template. That way you'll master the basics before you conquer the world.

What if I don't have a password? If you didn't assign yourself a password during the installation process, you can do so now. The following steps walk you through that process.

1. Select the Run option from the Windows Start button to launch the program **fpsrvwin.exe**, found in the folder where you installed FrontPage 97.

2. Click the <u>S</u>ecurity button in the FrontPage Server Administrator dialog box, as shown in Figure 1.8.

Figure 1.8

Accessing password controls

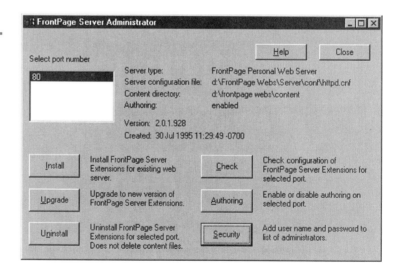

3. Enter your name in the Name area, and type a password in the Password area. Confirm your password by typing it again in the Confirm password area, as shown in Figure 1.9, and then click OK on the Administrator Name and Password dialog box.

4. Close the FrontPage Server Administrator dialog box.

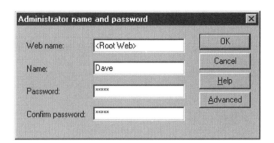

Figure 1.9

Assigning yourself
a password

To use FrontPage Explorer to examine a Web site:

1. Click the Hyperlink View button in the FrontPage Explorer, shown in Figure 1.10. This view shows links between pages in your Web site, but so far, you don't have any.

TIP   HTML files (you've just created one!) have the filename extension **.htm**.

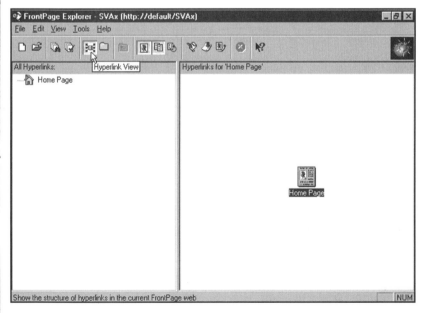

Figure 1.10

Your very own Web site
in Hyperlink View

2. Use the button shown at the bottom to switch to the side of the FrontPage Explorer Folder View (see Figure 1.11). Your embryonic Web site already has two folders. FrontPage created those folders for you and stores necessary files as you construct your Web site. You're not required to keep track of those files, the FrontPage Explorer does it for you. The Folder View also reveals a file named **index.htm**. This file is your Web site home page. It's blank, and waiting for you.

Figure 1.11

Your Web site in Folder View

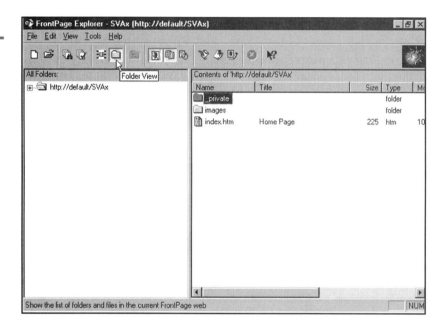

> So far, you haven't defined any links between files. But you will, and you'll note the change they make in the Hyperlink View.

3. Switch back to Folder View. You can drag the split bar between the left and right sides of the FrontPage Explorer window to the left or the right. Experiment with making minor changes in the sizing of Outline and Folder Views, as shown in Figure 1.12. Changing the size of the FrontPage Explorer windows comes in handy when you wish to see all the columns in FrontPage Explorer Folder View, or when you want to see many Web hyperlinks. You don't have many hyperlinks yet, but as your site grows like a spider web, you will. You'll see!

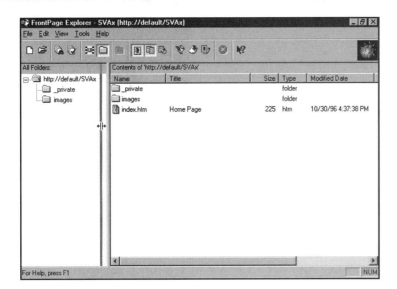

Figure 1.12

More information on your files

4. You can also adjust the Folder view by clicking and dragging on the split bars between columns. For example, in Figure 1.13, you're able to see the Modified column by narrowing the Title column.

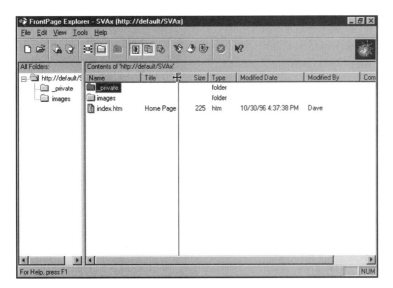

Figure 1.13

Making some space for folder names

So far, I admit, FrontPage Explorer hasn't been all that exciting. That's the way it does its job. It's there, in the background. It's the goalie in hockey, the shotblocker in basketball, the volleyball player who dives to the floor to set up the spiker. You get the picture. It's the unsung hero of FrontPage.

What exactly does it do? FrontPage Explorer makes sure that all the components of your Web site are organized, are put where they're supposed to be put, and all mesh together so that your visitors are greeted by a well-ordered, functioning Web site.

What does FrontPage Explorer ask of you in return? Simply that when you work on a Web page, you always open the Web site first in the Explorer. You've done that. Therefore, you can now forget about FrontPage Explorer and start creating your first Web page.

Your "normal" Web Page doesn't have anything on it yet. Change that by opening that blank page from FrontPage Explorer. Remember, keeping FrontPage Explorer open at all times ensures the integrity of your Web site. To open a page from FrontPage Explorer:

1. Double-click the file, either in Folder View or in Hyperlink View. Voilà! You're in the FrontPage Editor.

2. Notice that FrontPage Explorer is still open. It's being quiet and it won't bother you at all, but you know it's doing its job because you can see it in the taskbar.

Editing a Page with FrontPage Editor

Your word processing skills come in handy now. Most common word processing conventions apply, and the up and down arrows move your cursor around the text you create. CTRL + HOME moves you to the top of the page, and CTRL + END moves you to the bottom. The HOME key moves you to the left edge of the text, and the END key moves you to the end of the line of text.

Some things, though, are quite different from using a word processing program. Because Web browsers operate in all kinds of environments, only standardized text formats can be reliably viewed by everyone who visits your site. Rather than selecting from a wide variety of fonts and text sizes and styles, you are constricted to defined HTML styles. To enter heading text:

1. Type a heading. Figure 1.14 shows my heading, "Welcome to the SVA Web Site."

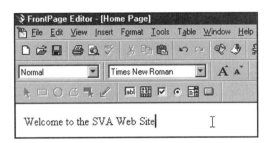

Figure 1.14

Creating a heading on a Web page

2. Click anywhere in the text you've typed with the FrontPage Editor insertion bar. Pull down the Change Style list from the Format toolbar (the lower one) in FrontPage Editor, and select Heading 1. See Figure 1.15.

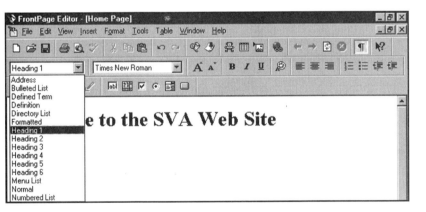

Figure 1.15

Assigning a Heading 1 style

To change styles:

1. Click in the paragraph to which you are assigning a new style.

2. Pull down the list of formats in the Change Style list, and select a different format style for the selected paragraph, as shown in Figure 1.16.

Figure 1.16

Changing styles

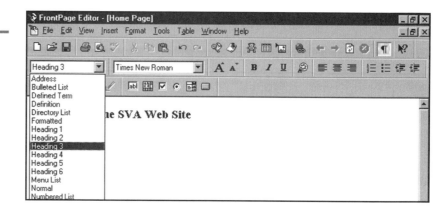

To edit text:

1. Place the insertion point where you want to delete the text.

2. To delete the character after the insertion point, press DEL . To delete the character before the insertion point, press ← .

You also can select the text you want to delete, and then press DEL ; the block of text is all deleted at one time.

3. To insert new text, make certain that the cursor is where you want the new text to begin and just type the text you want to insert, as shown in Figure 1.17.

Figure 1.17

Getting your message on your Web page

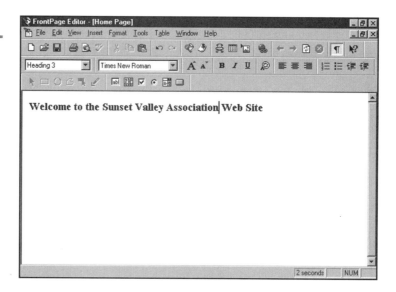

TIP

If you want to insert new text before or after text you've already typed, try using the HOME, END, CTRL + HOME and CTRL + END key combinations to move to the beginning or end of the text quickly.

To cut and paste text:

1. Right-click the text.

2. Select Cut or Copy from the pop-up menu, shown in Figure 1.18.

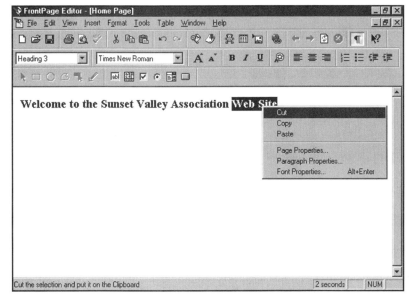

Figure 1.18

Slicing and dicing text

3. Place your insertion point where you wish to copy the image or text.

4. Right-click, and then select Paste from the shortcut menu as shown in Figure 1.19.

5. Take some time to practice cutting and pasting (or copying) text. An example of where copying (and a little editing) helps create a page quickly is shown in Figure 1.20.

Figure 1.19

Pasting text

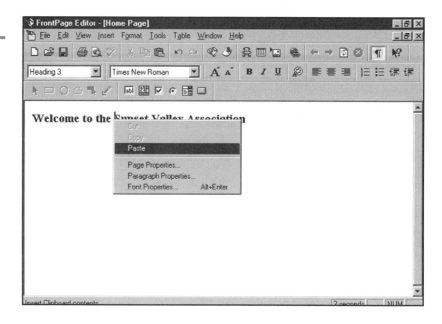

Figure 1.20

Why type when you can copy and paste?

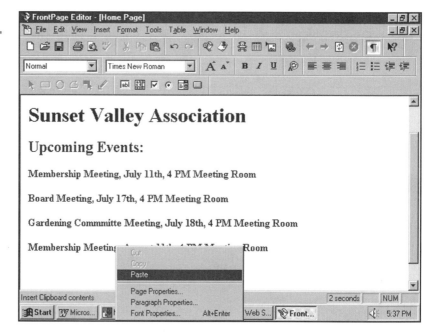

Inserting a Graphic in a Web Page

You can insert images in FrontPage Editor by copying them through the Windows 95 Clipboard, just as you would copy an image into any Microsoft Office application. You can also insert images from the Web site or from a file. To insert a graphic from the Web site:

1. Place your cursor where you want the image to appear on your page, and select Insert, Image.

2. Click the Clip Art tab in the Image dialog box.

3. Choose Icons from the Category list, as shown in Figure 1.21.

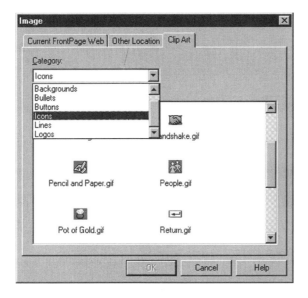

Figure 1.21

They're called icons, but they are actually cute little pictures.

NOTE   Later you'll learn to create your own images. For now, you'll borrow from FrontPage's clip art collection.

4. Double-click a clip art selection that fits your page. The selected image is placed on your Web page, as shown in Figure 1.22.

Figure 1.22

A graphic image on
your page

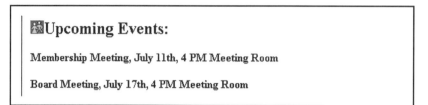

To cut and past text or graphic images:

1. Right-click the text or graphic.

2. Select Cut or Copy from the pop-up menu, shown in Figure 1.23.

Figure 1.23

Cut and paste works
for images

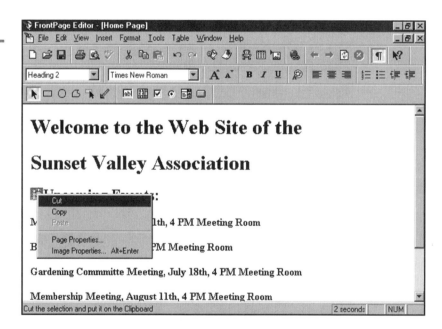

3. Place your insertion point at the place on the page where you wish to copy the image or text.

4. Right-click and select Paste from the shortcut menu.

5. Take some time to practice cutting, copying, and pasting text and graphic images.

TIP

If you're comfortable with the click-and-drag method of cutting and pasting from other Microsoft Office applications, feel free to click and drag text or graphics in FrontPage as well. Holding down the CTRL key when you click and drag selected text or images copies the selected object, as shown in Figure 1.24.

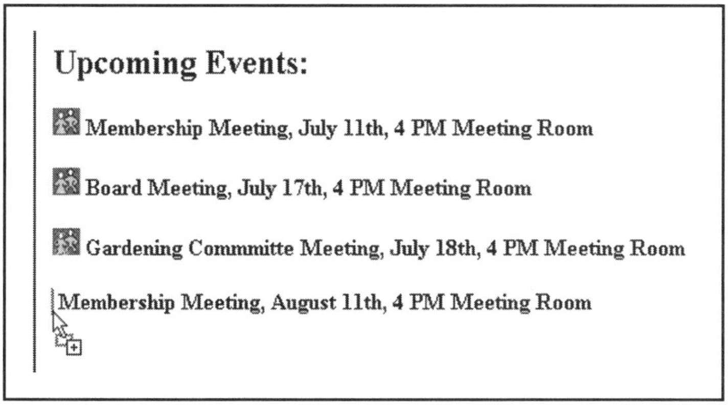

Upcoming Events:

🏃 Membership Meeting, July 11th, 4 PM Meeting Room

🏃 Board Meeting, July 17th, 4 PM Meeting Room

🏃 Gardening Committe Meeting, July 18th, 4 PM Meeting Room

Membership Meeting, August 11th, 4 PM Meeting Room

Figure 1.24

Click and drag to copy images

Touching Up the Page with Spell-Checking

Before you post your page, you should check the spelling. Nothing is more annoying to a visitor or embarrassing to a site host than having glaring spelling errors jumping off the page. It's the World Wide Web equivalent to having a big blob of ketchup on your nose when you meet an important client. First impressions are everything on Web sites.

Fortunately, FrontPage comes with a fine, built-in spell-checker that can catch your spelling mistakes before they display. To check spelling:

1. Click the Check Spelling button in the FrontPage Editor toolbar, as shown in Figure 1.25.

Figure 1.25

The spell-check tool

2. When the Spelling dialog box detects a word not in the FrontPage dictionary, it prompts you to change the spelling. If the word is spelled correctly, click Ignore All.

3. When the Spelling dialog box detects a word not in the FrontPage dictionary, it prompts you to change the spelling. If the word is spelled incorrectly, click Change if you want to change the spelling of only that occurrence of the word, or Change All if you want to change the spelling of that word throughout the entire page.

4. When the spelling check is complete, click OK in the FrontPage dialog box.

Taking a Peek at HTML

In the introduction to this book, I discussed how the FrontPage Editor translates the text and formatting you create to HTML code. For many people, the nice thing about this is that you don't even know it's happening. Still, take a quick peek at the code and see what you've accomplished. To view or copy HTML code in FrontPage Editor:

1. Select View, HTML and the View HTML window opens.

2. Use the vertical scroll bar to move up and down to view the Hypertext Markup Language. Notice that your text is surrounded by HTML markings such as <body> and </body> or <h1> and </h1>. Can you guess what the h1 tag stands for?

TIP   The code for Heading 1 is h1. Now you can figure out what h2 is on your own.

3. If you want to copy HTML code, you can use your mouse to select the HTML, right-click, and select Copy. You can also do some editing in the

HTML window if you wish. Cut, Paste, and Copy are similar to the way you copied in the Editor window, as shown in Figure 1.26.

Figure 1.26

A peek behind the curtain—HTML code

4. Click the <u>O</u>K button to save changes to your page made in HTML, or select <u>C</u>ancel to close the View or Edit HTML window without saving any changes you made.

> **TIP**
>
> For all of you hard-core coders, you can edit HTML code to your heart's delight in the View or Edit HTML window.

Saving Your Work

You've made some significant changes to your page! It was blank when you opened it from the FrontPage Explorer, and now you've added text and graphics. You've assigned styles to text and even checked the spelling. It is now time to save your work.

Titles, Filenames, and the Index.htm File

FrontPage Web pages are saved with both a filename and a title. The filename is how the page is identified in the Web site URL. URL (Uniform Resource Locator) is the address visitors use to find your site on the World Wide Web. When someone types in your Web address, the filename is the last part of that address.

Every page in a Web site needs a unique filename, but one filename is special. The file named **index.htm** is the page that visitors to your Web site go to by default, just by typing your Web site address. They don't need to include the page name because Web browsers automatically open the file named **index.htm** when a visitor comes to your Web site.

The **index.htm** file is, then, your Web site home page. It is the page people go to first. After you add new pages to your Web site, this will mean something. For now, **index.htm** will be your one and only file. It is the first (and for now, only) page visitors will see when they come to your Web site.

Web pages also have titles. Titles can be longer than page filenames and more descriptive. Filenames are constricted to eight characters and must have an **.htm** filename extension. They follow the old DOS file naming rules, and if you try to break those rules, FrontPage rejects your filename.

When you name a *new* page (and so far, you're just saving an existing one), you are prompted to enter a page title and a page name. Enter the title first, and FrontPage helps you out by coming up with the closest possible filename for you. To save a page in FrontPage Editor:

1. Click the Save button in the toolbar. You're not prompted to enter a filename or title for your page because the filename (**index.htm**) was assigned in FrontPage Explorer, where you opened the file. The title, "home page," was also generated for you.

2. When you place an image on a page that is not yet part of the Web site, FrontPage prompts you to save that file as part of the site. It's all part of FrontPage Explorer doing its thing quietly in the background. Click OK when prompted to save image files.

Viewing Your Site Using FrontPage Explorer

When you last looked at your site in the FrontPage Explorer, it had two files and no links between them. Look at the changes you've made. To view links in FrontPage Explorer:

1. Switch to the Explorer by clicking the FrontPage Explorer button in the Editor toolbar, as shown in Figure 1.27.

Figure 1.27

Switching to FrontPage Explorer

2. Click the (yellow) Hyperlink View button in the FrontPage Explorer toolbar. Hyperlink View then shows the link between the graphic image and the HTML page, as shown in Figure 1.28.

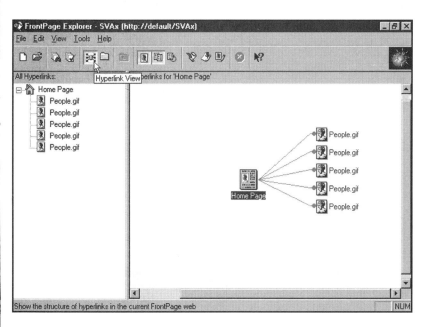

Figure 1.28

Hyperlink View

3. To hide graphic files, click the Links to Images button in the FrontPage Explorer toolbar, as shown in Figure 1.29.

Figure 1.29

Hiding Hyperlinks
to graphic files

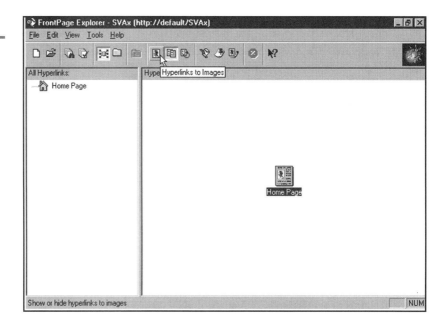

 TIP When your Web site gets large (and it will), it is sometimes helpful to get the graphic images out of the FrontPage Explorer views by hiding them.

4. Click the Hyperlinks to Images button again to see graphic files in the Outline and Links views.

Testing Your Site with the Personal Server

The Preview in Browser button in the FrontPage Editor toolbar launches the Web browser you have installed (Internet Explorer, Netscape Navigator or another one), and then opens your Web site using that browser. How handy!

What will your Web site actually look like when someone visits it? It will look a little different than it did in the FrontPage Editor, so that's one reason to use the Preview in Browser button.

Some browsers show Web pages somewhat differently. That's why some Web sites have messages that say things like, "Best Viewed with Microsoft Internet Explorer 3.0 or higher" or "Best Viewed using Netscape Navigator 3.0 or higher."

Until some universal standard is established, some browsers continue to display pages differently. Not totally differently, such as changing the words around, but text format, images, and other elements of your page do look different when viewed through some browsers.

At this level of sophistication (that's another way of saying you haven't done all that much yet), the Web sites don't look that different. But, even with what you've created, the display of backgrounds and word and line spacing will look different for AOL's visitors than visitors using Internet Explorer.

For your purposes, I use the Microsoft Internet Explorer to illustrate previewing your Web site. Microsoft's browser meshes smoothly with FrontPage-created Web sites. You didn't really expect them to acquire and develop a product that wouldn't work with their own browser, right?

NOTE

During your weekend sessions, you'll keep Microsoft Internet Explorer open quite a bit. I'll keep referring to it by its full name so that you don't confuse it with the Microsoft FrontPage Explorer (not to mention the Windows 95 Explorer!). It's like having three kids named "Beth." I will always use full names so that you don't get confused.

The reason you can "visit" your Web site without even logging onto the Net is that FrontPage includes its own server, the Personal Server. The Personal Server isn't adequate to run a Web site off your own computer, but it is fine to simulate placing your Web site on the Net.

The Personal Server has actually been running the whole time you've had the Explorer open. You may have noticed it on the taskbar —just sitting there quietly, doing its job of allowing the links you define in FrontPage Explorer to function.

You can maximize the Personal Web Server by pointing and clicking the Web Server Idle button in the Windows 95 taskbar. If you're not viewing the taskbar, you can press CTRL + until the Personal Web Server is selected.

There's really not a lot to see. The Server allows you to use a browser and test your Web site. There are no menus, options, and so on —it just runs, as shown in Figure 1.30.

Figure 1.30

FrontPage's Personal Web Server

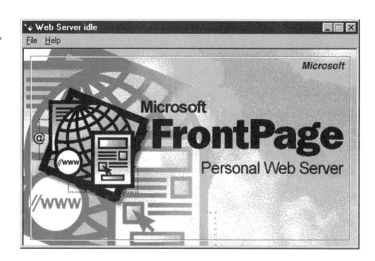

As you'll see, however, being able to test a Web site before posting it is an important job. As you develop your site over the weekend by adding more complex links and forms that allow for visitor input, you'll appreciate the ability to test all this out without consuming days of access time loading and unloading files to your (real Internet) site provider. To preview a Web site in your browser:

1. Before you preview your site, save your page! Only saved changes appear when you visit your site with a browser.

2. Click the Preview in Browser button in the FrontPage Editor, as shown in Figure 1.31.

Figure 1.31

The Preview in Browser button

3. View your Web site as a visitor would. Scroll down, if necessary, to see all the text, as shown in Figure 1.32.

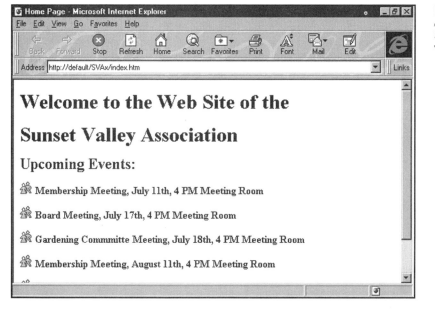

Figure 1.32

Scrolling through your Web site

As you enhance your Web site, you can refresh the connection between the Internet Explorer and the Web. To refresh your Web site in Internet Explorer:

1. Switch back to FrontPage Editor using the Windows 95 taskbar or ALT + ⬐.

2. Make an editing change to the page that you'll be sure to notice when you view it. I'm editing text and adding some new clip art—the little "Site Created in FrontPage" logo that is included in the clip art—as shown in Figure 1.33.

3. Save changes to the file by clicking the Save button in the toolbar. If you added image files, click OK on the prompt from FrontPage to save them as part of your Web site.

Figure 1.33

Editing a Web page

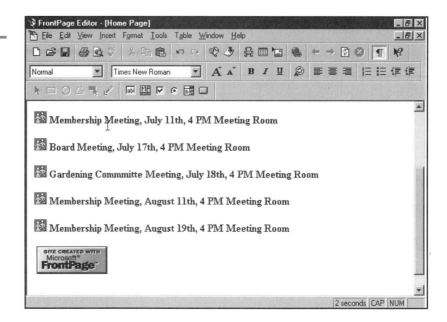

4. Switch back to your Web browser and notice that so far, the changes are not reflected on the Web.

5. Click the Refresh button in your Web browser, as shown in Figure 1.34.

Figure 1.34

When you refresh your browser view, changes appear.

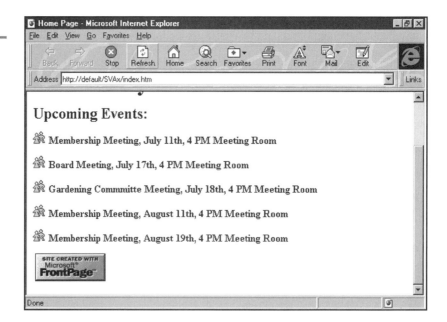

6. Take a fresh look at your Web site. The changes to the file have been uploaded to the Web site. The Microsoft FrontPage Explorer (the one you haven't been to for a while) tracked the changes to the file and integrated them into the Web site. All this appears just as it will on the Internet in Microsoft Internet Explorer using the Personal Server.

7. Save the changes. Notice the change in the Hyperlinks View in FrontPage Explorer.

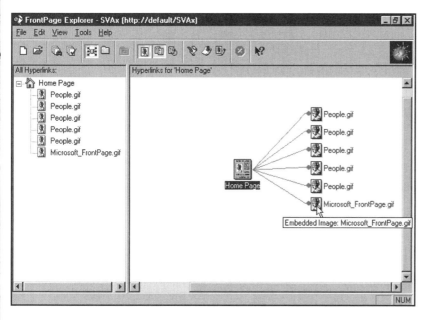

Figure 1.35

Scoping out Image Hyperlinks

8. When you've finished experimenting with the concepts and features I covered this evening, save changes to your page in FrontPage Editor, and then exit the Editor and FrontPage Explorer.

You've accomplished quite a bit in one evening. You created a real live Web site, added and deleted a graphic image, cut and pasted text, and formatted a heading. Not only that, you tested out your site by using a real Web Server, changed it, and retested it on the Server.

What's Next!

Of course, you've only scratched the surface. Tomorrow you'll explore a variety of ways to format and place your information on your page, including using tables, lists, and graphics (besides that "Under Construction" thing). After that, on Sunday, you'll explore the power of interactive forms that allow you to collect input from visitors to your site. So relax, take a walk if that's appropriate, and get a good night's sleep. You've taken your first big steps, and tomorrow you'll cover many miles.

CHAPTER 2

Saturday Morning:

Making Your
Site Look Good

Ahh, it's morning! Now what was that you did last night? Well, you created a Web site, added text to a Web page, formatted and edited the text, and even added a graphic image or two. You then checked out the site using a Web browser. In short, you created a Web site! Now, dive into what it takes to make that site look good.

Getting a Fresh Start

I have one note of caution to share before you start working. As you work through this morning's activity, you'll add quite a bit to your Web site. You will be adding and linking graphic files to the Web site, and before the day is over, you'll create links within a page, between pages, and even with other Web sites. FrontPage keeps track of all this for you, allowing you to focus on the creative aspects of designing your Web site. All you have to do is to cooperate by adhering to a few basic procedures:

❖ Always open FrontPage Explorer before opening pages in FrontPage Editor.

❖ Open existing Web pages *from the Explorer* by double-clicking on them in the Hyperlink View or Folder View.

❖ Save changes to pages in FrontPage Editor to update all links.

To open an existing Web site:

1. Start FrontPage from the taskbar.

2. The last Web you worked on has its own radio button in the Getting Started with FrontPage dialog box. This is handy. If you want to work on that Web, just click OK on the Getting Started…dialog box. If you're opening another Web site you created, select the Open Existing FrontPage Web radio button and OK the dialog box. If you choose to open an existing Web, you'll be prompted for the Web Server and your site's name.

Changing Heading Styles

On Friday evening, you created a nice Web site that included not only text, but also a heading. Before you experiment more with headings, it is helpful to understand how they work.

Defining type font, size, attributes, spacing, and alignment is done differently in FrontPage than in word processing programs. Unlike a word processing program in which you can define the exact appearance of headings as they appear on a printed page (or even onscreen), HTML documents are restricted to one of six types of headings: Heading 1, 2, 3, 4, 5, or 6. Different Web browsers interpret these different headings differently, but the headings have similar characteristics, regardless of which browser is displaying them. Table 2.1 summarizes the characteristics of the six heading types (see Figure 2.1).

Table 2.1	HTML Headings
Types	Characteristics
Heading 1	This heading is the largest one and is used for major statements. It's normally left aligned, 24 point boldface type, with one line of spacing before and after the paragraph.
Heading 2	There's no rule against starting a page with a Heading 2 paragraph. It's normally 18 point boldface, left aligned with one line of spacing before and after the paragraph.
Heading 3	This heading is normally used for subheadings within a page. It's normally left aligned, 14 point boldface type with one line of spacing before and after the paragraph.
Heading 4	This heading is normally used for subheadings within a page. It's normally left aligned, 12 point boldface type with one line of spacing before and after the paragraph.

Types	Characteristics
Heading 5	This heading is actually smaller than Normal text and is used for effect. It's normally left aligned, 10 point boldface type with one line of spacing before and after the paragraph.
Heading 6	This heading is the smallest one. It's often used for footers and fine print in general. It's normally 8 point boldface, left aligned, with one line of spacing before the paragraph.

Figure 2.2 shows a page with the top paragraph assigned a Heading 1 style, the second paragraph with a Heading 2 style, the third paragraph a Heading 3 style, the fourth paragraph a Heading 4 style, and the list of events formatted with a Heading 5 style.

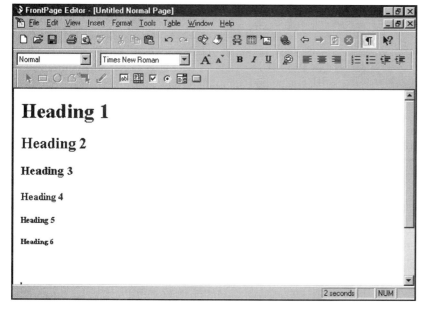

Figure 2.1

Six heading sizes

When the cursor is placed in a paragraph, the Change Style list box displays the heading style for that paragraph, as shown in Figure 2.2.

Figure 2.2

Heading size is displayed in the Change Style list.

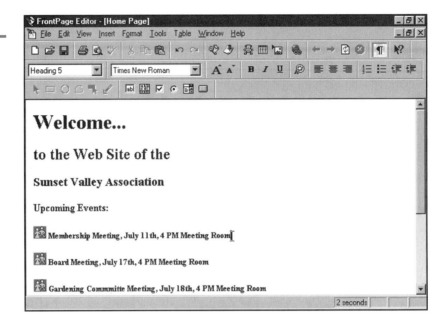

Does the limitation of six predefined headings mean you have no control over how your heading appears when someone visits your page? In part, the answer to this depends on what browser a visitor to your site is using. Visitors who are armed with the latest from Netscape or Microsoft can see the exact fonts that you assign to text. You'll explore formatting text font a little later in this chapter, but it is useful to be aware that older browsers do not interpret all the fonts that you can assign in FrontPage 97.

What *do* visitors see when they visit your site with an older browser? Some Web browsers center Heading 1 paragraphs. Some don't. If different browsers interpret Heading 1 paragraphs differently, how are you supposed to know what they will view? The rules for this are becoming standardized, but for now, the basic rule to remember is that in *any* browser, Heading 1 paragraphs are more prominent than Heading 2 paragraphs, and so on—with Heading 6 being a very small heading that is actually smaller than normal text. All browsers display Heading 1 in a large, bold-face font, for example, with some spacing above and below the paragraph. To change heading styles:

1. Select the paragraph(s) you wish to redefine.

2. Click the down arrow beside the Change Styles list and select a new style to apply, as shown in Figure 2.3.

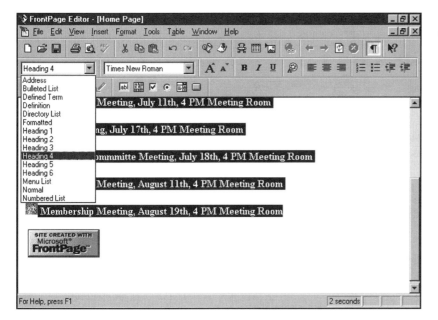

Figure 2.3

Changing heading style

The Paragraph Properties dialog box allows you to assign a style to a selected paragraph or paragraphs. This dialog box also enables you to select paragraph alignment. Paragraph alignment can be default, left, centered, or right. Left, center, or right alignment aligns the paragraph with the left, center, or right of the Web page (or table cell, but you'll explore that later in this chapter). The default setting just basically leaves the paragraph the way it is. To change heading styles using the Paragraph Properties dialog box:

1. Select Format, Paragraph.

2. Select the style you want to use from the Paragraph Properties dialog box.

3. Pull down the list of paragraph alignments and select one, as shown in Figure 2.4.

Figure 2.4

Changing paragraph
alignment

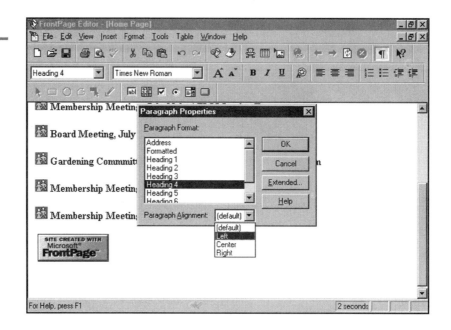

4. Click OK on the Format Paragraph dialog box.

Changing the Formatting of Characters

How can you customize your headings? You can apply font characteristics such as Boldface, Italic, and Underline to heading styles, depending on inherent characteristics of the style. For example, you can apply underlining or italics to a Heading 1 style, but you cannot remove the boldface. Figure 2.5 shows a Heading 1 style with italics applied.

You can also select from a large variety of font styles. Just keep in mind that visitors using older browsers do not see them. It is a good idea to assign different font styles (like Arial, Courier, and so on) to text in your Web site. Visitors who come to your site via Navigator 3.0 or higher, or Internet Explorer 3.0 or higher, see your fonts as you assigned them. Visitors with older browsers miss out, but they'll still be able to read your text—it appears in Times Roman font instead of the one you selected. Heading styles (like Heading 1, Heading 2, and so on) will be interpreted by *every* browser.

Font styles, however, make letters larger or smaller. A line that just barely fits on a page using Arial Narrow font becomes two lines when a browser interprets it as Times Roman. This may disrupt the careful symmetry and aesthetic ambiance you so carefully cultivated for your Web site. That's the price you pay when you use different font styles. They look great with current browsers, but your page suffers a little when viewed with older browsers. Those older browsers display most text as Times Roman.

Along with defining character fonts, you can assign boldface, underlining, and/or italics to text. You can change type size (choosing from a list of seven sizes), and you can assign colors to fonts. All this gives you tremendous control over the look of your Web site page.

Character styles override the default heading styles. They stay with the text, even if you assign a different heading style. Removing heading format can get confusing, especially if you assigned character attributes that do not go away, even when you assign different heading styles or assign a normal text style to a paragraph. To change a heading to a default heading style, you need to remove all character formatting from the heading, as shown in Figure 2.5.

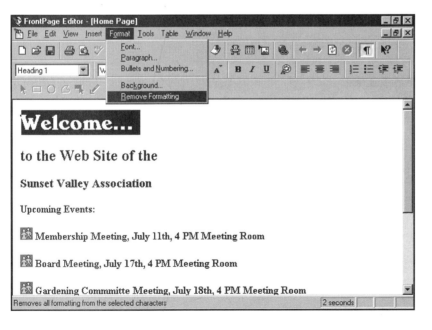

Figure 2.5

Removing character formatting

To enhance characters:

1. Select *all* the text to which you want to assign special formatting attributes.

2. Select Format, Font.

3. Select a font style from the Font list.

4. Select boldface and/or italics from the Font Style list.

5. Select one of the available text sizes from the Size list.

6. Choose underline, strikethrough, or typewriter style font display by clicking on checkboxes in the Effects area of the dialog box.

7. Choose a color for your text from the Color list.

8. Check out the text in the Sample area of the dialog box. You can try different text attributes and see how they look.

9. When everything looks fine, click OK on the Font dialog box (see Figure 2.6).

Figure 2.6

Applying font formatting

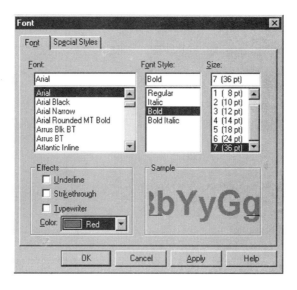

TIP A note on text color. Internet Explorer will do a fine job of showing off any font color you select to visitors who come using that browser. Netscape Navigator and other browsers may not support all of the color magic that FrontPage will create. Keep this in mind when you use color in general on your Web site.

About Special Style Attributes

You may notice that the Font dialog box has a Special Styles tab. These special style attributes are mainly a holdover from the days when Web browsers couldn't interpret the variety of font styles that most of them now read. Because the Font tab in the Fonts dialog box gives you much more control over font display, there's not that much you need from the Advanced tab.

There are a few interesting font features in the Advanced tab. You can make text blink—which makes it flash on and off when viewed in a browser. Text formatted to blink won't blink in the FrontPage Editor, but most browsers display the text as blinking. Besides being able to add blinking to your text, you can also make text superscript (raised) or subscript (lowered).

Make selections from the Special Styles tab by first selecting the text to which you wish to apply the special style. Then, open the Font dialog box, choose the Special Styles tab, and select features by using the checkboxes, as shown in Figure 2.7.

To remove formatting:

1. Select *all* the text from which you want to remove formatting.
2. Select F<u>o</u>rmat, <u>R</u>emove Formatting.

All *additional* character formatting is stripped from the text, leaving only the format characteristics that come with the assigned heading style. To change text for a selected paragraph back to normal, pull down the Change Style list and select Normal.

Figure 2.7

Selecting special
text features

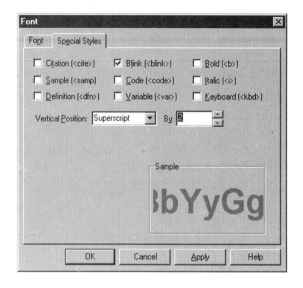

Having Fun with Fonts and Colors

I get a lot of feedback on the Web sites I create, and one of the things people seem to like the most is a variety of fonts and colors. Of course, you can overdo any good thing, but in general, folks are pleasantly surprised to find a Web site that uses plenty of color and font styles.

One thing you should avoid is using blue or purple for text colors. Those colors are reserved for hyperlink text—something you'll explore in the Saturday Afternoon session.

You need to test your fonts using the Preview in Browser button in FrontPage Editor. Some fonts don't look the same in the Editor as they do in a browser. Stay away from the Food font unless you want strange blurry lines to cryptically disguise your text. Again, the basic rule is to have fun, but check your page using your browser before finalizing your font selection. Figure 2.8 shows some font variety and color to spice up a Web page.

Figure 2.8

Fonts! Fonts! Fonts!

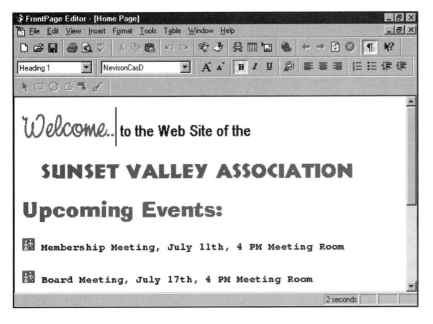

NOTE

Sometimes when you make a number of font changes to your page, the display in FrontPage Editor goes a little haywire. Fix this by selecting View, Refresh.

You can change text font using the Change Font list in the Formatting toolbar. You can also make text larger or smaller, boldface, italic, underlined, and change color by using buttons in the Formatting toolbar. In Figure 2.9, I use the Change Text Color button to assign a new color to selected text.

Figure 2.9

Selecting colors from
the color palette

Creating Bulleted and Numbered Lists

Long lists can get boring, so bullets help each list item stand out. Bullets add emphasis to each point and help the visitor scan the list and pick out points of interest.

Numbering can also help visitors get more out of lists. For one thing, they can quickly tell how many items are in a list. In the Saturday Afternoon session, when you add hyperlinks to your site, you can use numbered or bulleted lists to serve as a table of contents for your Web site. Bullets and numbering are assigned from the Format toolbar in FrontPage Editor.

❖ *Bulleted lists* create hanging indent paragraphs with bullets, as shown in Figure 2.10.

Figure 2.10

Bulleted list

❖ *Numbered lists* create hanging indent paragraphs also, but with automatically assigned numbers instead of bullets, as shown in Figure 2.11. When you cut and copy paragraphs within a numbered list, the paragraphs are automatically renumbered.

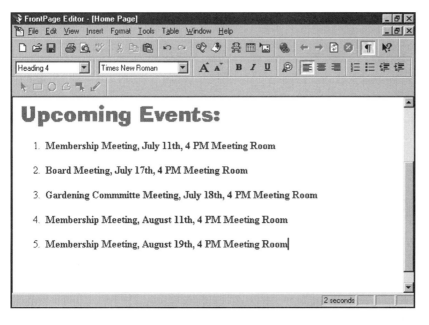

Figure 2.11

Numbered list

To create a bulleted list:

1. Place your insertion point in the page where you want to start the bulleted list and type the first item.

2. Press Enter at the end of the first item, and type more items.

3. Select all the paragraphs to which you want to assign bullets, and click the Bulleted List button in the Formatting toolbar, as shown in Figure 2.12.

Figure 2.12

The Bulleted List button

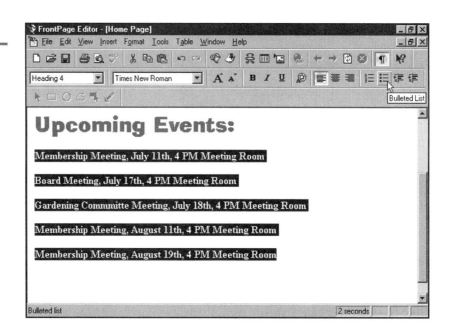

4. Press Enter twice when you are finished typing the list.

To create a numbered list:

1. Place your insertion point in the page where you want to start the numbered list and type the first item.

2. Press Enter at the end of the first item, and type more items.

3. Select all the paragraphs to which you want to assign numbers, and click the Numbered List button in the Formatting toolbar, as shown in Figure 2.13.

FrontPage Editor - [Home Page]
File Edit View Insert Format Tools Table Window Help
Numbered List
Times New Roman
Numbered List
Upcoming Events:
1. Membership Meeting, July 11th, 4 PM Meeting Room
2. Board Meeting, July 17th, 4 PM Meeting Room
3. Gardening Commmitte Meeting, July 18th, 4 PM Meeting Room
4. Membership Meeting, August 11th, 4 PM Meeting Room
5. Membership Meeting, August 19th, 4 PM Meeting Room
Numbered list
2 seconds

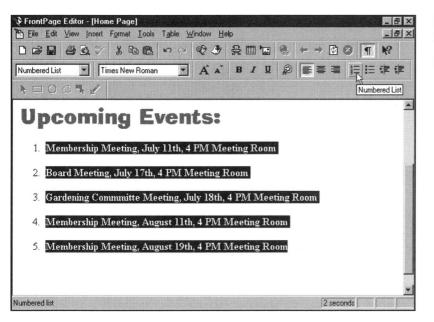

Figure 2.13

The Numbered List button

4. Press Enter twice when you're finished with the list.

To reorder a list, use the cut, copy, and paste techniques you learned in the Friday Evening session, as shown in Figure 2.14.

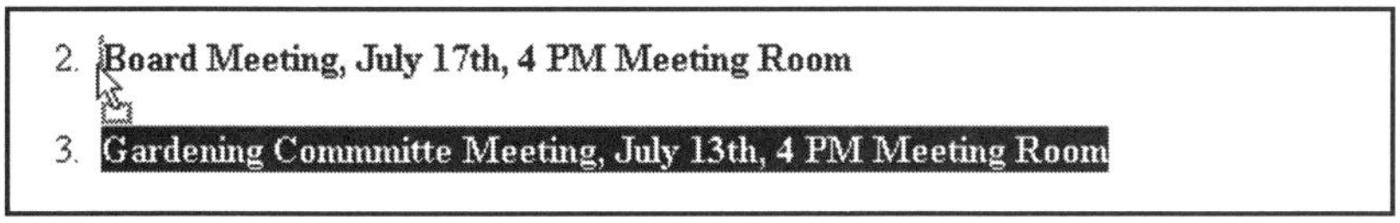

2. Board Meeting, July 17th, 4 PM Meeting Room
3. Gardening Commmitte Meeting, July 13th, 4 PM Meeting Room

Figure 2.14

Reordering a list with click-and-drag editing

When you cut, copy, and paste within a numbered list, the numbering is automatically revised to keep the list items in order. When you use the ENTER key to create new lines, they are automatically assigned sequential numbers.

TIP

You can select an *existing* list of paragraphs and assign bullets or numbers. Select the existing paragraphs and click the Numbered List or Bulleted List button on the Formatting toolbar.

When you place your cursor at the end of a numbered or bulleted list item and press ENTER, FrontPage 97 automatically assigns the list formatting to the next paragraph. This is a nice feature if you're continuing a list. However, sometimes it can seem like you're trapped in a list. It's annoying if you're finished with the list and you can't seem to get back to normal type. The trick to escaping the automatic formatting is to press ENTER twice.

A small variety of bullet formats is available. To change or remove bullets:

1. Select the bulleted list paragraphs to be reformatted.

2. Choose Format, Bullets and Numbering.

3. From the Bulleted tab in the List Properties dialog box, select a different bullet format, or select the upper-left square to remove bullets.

4. Click OK on the List Properties dialog box.

You can also choose from a variety of numbering formats, including roman numerals and letters, and reset the starting number so that the first item is not number 1. If you interrupt a list (for example, with a subheading), you may want to start the continued list with a number other than 1 to make it sequential with the preceding list. See an example in Figure 2.15.

To change or remove numbering:

1. Select the numbered list paragraphs to be changed.

2. Choose Format, Bullets and Numbering.

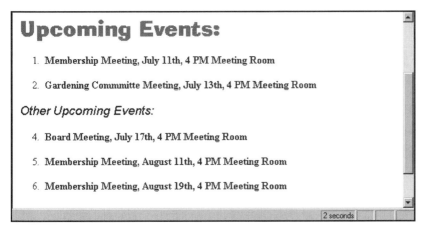

Figure 2.15

Starting a numbered list with 4

3. From the Numbering tab in the List Properties dialog box, select a different number format, or select the upper-left square to remove numbering.

4. You can change the starting number using the Start At spin box, as shown in Figure 2.16.

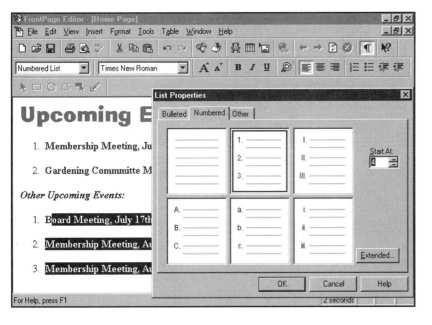

Figure 2.16

Changing the starting number

5. Click OK on the List Properties dialog box.

Indenting and Outdenting—and Those Other Lists

You can indent paragraphs in FrontPage using the Increase Indent button in the Formatting toolbar. You can outdent a paragraph—move its left margin farther to the left—with the Decrease Indent button. Using these two buttons, you can create lists with indented definitions where a site with indented paragraphs is viewed using Internet Explorer (see Figure 2.17).

Figure 2.17

Indented paragraphs

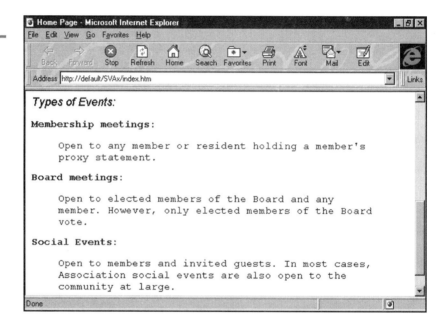

It doesn't work to indent the first line of a paragraph by using the ⊞ key. Indenting paragraphs is often done on Web sites to create lists of defined terms and definitions.

Indenting Paragraphs

The Increase Indent button moves the left margin for the selected paragraph. You can also use this button to indent a numbered or bulleted list paragraph. FrontPage 97 lets you indent as much as you like—although the practical limit is three or four levels of indenting. To indent a paragraph:

1. Select the paragraph(s) you wish to indent.

2. Click the Increase Indent button in the Formatting toolbar, as shown in Figure 2.18.

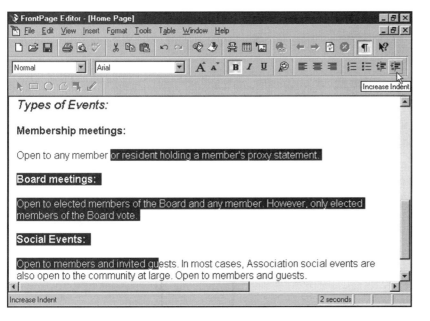

Figure 2.18

Indenting a paragraph

To decrease the indentation of a paragraph:

1. Select the paragraph(s) you wish to move to the left.

2. Click the Decrease Indent button in the Formatting toolbar, as shown in Figure 2.19.

Figure 2.19

"Outdenting" a paragraph

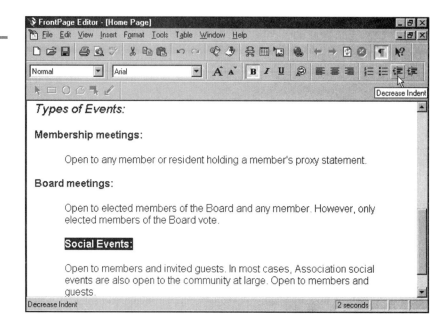

You can increase the indent on any paragraph, even one that is already indented. Figure 2.20 shows an entire list with defined terms and indented definitions, indented farther. To indent an indent:

Figure 2.20

Several levels of indenting

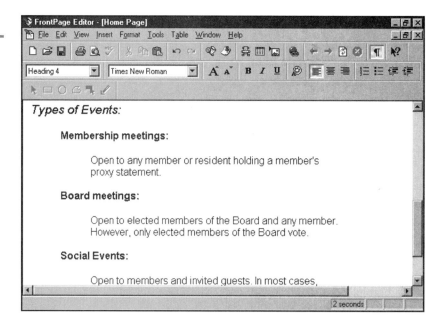

1. Select all the paragraphs to be indented.

2. Click the Increase Indent button in the Formatting toolbar.

What's with Those Other Lists?

You notice other list formats available in the Change Styles list. Directory lists, menu lists, definitions, and defined terms are all styles that incorporate features that are more easily assigned other ways.

Directory Lists and Menu Lists are similar to Bulleted Lists. Defined Terms and Definition Lists are styles that assign indenting to paragraphs with definitions. These styles reflect the limitations of older browsers and apply list and indenting paragraph attributes that are more easily assigned using numbered lists, bulleted lists, or indenting.

Breaking Up the Page

FrontPage allows you to insert horizontal lines to create aesthetic breaks between sections of your page. Remember that unlike a sheet of paper, pages attached to your Web site are endless. Horizontal lines can identify breaks between topics or sections of a page. To insert a horizontal line:

1. Place your cursor at the spot where the line is to appear.

2. Select Insert, Horizontal Line, as shown in Figure 2.21. A horizontal line appears.

To remove a horizontal line:

1. Place your cursor to the left of a horizontal line, and click.

2. You can press the [DEL] key on your keyboard, or right-click and select Cut from the shortcut menu, as shown in Figure 2.22.

Figure 2.21

Breaking up a page is easy to do.

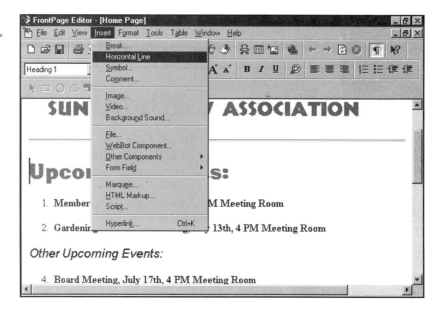

Figure 2.22

Poof! It's gone.

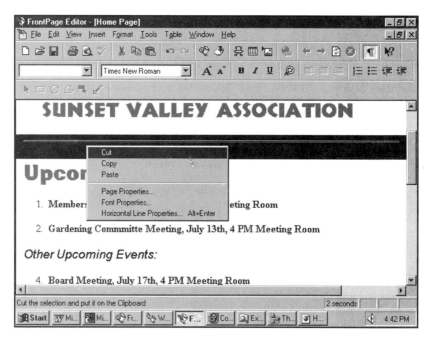

Creating Tables Magically

Tables allow you to organize text (and later, graphics) on a page in columns. FrontPage allows you to use tables the same way you use them in word processing programs—to organize information in rows and columns (see Figure 2.23).

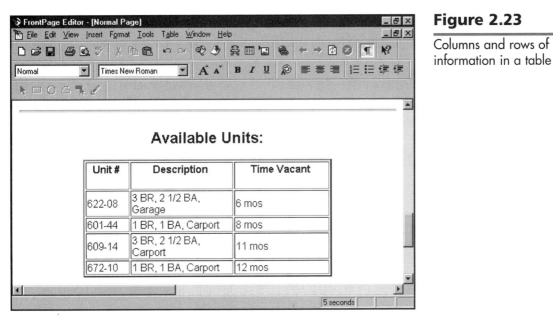

Figure 2.23

Columns and rows of information in a table

You can also use tables to place blocks of text side by side, as shown in Figure 2.24. Placing blocks of text side by side with tables helps you pack more information on a single screen and creates many possibilities for creative layout. There's no rule that tables must have visible borders, so it can look like your page is arranged in columns. Explore both of these ways to use tables. To insert a table:

1. Place your cursor where you want the table to appear.

2. Click the Insert Table button in the FrontPage Editor toolbar.

3. Click and drag in the grid to select the number of rows and columns you want in your table, as shown in Figure 2.25.

Figure 2.24

Using a table to create page layout columns

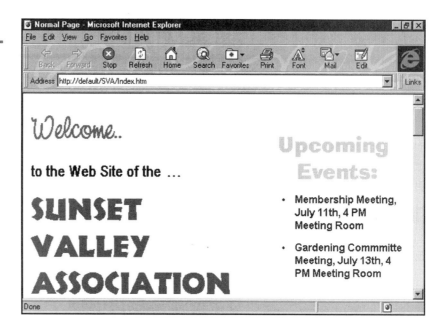

Figure 2.25

Designing your table

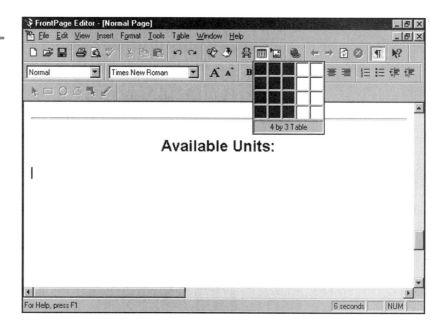

To change table properties:

1. Right-click anywhere in the table and select Table Properties from the shortcut menu.

2. Change settings in the dialog box. For example, the settings in Figure 2.26 are changing the table width to two-thirds of the page (66 percent), and aligning the table in the center of the page.

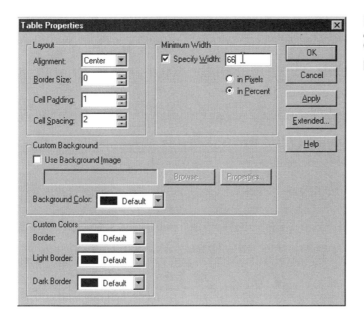

Figure 2.26

Changing table properties

3. Choose the alignment of the table in the Alignment drop-down list. You can left align, right align, or center your table. The default selection from this list leaves the table aligned as it was when the table was created.

4. Enter the Border Size using the spin box in the Layout area. Unlike page-based layout programs, FrontPage measures border width in screen pixels. If you select 0 in the Border Size area, your table appears without gridlines when your site is visited.

NOTE Don't be fooled by the appearance of gridlines in FrontPage Editor. If you don't assign a Border Size greater than 0, no gridlines appear when visitors view your site.

5. Assign Cell Padding using the spin box in the Layout area. Like border size, cell padding is measured in pixels. Cell padding applies to all cells in a table. If you are using borders in your table, cell padding keeps your cell contents from smashing up into the cell border.

6. Use the Cell Spacing spin box in the Layout area to control the space between rows in your table. This measurement, too, is in pixels. The default setting of 2 insures that there are spaces between cells.

7. Click the Percent radio button in the Width area of the Insert Table dialog box to determine how much of the screen the table should take up. If you want your table to fill the entire screen, set the Width at 100 and select the in Percent option button.

TIP You can define the width of your table in pixels or in percent. Setting table width to 75 percent causes the table to fill 3/4 of the width of the page.

8. You can set custom colors for the entire table background. You can also set a variety of coloring for cell borders. Light border color defines the coloring in the upper- and left-hand borders of the cell. The Dark border color defines the coloring for the lower and right borders. You can mix and match border colors to define shadowing effects in the cells. The border color for list sets a default color for cell borders that gets overridden by Light or Dark border colors.

9. When you have defined your table, as shown in Figure 2.27, click OK in the Insert table dialog box.

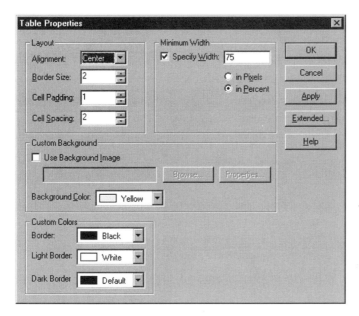

Figure 2.27

Table properties OK!

10. Take a look at your creation. You defined the alignment, borders, colors, and width of your table. You'll explore adding cells shortly.

To enter text in a table:

1. To enter text in the first cell of the table, just begin typing.

2. To move from cell to cell, use your mouse pointer or press the up-, down-, right- or left-arrow keys. You cannot use the 🔳 key to move from cell to cell. Are you used to moving from cell to cell in other programs with the tab key? So am I. It won't work here though.

The column property you are most likely to want to change is the column width. The logic for doing this is different than when you are working with a spreadsheet, database, or word processing program table. Rather than define columns in terms of inches, it's easier to define column width by percent (unless you want to count pixels). To define relative column widths:

1. Hold your cursor over the top of the column you wish to make wider or narrower. The cursor changes to a down arrow, as shown in Figure 2.28. When it does, click to select the row.

Figure 2.28

Selecting a column with that little down arrow

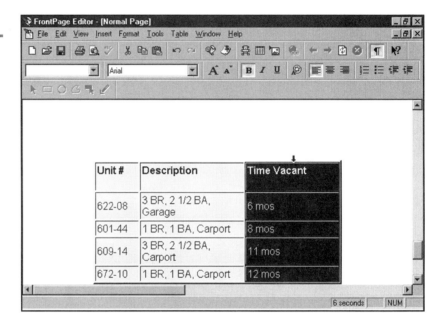

2. With the highlighted column you want to reformat, right-click it and select Cell Properties, as shown in Figure 2.29.

3. Change any cell properties you wish. Those properties are applied to all selected cells—in this case, the column. For example, you could make a column take up 25 percent of the width of the entire table by using the settings shown in Figure 2.30.

You can format text within a cell by simply using the text formatting techniques you've already explored in this session. Select text and change fonts, text colors, text size, and alignment.

You can also change some of the table properties for a specific cell, such as background and border colors. To change cell format:

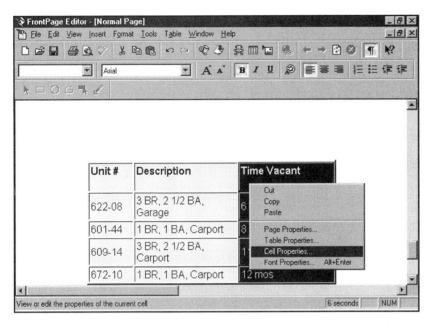

Figure 2.29

Changing properties for selected cells

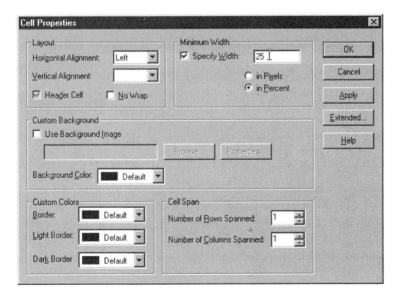

Figure 2.30

Redefining cell properties

1. If you want to format more than one cell, select the cells by clicking and dragging. You can select an entire row or column by moving your cursor to the right of the row or on top of the column, and clicking when the cursor becomes an arrow. After you select the cell(s) you wish to format, right-click.

2. Select Cell Properties by clicking in the shortcut menu.

3. Change background or border color, as shown in Figure 2.31.

Figure 2.31

Changed cell background colors

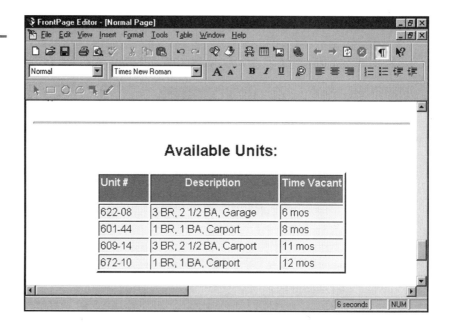

You can define some properties for a selected cell; however, row and column properties take precedence. Don't expect to be able to change the width of a single cell if you already defined the width of that cell's column.

To delete a row, column, or an entire table:

1. Select the row, column, or table you wish to delete.

2. Press the `DEL` key.

To insert a row or column:

1. Click (not right-click) in a cell next to where you want to insert the row(s) or column(s).

2. Select Table, Insert Rows, or Columns.

3. Click either the Rows or Columns radio button.

4. Enter the number of new columns or rows in the Number of... spin box.

5. Choose Above, Below, Right, or Left of the selection and click OK on the Insert Rows or Columns dialog box.

Adding Captions to Tables

You can add captions to annotate or provide a title for a table. If you have a line of text you wish to associate with a table, captions solve the problem of having to reformat the text each time you reformat the table. Captions stay connected to the table and inherit the alignment properties assigned to the table. Captions are just like titles. To assign a caption to a table:

1. Click inside the table to which the caption will be attached.

2. Select Table, Insert Caption.

3. Type the Caption text.

TIP If you are creating a two-line or multi-line caption, use CTRL + ENTER to create a line break instead of using ENTER. Figure 2.32 has a two-line caption. When viewed with a browser, the carriage return symbol won't show up.

Figure 2.32

A table and caption

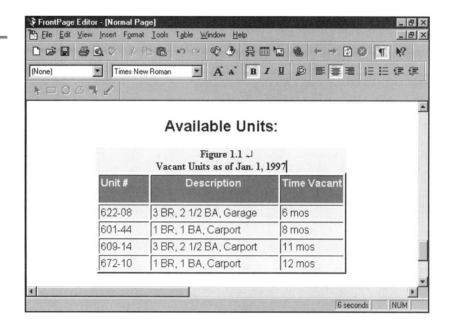

Coloring a Web Page

You can change the background color for your site, and you can change the colors of text in your site. Before you go wild with redecorating your Web site, pause to appreciate how effective the clear black text is against the default beige background. If you're the least bit unhappy with those colors and think you may change them, here are three simple rules:

❖ Avoid choosing a background color that makes it difficult to read your text or appreciate your images.

When you change background color, you may find your text colors clash with, or fade into, the background. You can change the text color assigned to any text. Again, just because you can doesn't mean you should. Black text on a light background is easy to read and pleasant to look at. The trick is to experiment, get objective opinions, sleep on it, and make a final decision in the morning. But first, do a lot of experimenting just so you know what's possible.

❖ Avoid using blue or purple as text colors. These colors are associated with links, as you will see this afternoon.

❖ Because you haven't examined links yet, leave this topic alone until you know enough to stay out of trouble.

Now that you've appreciated the existing colors and read the rules, redo your Web page. Have fun experimenting with background and text colors before you settle on the one you want. To change background color:

1. Right-click anywhere on your page in FrontPage Editor and select Page Properties... .

2. In the Background tab, select a color from the Background list.

 TIP I strongly advise against changing the hyperlink colors until you have some idea of what a hyperlink is.

3. When you have selected a new background color for your page, click OK on the Page Properties dialog box.

4. Take a careful look at how the text and graphic images contrast with your new background color. If you hate it, read on.

To remove background color:

1. Right-click the page and select Page Properties from the shortcut menu.

2. Select a different color from the Background list in the Background tab of the Page Properties dialog box. Click OK.

FrontPage 97 comes with a nice selection of background images that you can use to give your site that classy, professional look. Background images can liven up your page, or create the look of a quality sheet of paper. To assign a background image:

1. Right-click anywhere on your page in FrontPage Editor, and select Page Properties....

2. In the Background tab, click the Background Image checkbox, as shown in Figure 2.33.

Figure 2.33

Selecting a background image

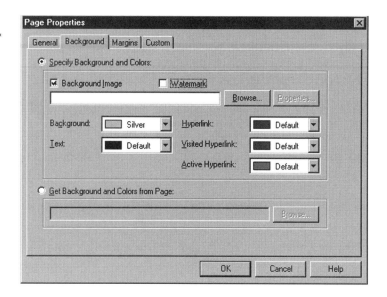

3. Click the <u>B</u>rowse button.

4. Click the Clip Art tab in the Select Background Image dialog box, and Backgrounds from the <u>C</u>ategory list.

5. Select one of the background patterns and click OK on the Select Background Image dialog box.

6. Click OK on the Page Properties dialog box and see how you like the background image. To really see what it will look like, save your page and preview the page in your browser, as shown in Figure 2.34.

7. You can always go back to the Page Properties dialog box, find the Background tab, and uncheck the <u>B</u>ackground Image checkbox if you decide you can do without a background image.

TIP
The background image is a separate graphic image file that is attached to your Web site when you save the page. Save the image file when you are prompted.

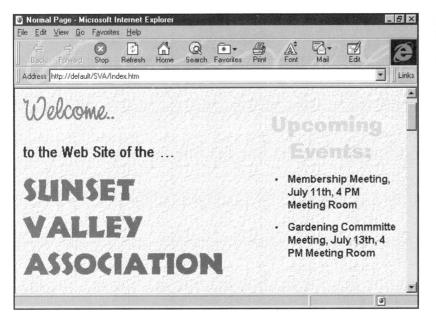

Figure 2.34

How's this background image?

Lunch Break!

Wow, that was a lot to accomplish before lunch! Before getting up, remember the necessary steps to ensure that your files are saved and your hyperlinks are intact:

1. Save your page in FrontPage Editor.

2. Click OK in the dialog boxes to refresh or create hyperlinks and saved files.

What's Next!

The formatting features you used this afternoon are all the tools you need to create attractive, easy-to-read Web pages, but there's so much more that can be done to enhance the site.

The next step in creating a professional page is to create and import customized graphic images. The selection of clip art that comes with FrontPage 97 is OK, but a professional Web site needs unique graphic images.

Saturday, you create hyperlinks—those zany bits of charged-up text and images that send your visitors off to their destination with a quick click of a mouse. Sunday, you'll automate your page with robots, add interactive forms, and explore the process of copying your Web to a server. That's quite a bit.

You're well on your way to creating an attractive, useful, fun, and professional Web site. And the weekend's just beginning!

CHAPTER 3

Saturday Afternoon:

Designing Graphics with Image Composer

I n your Friday Evening session, you learned how to insert image files into your FrontPage Web site. FrontPage comes with clip art, which you can use to liven up your pages without creating original art of your own.

For most Web site designers, that's not quite good enough. Original art can give a whole new dimension to your Web site. Unique logos can identify your company and give your site a special look and feel. There are fun things you can do to stretch, bend, and warp text to make your Web site a real eye-catcher. In Figure 3.1, I combined text with shapes, fills, and shading to create customized buttons to let visitors jump to Events, to Join up, and to see a list of Available Units. To create graphic images like this, you need a graphic design package.

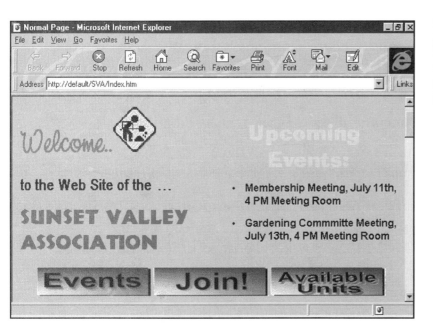

Figure 3.1

Text, shapes, shading, and shadows can be combined to make buttons.

FrontPage 97 comes bundled with its own, first-class graphics package—Microsoft Image Composer. Image Composer allows you to create graphic images with zillions of effects. If you're graphically inclined, the brief introduction to Image Composer in this book may inspire you to further explore the program on your own, or with a book that only addresses Image Composer. For graphically-challenged folks, a little knowledge can be a *good* thing—you too can create smooth, sophisticated, or flashy graphic images for your sites in Image Composer. If you wish to use a different graphics package, skip ahead to the section in this chapter on Editing Graphics in FrontPage. Use your own graphics program, and then catch up there.

Welcome to Image Composer

Microsoft Image Composer is included free of charge in the FrontPage 97 Bonus Pack. It's a handy, helpful, and very utilitarian graphics package. Those of you who will explore all of its features will be impressed with the collection of tools in Image Composer to modify or enhance scanned photos. Those particular effects, however, are beyond the scope of this book.

You'll concentrate on working with shapes and text in Image Composer. Why work with graphical text? After all, FrontPage Editor allows you to format text in dozens of fonts and with a full palette of colors. There's two reasons to use graphical text created in Image Composer:

❖ Many browsers still won't interpret all the available fonts in FrontPage Editor.

❖ Graphical text can be warped, stretched, filled with sophisticated shading, and combined with shapes to make logos, buttons, signs, and artistic presentations.

In short, graphical text is a lot of fun! You'll also combine text with shapes. After you get proficient at combining text and graphics, you'll create something called *image maps*. Image maps are graphical objects that provide hyperlinks to areas in your Web site or other people's Webs. In the Saturday Night session, you'll combine the graphic images you learn to create with hyperlinks to put together image maps.

Starting Microsoft Image Composer from FrontPage

If you did not install Image Composer when you first ran the setup program for FrontPage 97, you can install it now by running the setup program again and selecting Image Composer from the installation menu.

After Image Composer installs, launch Image Composer from either FrontPage Editor or FrontPage Explorer. Typically, you will be working in FrontPage Editor, and then decide that it would be nice to include a graphic image. Follow these steps to add one:

1. From FrontPage Editor, select Tools, Show Image Editor, as shown in Figure 3.2.

2. You can also view or open Image Composer from the FrontPage 97 Explorer by clicking the Show Image Editor button in the toolbar shown in Figure 3.3.

3. If you have installed Image Composer, either of the two preceding steps will launch Image Composer, as shown in Figure 3.4.

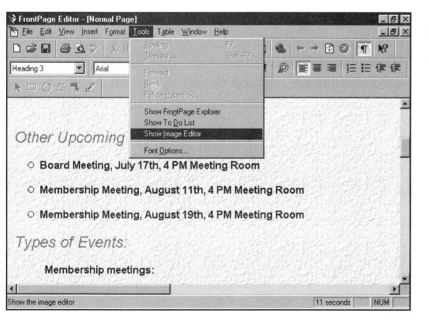

Figure 3.2

Launching Image Composer from FrontPage Editor

Figure 3.3

Starting Image
Composer from
FrontPage Explorer

Figure 3.4

Image Composer—the
canvas awaits

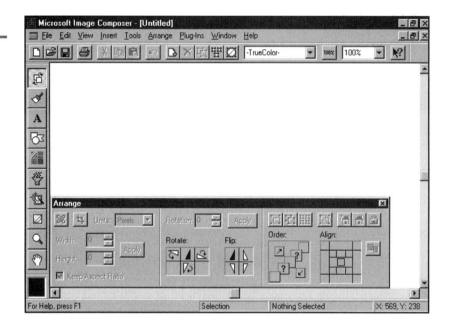

After you launch Image Composer, use the taskbar to switch back and
forth between FrontPage and Image Composer. The two options you
just explored for starting Image Composer directly from FrontPage
open a new copy of Image Composer each time you use them. If you
click on the Show Image Editor button in FrontPage Explorer four
times, you end up with four copies of Image Composer running, and
that's not a good idea.

Microsoft recommends against having more than a couple of copies of
Image Composer open at a time to save memory. If you have opened
Image Composer once, that's enough. After that, use the taskbar to
switch back and forth between FrontPage and Image Composer.

Getting Your Bearings in Image Composer

Sprites are the basic elements of Image Composer graphic objects. A sprite can be text, a circle, an imported photograph, or a wavy line. Sprites can be created in Image Composer, and then edited. Sprites can be combined, but most of the effects available in Image Composer—ranging from color fills to outlines and resizing—are applied to one sprite at a time.

The Image Composer screen isn't very entertaining when you open the program. It does, however, have a lot of potential, but it helps to know your way around. It is like a big, empty canvas with many art tools available. You won't work with every tool, but you'll use several of them to get you off to a good start. Understanding the Image Composer layout starts with the relationship between the main elements of the screen (see Figure 3.5):

* ❖ The toolbar
* ❖ The toolbox
* ❖ The palette
* ❖ The color swatch
* ❖ The workspace

The toolbar shouldn't be too mystifying if you've used other Microsoft Office products. Even your experience with FrontPage should help you recognize tools to open, save, and print files. The other tools in the toolbar will be identified as needed.

The workspace is where you compose and edit sprites. The color swatch lets you pick a default color that will be assigned to sprites you create.

Check Out the Toolbox

The heart of working with Image Composer is using tools in the toolbox. The toolbox is the set of buttons on the left side of the screen. When you point to a button in the toolbox, a helpful tool tip identifies that tool. When you click a tool in the toolbox, a palette appears at the bottom of the workspace that has features associated with it. You won't use all the tools listed in Table 3.1, but at least get a sense of what they do.

Color Swatch   Toolbar   Workspace

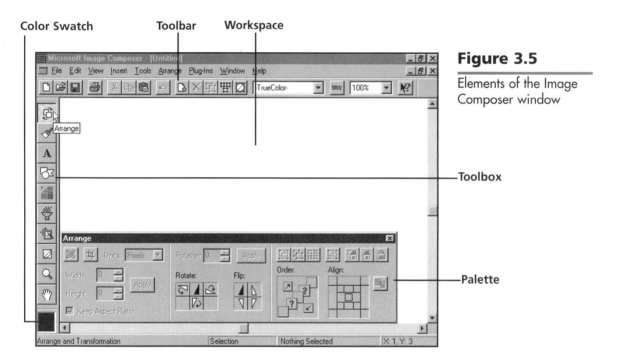

Figure 3.5

Elements of the Image Composer window

Toolbox

Palette

Table 3.1	Tools
Tool Name	What It Does
Arrange	This tool lets you move sprites front to back and aligns them.
Paint	Adds paint type effects to sprites.
Text	Composes lines of text that are transformed into graphic images.
Shapes	Draws rectangles, ovals, polygons, and a variety of lines and shapes that Image Composer refers to as *Splines*.
Filters and Warps	Assigns a fun variety of effects that can be applied to reshape and emphasize sprites.

Tool Name	What It Does
Art Effects	An arsenal of effects used mainly to transform scanned photos into drawings, watercolor paintings, charcoal sketches, and over a dozen other art media.
Color Tuning	Tools to adjust colors in scanned photos and other images.
Zoom	Click to zoom in and see your image larger and close up. Use CTRL + click to Zoom out and see more of the screen.
Pan	Using the hand cursor, click and drag to scroll around your screen.

To get familiar with the Image Composer interface, click on different tools in the toolbox and take a peek at the different palettes that appear.

Creating Text Sprites with the Image Composer

The Text tool allows you to enter text, and then transforms it into a graphic image. This enables you to apply the whole range of Image Composer effects to the text. You can give the text a vanishing point (see Figure 3.6).

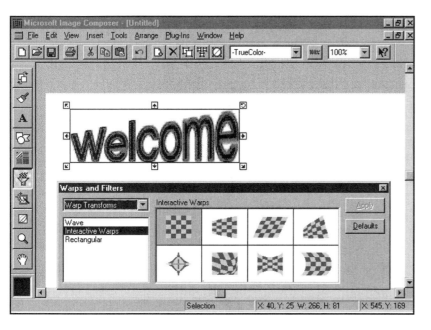

Figure 3.6

Text with a vanishing point

You can also apply shadows as shown in Figure 3.7.

Figure 3.7

Text with shadows

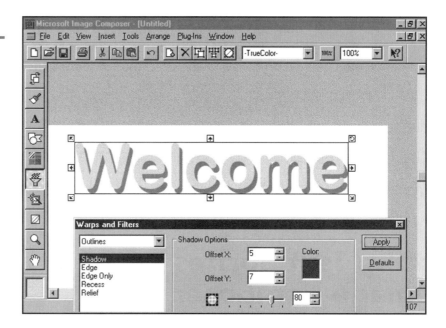

After you start working shapes, graphical text can be combined with shapes to create artistic presentations, like in Figure 3.8:

To create text sprites:

1. Click the Text tool in the Image Composer toolbox, as shown in Figure 3.9.

2. When you select the Text tool, the Text palette appears. Type some text into the Text area of the Text palette. If you have typed text before, the previous text shows. You can delete it and enter new text.

3. Click the Select Font button in the Text palette. Select a text font, choose bold and/or italics if you wish, and choose a font size. You can try 18 point Arial in bold, as shown in Figure 3.10.

4. After you define the text font, click OK on the Font dialog box. A sample of your text displays in the Font palette, as shown in Figure 3.11.

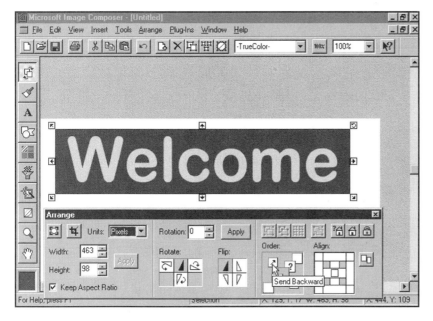

Figure 3.8

Text with a rectangle

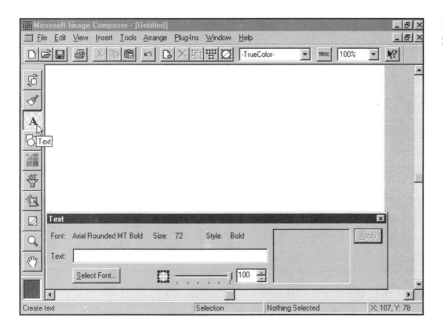

Figure 3.9

The Text tool

Figure 3.10

Making a large, bold
statement in Arial

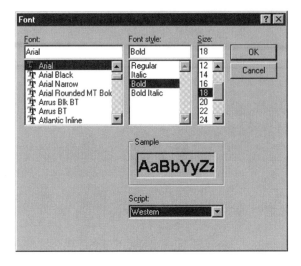

Figure 3.11

Text in the Text palette—
just waiting to get put
on the screen.

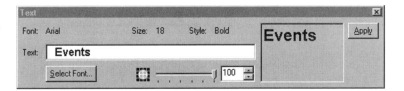

TIP

The Opacity slider is the adjustable slider in the middle of the Font
palette that determines the amount of transparency or opaqueness of
your image. Normally, you will want text to be completely opaque, so
leave the slider at 100 percent.

5. Click the Apply button in the Text palette. Your text becomes a graphic
image in the workspace, as shown in Figure 3.12.

You created a sprite! It is surrounded by sizing handles on the top, bottom, right, left,
and on three corners. The upper-right corner handle is the rotation handle and can
be used to rotate the sprite. You'll explore sizing later.

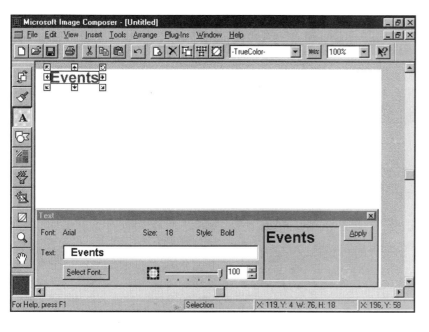

Figure 3.12

Poof! A text sprite appears.

Because your text sprite is a graphic image, you cannot edit text within it. You can, however, change the text in the Text palette and create a new sprite. To edit text sprites:

1. Delete the old sprite by pressing the [DEL] key.

2. Edit, or completely retype, the text in the Text palette.

3. Click Apply to generate a new graphic image with your new text.

TIP

You were hoping for spell-checking and Search and Replace? A Thesaurus maybe? It's not quite like that. Remember, after you click the Apply button in the Text palette, your text converts into a graphic image.

And don't try editing sprite text. You can't change the letters, make your text boldface or italic, or change from lowercase to uppercase no more than you can edit text chiseled into a stone wall. If you want to edit the text in a sprite, delete it, and create a new one.

Moving, Sizing, and Rotating Sprites

So what *can* you do with text sprites. Tons! After they are generated, you can move, resize, and rotate sprites. You should do your best to create the sprite in the size you want before you generate it. With text sprites, that means selecting the font before you generate the image with the Apply button.

Rotating text is fun. Visitors to your Web site will wonder how the text became rotated. Don't overdo it, though—a little rotated text goes a long way.

When you're just working with one sprite, there's no need to move it. When it comes time to place your sprite in a Web site, you'll copy it from Image Composer so its location in the workspace won't matter; but soon, you'll be working with more than one sprite, so practice moving them now. To move a sprite:

1. Move your cursor directly over the sprite. The cursor becomes a four-sided arrow, as shown in Figure 3.13.

Figure 3.13

Getting ready to move a sprite

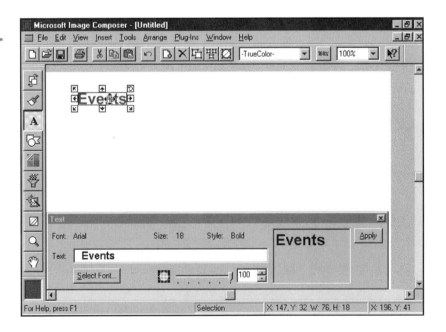

2. Click and drag to move the cursor to a new location, as shown in Figure 3.14.

3. Release the mouse button at the spot you want to move the selected sprite.

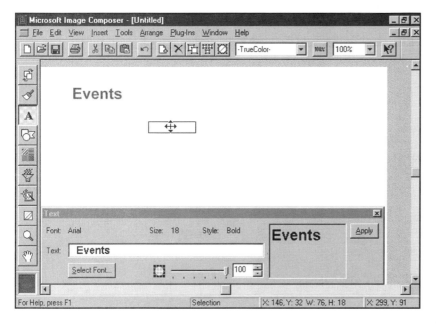

Figure 3.14

A sprite on the move

To resize a sprite:

1. Place your cursor over one of the seven arrow cursors.

2. Click and drag the arrow in to shrink the sprite (or out to enlarge the sprite), as shown in Figure 3.15.

3. When you have resized the sprite to your satisfaction, release the mouse button and the sprite will be recomposed at the new size.

 TIP

If you try to enlarge a text sprite too much, you will be warned by Image Composer's quality police that your image quality will suffer. That warning is trying to tell you that you can create crisper, sharper looking text if you select a larger font before you generate the image.

To rotate a sprite:

1. Click the Rotation Handle in the upper-right corner of a selected sprite.

Figure 3.15

Shrinking the sprite

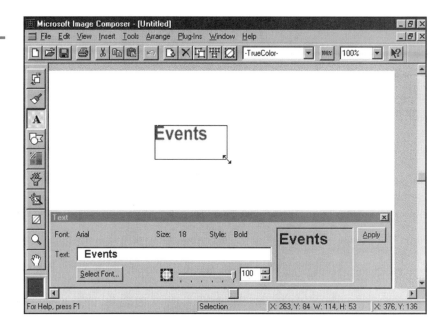

2. Click and drag up, down, and to the right to rotate the sprite clockwise, and up and to the left to rotate the sprite counterclockwise, as shown in Figure 3.16.

Figure 3.16

A tipsy sprite

3. Release the mouse, and the sprite will be recomposed at a tilt, as shown in Figure 3.17.

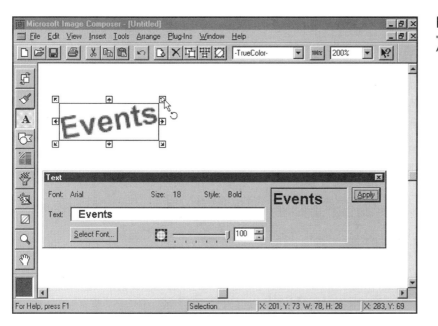

Figure 3.17

A sprite at a tilt

Warped Text Sprites

The Warps and Filters palette is loaded with effects that enhance text with shadows, outlines, edging, relief, and more. This palette is also stocked with some warp effects that allow you to stretch, twist, distort, and reshape your text in many different ways. To outline text:

1. You must select the text sprite you wish to outline. Then, click the Warps and Filters tool in the toolbox. The Warps and Filters palette appears, as shown in Figure 3.18.

2. From the Warps and Filters Group list on the left of the palette, choose Outlines if that group is not selected.

3. With Shadow selected from the list of outlines, click the color swatch *inside* the Warps and Filters palette.

Figure 3.18

The Warps and
Filters palette

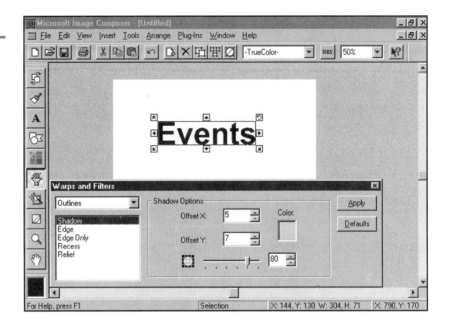

TIP

There is another color swatch at the bottom of the toolbox. The color
swatch inside the palette affects coloring of edges and shadows. You'll
explore the other color swatch shortly.

4. In the Color Picker dialog box, select a color from the palette on the left, as
shown in Figure 3.19, and a hue (degree of darkness) from the scale just to
the right of the palette. When you have selected an outline and shadow color,
click OK from the Color Picker dialog box.

5. Select one of the five outline options from the list of outlines and click the
Apply button in the Warps and Filters palette.

TIP

The Opacity slider comes in handy in setting shadows. A 60 percent opaque
shadow gives off a shadowy, ethereal vibe, as shown in Figure 3.20.

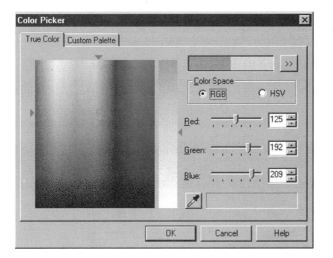

Figure 3.19

Selecting a color and hue from the Color Picker

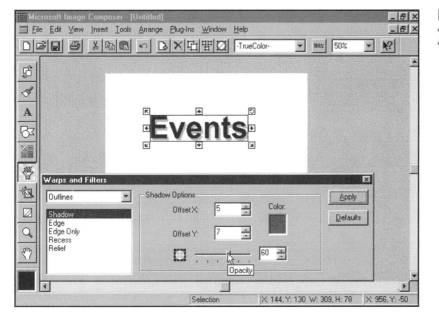

Figure 3.20

A semi-opaque shadow

TIP

If you don't like an effect, use CTRL + Z or Edit, Undo... from the menu. If you apply a second effect, that effect is *added to* the existing effect and does not replace it. You'll get plenty of use out of the Undo command as you experiment with effects. You can use Undo after you have applied an effect.

The Warps and Filters palette has two groups of warps—Warps, and Warp Transforms. The Warps are strange and fun, but there's no need for a discussion of them. Try them out and keep the Undo keystrokes handy—[CTRL] + [Z]. In Figure 3.21, an Escher warp is applied to some text. There must be a time and a place for an intriguing effect like this.

Figure 3.21

Trippy events

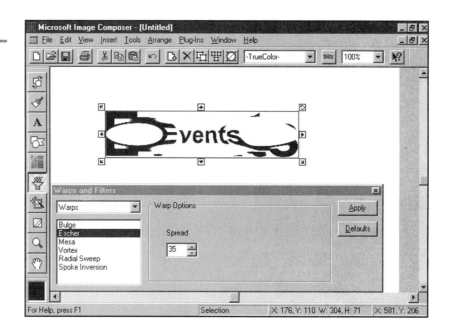

Interactive warps allow you to reshape your text. To apply interactive warps:

1. Make sure to select the text sprite to be reshaped.

2. Click the Warps and Filters tool, if it is not selected, and choose the Warp Transforms Group from the list of Warp and Filter groups to the left of the palette.

3. Select one of the model warps and read the help message that appears: **"Move the pointer to a view and drag to manipulate the warp control points."** Click OK.

4. Each warp transform model works differently, but they all allow you to reshape your sprite by clicking and dragging with your cursor. In the example

in Figure 3.22, the second warp transform model was selected and the trapezoidal cursor appears and creates a "comin' at ya" type of perspective effect.

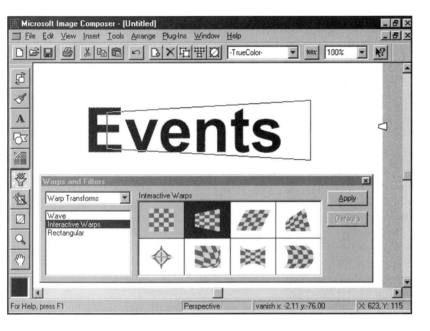

Figure 3.22

Warped events

5. After you reshape the selected sprite, release the mouse button and use the <u>A</u>pply button in the palette to regenerate your sprite with the selected effect. The regenerated sprite appears in the workspace, as shown in Figure 3.23.

Working with Shape Sprites

Shape sprites are handy in creating buttons and tools for your Web site. Here, you'll create and fill some shapes. In a bit, you'll combine those shapes with text to make buttons. Tonight, in the Saturday Night session, you'll use those buttons as hyperlinks. To create a rectangle sprite:

1. Click the Shapes tool in the toolbox. The Shapes-Geometry palette appears, as shown in Figure 3.24.

Figure 3.23

An applied warp

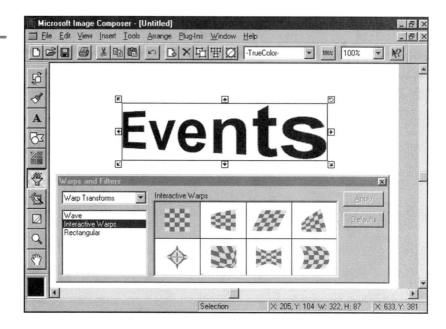

Figure 3.24

The Shapes-Geometry palette

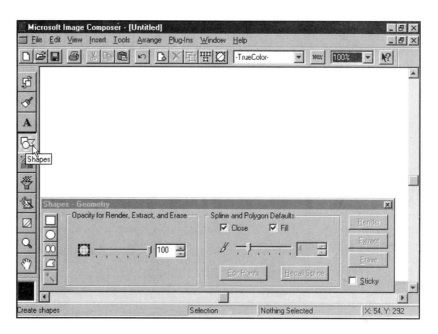

2. Select the square icon from the shape tools on the left side of the Shapes-Geometry palette.

TIP

If it is a square you want, hold down the [Ctrl] key while you draw the rectangle. That will keep the sides equal.

3. Then, click and drag to adjust the lengths of the sides to become a rectangle, as shown in Figure 3.25.

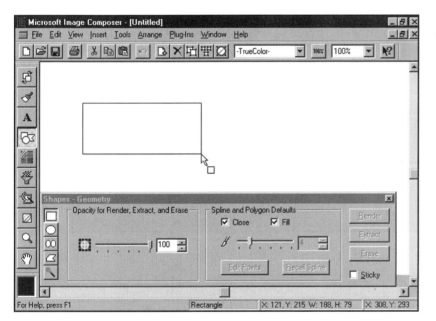

Figure 3.25

Drawing a rectangle

TIP

If you need several tries to get your shape right, click the Sticky checkbox in the lower-right corner of the Shapes-Geometry palette. This feature keeps your selected shape until you pick a new one.

To create an oval sprite:

1. If not selected, click the Shapes tool in the toolbox. The Shapes-Geometry palette now appears.

2. Select the oval from the shape tools on the left side of the Shapes-Geometry palette. Then click and drag to draw the parameters for your oval in the workspace. The parameters of your oval will appear as a rectangle as you draw, as shown on the right side of Figure 3.26.

Figure 3.26

Outlining an oval

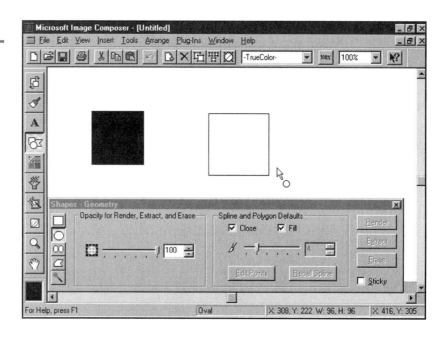

TIP

To draw a circle, hold down the `CTRL` key while you draw the oval.

Splines and polygons are more flexible and powerful shape tools. Splines are lines, but with an "S" (for shape). You can use the Spline tool to draw wavy lines, straight lines, shapes, closed shapes, and zigzag lines. Polygons can be of any shape.

When you create a spline or polygon, you can elect to have the resulting sprite be a closed shape or a line. If you select the Close checkbox in the Shapes-Geometry palette with one of these two shape tools, your sprite will be closed, as shown in Figure 3.27. An example of an open spline is shown in Figure 3.28.

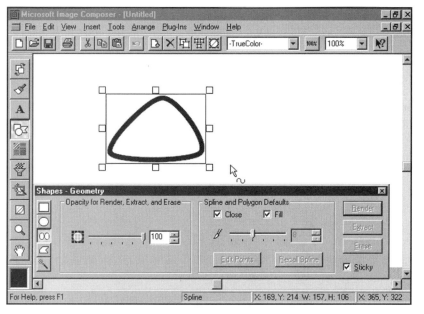

Figure 3.27

A closed spline

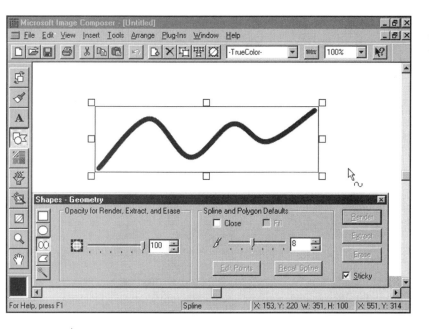

Figure 3.28

An open spline or the design for a roller coaster?

To create an open spline:

1. Select the Shape tool and click the Spline tool in the Shape palette.

2. Deselect both the Close and Fill checkboxes in the palette.

> **NOTE**   These checkboxes are only available for splines and polygons.

3. With the "S" shaped cursor that appears, click in the workspace where you wish to start your spline.

4. Continue to click each nodal point for the spline.

5. When you have traced the shape of your spline, click the Render button in the Shapes-Geometry palette.

Polygon sprites can be used to create fun shapes to use behind text in buttons. To create a polygon sprite:

1. Select the Shape tool and click the Polygon tool in the Shapes-Geometry palette.

2. Deselect both the Close and Fill checkboxes in the palette if you wish to draw an unfilled polygon. Select both checkboxes for a filled polygon. On the left is a filled, closed polygon. Figure 3.29 shows a closed, filled spline and an open spline. On the right is a polygon that is unclosed and unfilled.

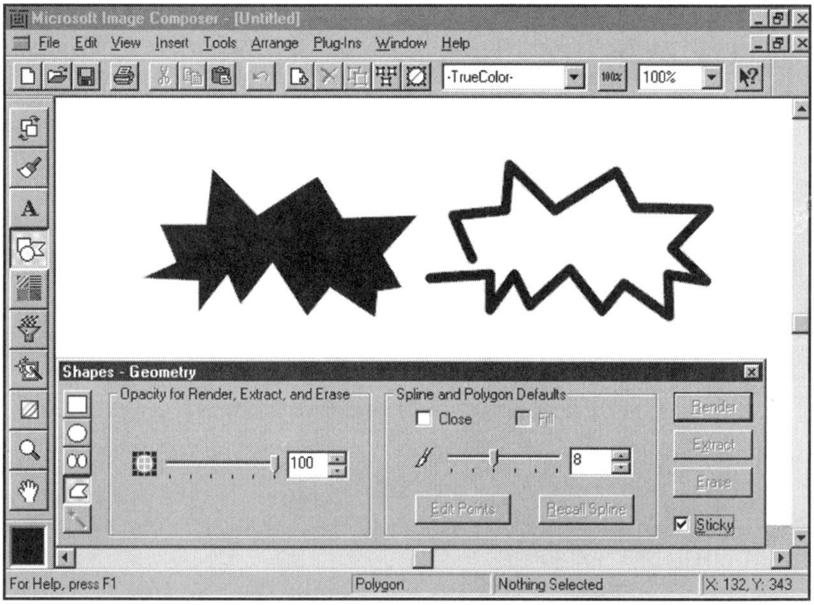

Figure 3.29

Spline vs. spline

> **NOTE**
>
> A closed polygon can be filled or unfilled. A polygon that isn't closed can't be filled.

3. With the polygonal-shaped cursor that appears, click in the workspace where you wish to start your polygon.

4. Continue to click each nodal point for the polygon.

5. When you have traced the shape of your polygon, click the <u>R</u>ender button in the Shapes-Geometry palette.

Filling Sprites

Fill colors for sprites can be changed. Image Composer comes with a full supply of colors and hues, shades, and gradient ramps. Image Composer also does a good job of creating color fills that move well into the FrontPage Editor and on your Web site. To change fill color:

1. Select a sprite by clicking it.

2. Click the Patterns and Fills tool in the toolbox, as shown in Figure 3.30.

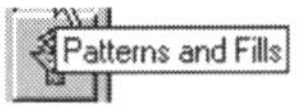

Figure 3.30

Patterns and Fills tool

3. Click the color swatch in the lower-left corner of the Image Composer window to display the Color Picker.

4. Click a color in the color palette area of the Color Picker window (the large palette on the left). Select a hue from the bar to the right of the palette. You can also create a color using the Red, Green, and Blue sliders in the Color Picker dialog box.

5. When you have selected a fill, click OK on the Color Picker dialog box.

6. Make sure you have the sprite selected in the workspace to which you want to apply a color.

7. Click Current Color Fill from the list of fills, and click <u>A</u>pply. The fill color of the selected sprite is now changed.

Gradient ramps are color fills that blend up to four colors together. You can select separate colors to start in the upper-left, upper-right, lower-left, and lower-right corners. To apply gradient ramp fills:

1. Select the sprite to which you will apply the gradient ramp fill.

2. Click the Patterns and Fills tool, if it is not selected.

3. Select Gradient Ramp from the list of Patterns and Fills.

4. Select a color for each corner of the gradient ramp, using the four color swatches that appear. Each color swatch opens the Color Picker when clicked.

5. After selecting your four colors, click the <u>A</u>pply button to assign the defined fill to your selected sprite, as shown in Figure 3.31.

Arranging Sprites

You can move a text sprite onto a shape sprite to create a button. Create a button? You are used to clicking *on* buttons when you use programs. But when it comes to designing your Web site, *you* are the program designer. You can combine text and shapes to design your own custom buttons. When these graphic images are combined with hyperlinks, they will work like buttons for your Web site visitors. Ah, but I'm jumping ahead just a bit. You need to create the button first.

Combining text and graphics to create a customized button requires being able to move the text sprite to the *top* of the shape, so it isn't hidden behind it. You can also align sprites so that, for example, the text sprite is centered over the shape sprite. Try that, and create an image that can be used as button, such as the one in Figure 3.32.

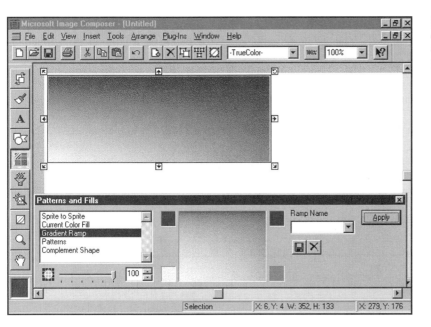

Figure 3.31

Assigning a gradient ramp fill

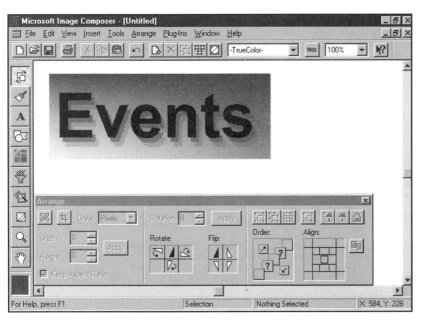

Figure 3.32

Someday this will be a button.

To move sprites front to back:

1. Move a shape sprite on top of a text sprite—as shown in Figure 3.33.

Figure 3.33

Moving a shape on top of text

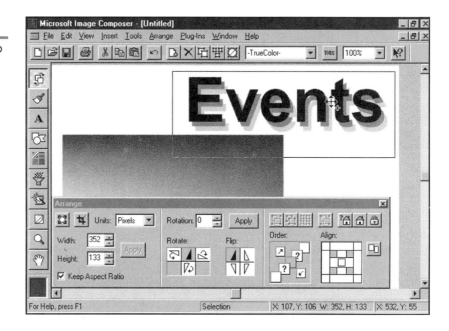

2. This causes the text to disappear.

To move the shape behind the text, and to make the text visible, click the Arrange tool. With the shape selected, click the Send Backwards button in the Order area of the Arrange palette, as shown in the Arrange palette at the bottom of Figure 3.34.

To align edges, or centers, of two or more selected sprites:

1. With the Arrange tool selected from the toolbox, draw a marquee (border) around all the sprites you wish to align.

2. Select one of the alignment options in the Align area of the Arrange palette. In Figure 3.35, a marquee is drawn around a text sprite and a shape, and the Center Vertically option in the Align area is selected.

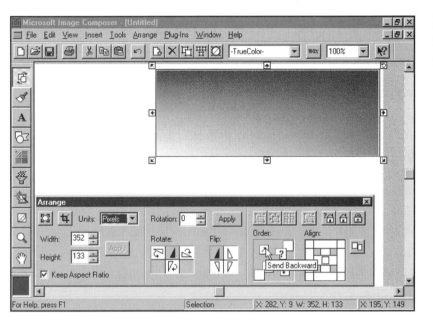

Figure 3.34

Hey, what happened to the text?

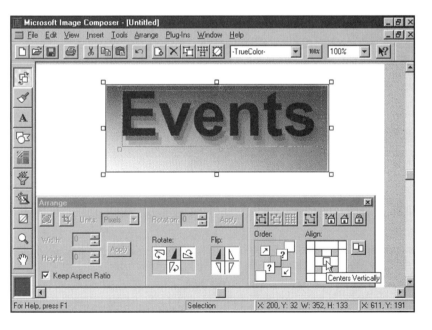

Figure 3.35

Getting vertically centered

Image Composer Files and Web Graphic Images

When you have put together a combination of sprites, and you want to place them in your Web site, the easiest way to do that is to simply copy them from Image Composer to FrontPage Editor. You'll walk through that process in a bit, as well as explore other options for sending an Image Composer graphic to FrontPage.

You can save your sprites in an Image Composer file so that you can use the saved sprites again and again, or go back and edit them and bring them back into your FrontPage Web site. Image Composer files, saved in Image Composer format, cannot themselves be imported into a Web site, but they can be opened in Image Composer and sprites can be copied from them to FrontPage Editor. To save an Image Composer file in Image Composer format:

1. Click the Save button in the Image Composer toolbar.

2. Use the Save in list to navigate to the folder in which you want to save your file. Make sure Microsoft Image Composer (*.**mic**) is selected from the Save as type list, and enter a filename in the File name area of the Save As dialog box, as shown in Figure 3.36.

Figure 3.36

Saving an Image Composer file

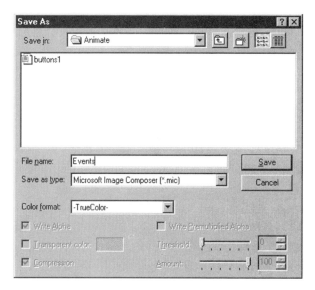

3. Click the Save button to save your file. The next time you wish to re-save the file, click the Save button in the toolbar and the file re-saves without opening the Save as dialog box.

Placing Graphic Images in FrontPage 97

Now that you've created a graphic image, how do you get it into FrontPage? It is simple, and it doesn't matter what program you used to create or edit your graphic image. Microsoft Image Composer is a fine graphics package, but any program can be used to place images in a FrontPage Web.

The process is as easy as copying the file into FrontPage through the Clipboard—just copy and paste an object within FrontPage or any other Microsoft Office application. To copy a graphic onto your page:

1. Select a graphic image in any graphics program and click the Copy button in your graphics program, as shown in Figure 3.37.

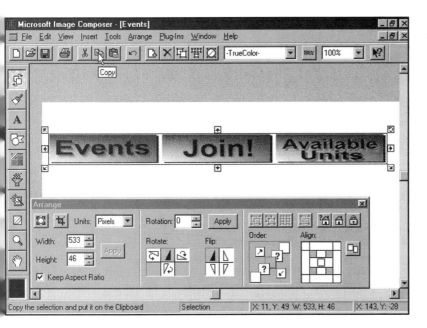

Figure 3.37

Copying an image

TIP   CTRL + C copies a selected object to the Clipboard in any Windows application.

2. Switch to FrontPage Editor and place your insertion point where you want the graphic to be inserted.

3. Click the Paste button in the FrontPage Editor toolbar.

The image appears on your FrontPage Editor Web page, as shown in Figure 3.38.

Figure 3.38

A copied image from Image Composer to FrontPage Editor

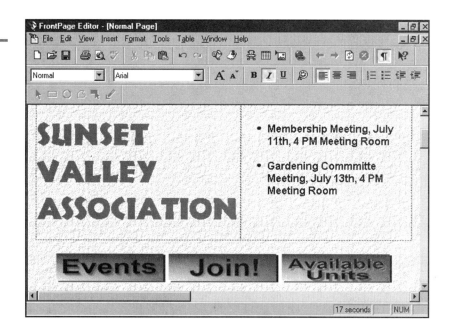

GIF and JPEG—Graphic File Formats for the Web

Computer graphics come in many formats. Image Composer saves graphic image files in its own *.mic format. Your scanner may create files using a TIF format. Your paint program may create PCX files, and the default for CorelDRAW is yet another type of graphics file. Web browsers, however, don't interpret any of the popular graphic formats. Instead, they have their own. Most World Wide Web browsers recognize graphics in either the JPEG (also known as JPG) or GIF format.

The GIF file format was developed by CompuServe. Images are limited to 256 colors, but this graphic format is the most widely recognized on the Web.

The JPEG (Joint Photographic Experts Group) format is becoming universally recognized by most Web browsers. JPEG images can display 16.7 million colors.

Table 3–2	The Match of the Century: GIF vs. JPEG	
Format	**Feature**	**Reason to Use**
GIF	Transparent color option	You are importing an image with a background you do not want to display.
GIF	Interlacing	You want large, slow graphic images to "phase in."
GIF	Universally Accepted	You want to make sure every visitor can see your image.
JPEG	More colors to display: up to 16.7 million vs. 265 for GIF files	Ideal for scanned color photos and other artwork.
JPEG	Compression system cuts file size	Some programs allow you to define the amount of compression—more is faster, but there is a loss of quality.

FrontPage can handle *any* graphic image that can be cut and pasted through the Windows 95 Clipboard. Therefore, all you have to do is open or create your graphic image in your favorite graphics program, and copy it onto your page in FrontPage Editor. Note, however, that you cannot use FrontPage to edit a graphic image.

Saving Image Composer Files as GIF or JPEG files

You can assign either GIF or JPEG formatting to images after they've been copied into FrontPage Editor.

TIP
You should also know that Image Composer files can be saved as GIF or JPEG files. Both options are available from the Save as type list in the Save as dialog box. Because you can assign these attributes within FrontPage Editor, that's the easier way to do it. If you are prepared to tweak your JPEG compression yourself, you will have more control if you save your image as a JPEG file in Image Composer. For most of us, most of the time, FrontPage Editor works fine as a place to assign GIF or JPEG format to an image file.

I think you'll find copying selected sprites from Image Composer to FrontPage Editor works fine for your weekend session, and it really gives you enough control over your images to do plenty of high-powered image editing.

Editing Graphic Images in FrontPage

After you copy an image into FrontPage Editor, you should save your page right away. Saving the page also prompts you to save any images you've copied onto the page. When you do save those images, they're part of your Web site and can be inserted onto other pages. To save an image as part of a page:

1. Copy the image onto the FrontPage Editor page and click the Save button in the FrontPage Editor toolbar.

2. FrontPage assigns names to any images on the page that have not yet been saved to the Web site. Select Yes to <u>A</u>ll in the Save Image to FrontPage Web dialog box, as shown in Figure 3.39.

NOTE
Copied image files are saved in GIF format. You'll examine how to change this, if necessary, in a moment.

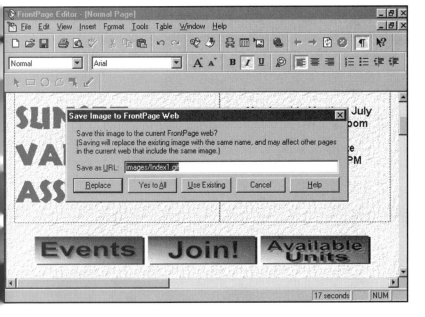

Figure 3.39

Saving Linked
Image files

Sizing Images

You can't change the content of an image in FrontPage Editor—that's the job of Image Composer or other graphics packages—but you can resize images. To change the size of an image:

1. Click the image to select it.

2. Click and drag in to shrink or out to expand on any of the selected images, as shown in Figure 3.40.

Making Images Transparent

Some imported images have backgrounds you do not wish to display. For example, the clip art in Figure 3.41 was copied into FrontPage Editor with a white background that clashes with the gray page background.

Figure 3.40

Resizing an image in
FrontPage Editor

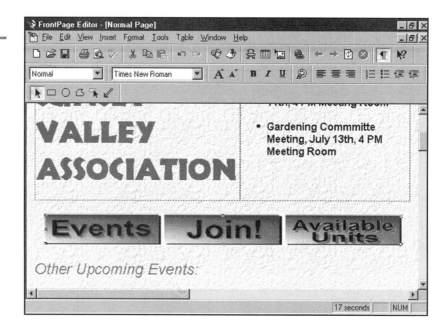

Figure 3.41

This image background
clashes with the page
background.

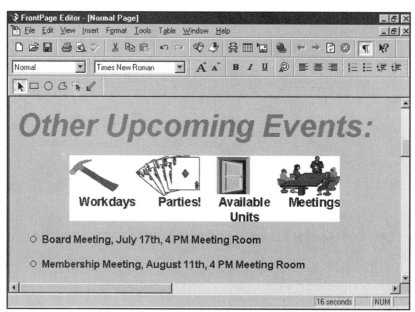

If the image is in GIF format, you can make one color transparent using the Make
Transparent tool in the Image toolbar. To make a GIF image color transparent:

1. Select the graphic image in FrontPage Editor. When you select the image, the Image toolbar becomes active.

2. Click the Make Transparent button in the Image toolbar as shown in Figure 3.42.

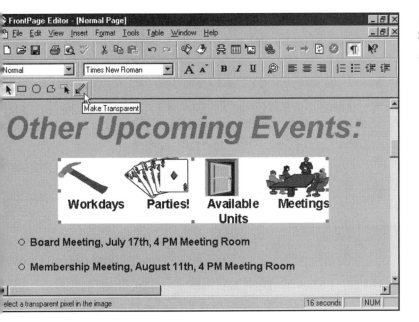

Figure 3.42

The Make Transparent tool

TIP

The Image toolbar is active only when you select a graphic image.

3. Point the eraser-shaped cursor at the color you wish to make transparent and click (see Figure 3.43). The selected color becomes transparent.

You can assign one color in an imported image to be transparent. Only GIF files can have a transparent color (one good reason to choose GIF over JPEG format for your graphic). Making a background color transparent helps an image blend into the Web page, as shown in Figure 3.44.

Figure 3.43

Selecting a color to make transparent

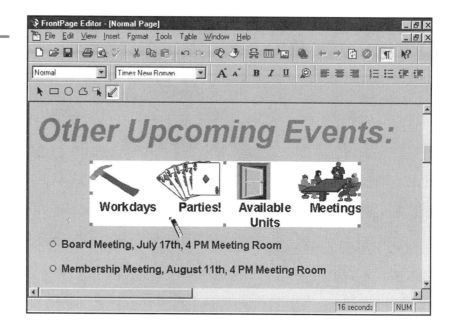

Figure 3.44

Now the images fit in

Changing Image File Types in FrontPage Editor

I've discussed some of the pros and cons of the two image formats. FrontPage makes your imported image a GIF file by default, and that usually works well. GIF files can be "phased in" using interlacing, and they can have one color designated as transparent to help them blend into a Web page.

Imported photos are sometimes best displayed in JPEG format. If you want to change an image file format, FrontPage lets you do that. To save a graphic as a GIF or JPEG file:

1. Save the page with the file in FrontPage Editor. If your image hasn't been saved to the Web site yet, you will be prompted to save your imported graphic image file as you discovered earlier.

2. Right-click the image and select Image Properties from the shortcut menu.

3. Click the JPG radio button in the General Tab of the Image Properties dialog box (see Figure 3.45). Remember, JPG and JPEG are two ways to refer to the same file format.

Figure 3.45

Assigning JPEG format

TIP

The Quality spin box determines the relationship between speed and quality of your image. The higher quality number you select, the slower your image is in appearing, but the better it looks. Choose between 1 and 99—with 1 being the lowest/worst quality. Normally, the default of 75 works well.

4. Select <u>OK</u> to re-save the image. You can change the properties of the image file as often as needed.

Remember, your image is actually a separate file that has been linked to the page you're editing in FrontPage Editor.

Watching Your Graphics Speed

Have you ever waited seconds, minutes, or seemingly hours while a graphic resolves itself on the screen only to conclude grumpily that it wasn't worth the wait? Think back on that experience and let it guide you in placing graphics on your own site.

FrontPage helps you keep tabs on how long your Web site will take to load in a visitor's browser. On the right side of the status bar, FrontPage Editor displays an estimate of how long your page will take to load if your visitor has a 28.8 speed modem. As you add graphics, you'll see the number of seconds grow.

Graphics are great, but they do slow down the process of interpreting your page. There are things you can do to mitigate the wait. One is to use smaller graphics. The larger the graphic, the longer it takes to resolve on the visitor's screen. Another option is to interlace the graphic. This option is available for GIF files. Interlaced graphics "fade in" on the page, first displaying as a fuzzy outline, and then filling in.

Interlacing an image file allows your visitors to see the entire image immediately, albeit in a grainy and blurry form. Is that better than having them gnash their teeth while your images flow onto the screen one line at a time from top to bottom? You be the judge. This is hard to test without opening your file with a Web browser—the procedure you experimented with at the end of the Friday Night session. To make a GIF file interlaced:

1. Right-click the image and select Properties from the shortcut menu. The Image Properties dialog box appears.

2. To interlace a graphic image, select <u>G</u>IF in the Type area.

3. Click the <u>I</u>nterlaced checkbox in the Type area, as shown in Figure 3.46.

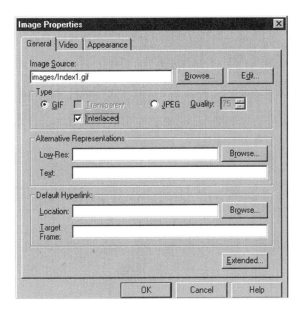

Figure 3.46

Interlacing a graphic image

4. Click OK in the Image Properties dialog box.

Providing Alternative Text

Alternative text displays when your visitor's browser cannot read your graphic image. There's another benefit to alternative text—it displays while the image resolves. It gives the visitor something to read while waiting for the picture, and it helps visitors decide whether they want to wait and see the image or scroll down the page in search of other items. To assign a text alternative:

1. Right-click the image and select Properties from the shortcut menu. The Image Properties dialog box appears.

2. Type some alternative text in the Te<u>x</u>t area of the Alternative Representations area in the General tab of the Image Properties dialog box, as shown in Figure 3.47.

Figure 3.47

Assigning alternative text

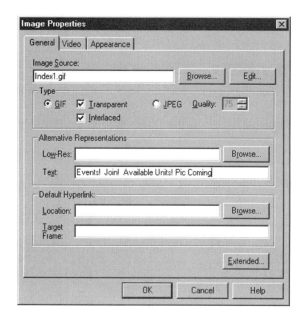

3. Click OK in the Image Properties dialog box.

To place a border around an image:

1. Right-click the image and select Properties from the shortcut menu. The Image Properties dialog box appears.

2. Click the Appearance tab in the Image Properties dialog box.

3. Use the <u>B</u>order Thickness spin box to assign a border to the selected image, as shown in Figure 3.48. Border thickness is measured in screen pixels.

4. Click OK in the Image Properties dialog box. Your image has a border, as shown in Figure 3.49.

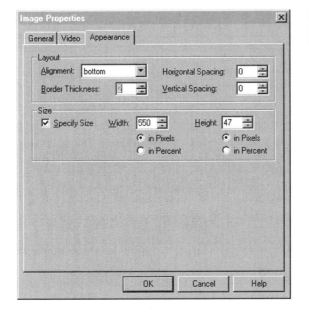

Figure 3.48

Defining border thickness

Figure 3.49

A nice border helps the image stand out

Image Hyperlinks in FrontPage Explorer

You've defined links between graphic images and a page in your Web site. Each image you copy into FrontPage Editor is saved as part of your Web site when you save your page. Remember, you were prompted to save the image file along with your page. What appears to be one "page" is actually an HTML file and linked image files. The FrontPage Explorer has kept track of all these files and their hyperlinks. To examine image links:

1. Click the FrontPage Explorer button in the FrontPage Editor toolbar.

2. Examine the Web in Folder View. Notice that the window shows new image files. FrontPage has assigned the filenames, as shown in Figure 3.50.

Figure 3.50

Image files in
Folder View

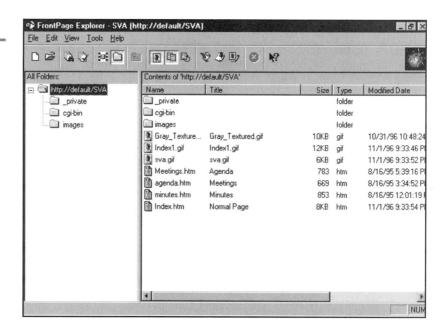

3. Select Hyperlinks View and show Hyperlinks to Images. My site has some additional hyperlinks, but you can see the links to graphic images in Figure 3.51. Notice that the image files are linked to the Normal page.

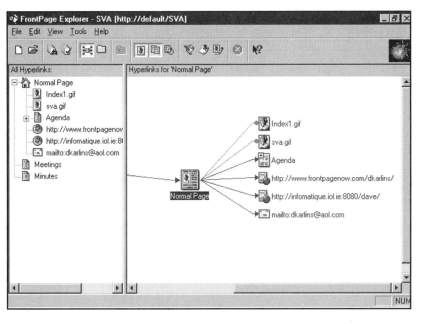

Figure 3.51

Tracking image
hyperlinks

Optional: Importing Graphic Files

Although cutting and pasting directly into a page in FrontPage Editor is the easiest
way to place a graphic image in your Web site, you may not be satisfied with how the
images are handled when they are converted automatically. In that case, your option
is to convert the graphic file to a GIF or JPEG file using a graphics program. Microsoft
Image Composer, for example, provides an export option to both of these formats.

If your graphic image is already in GIF or JPEG format, you can attach it to the Web
through FrontPage Explorer, and then link it to any page in the Web. Here, again, by
working through the Explorer, you are ensuring that all linked files are organized in
the Web and links are protected by FrontPage. To import a JPEG or GIF file directly into FrontPage Explorer:

1. From the FrontPage Explorer menu, select File, Import.

2. In the Import File to Web dialog box, select Add File.

3. From the Files of type list, select images files (*.**gif, jpg**), as shown in
   Figure 3.52.

Figure 3.52

Importing an Image File

4. Navigate to the folder with your saved image file.

5. Double-click the graphic filename.

6. Click OK in the Import File to FrontPage Web dialog box.

TIP   The image file is visible in Folder View, as shown in Figure 3.53. When you link the image to a page, the link will be visible in Hyperlink View.

Figure 3.53

Imported Image File
in Folder View

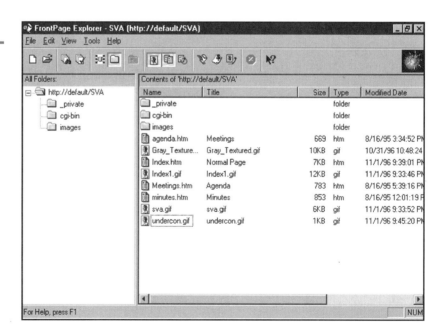

If you have a file that is in JPEG or GIF format, it is not necessary to copy and save the file through the Clipboard. After you have added the image to the Web (which you just walked through), you can insert that image onto any page in the Web. To import a graphic file using FrontPage Editor:

1. Place your cursor on the page at the location where the image should be placed.

2. Select Insert, Image.

3. Double-click the graphic image you wish to import in the Current FrontPage Web tab of the Image dialog box, as shown in Figure 3.54.

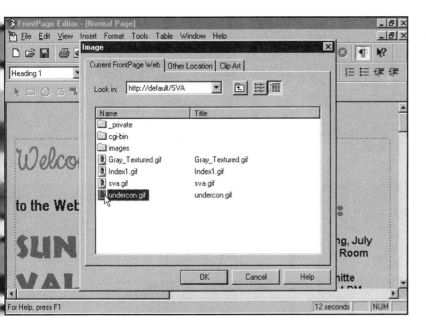

Figure 3.54

Inserting a previously imported image in FrontPage Editor

4. Save your page in FrontPage Editor.

TIP

When you save your page in FrontPage Editor, FrontPage prompts you to confirm changes in any image files.

What's Next!

Between font formatting, tables, and images, you've got the tools to create a fine looking Web site. As you experiment with the tools I've shown, you'll find your own tricks to create unique and entertaining Web sites.

The real magic of Web sites is hyperlinks—special text and graphic objects that, when clicked on, link the visitor to other parts of your Web site, or other sites on the World Wide Web.

When you resume your adventure, you'll hyperlink to the max. So stay tuned, the real excitement is yet to come!

CHAPTER 4

Saturday Night:

Live and Hyperlinked

A lready this weekend, you've explored the tools to create an attractive Web page with formatted headings, text, and tables. You also got graphical with horizontal lines, inserted images, and altered background colors and patterns for your page.

Now it's time to introduce one of the most powerful features of World Wide Web sites—hyperlinks. Hyperlinks provide the ability to click text or an image, and zoom to another place. A hyperlink may lead to another spot in the current Web page, to another page in the Web site, or even to another site on the World Wide Web. With hyperlinks, your Web site becomes far more navigable and friendly. Hyperlinks could be thought of as an instant index, allowing your visitors to find exactly what they're looking for with the click of a mouse.

Microsoft FrontPage makes defining and assigning hyperlinks a breeze. Of course, you need to think about the kinds of hyperlinks that are appropriate for your visitors. What are they looking for? Are they really interested in reading a long introduction to your Web site before they zip to the area of their interest? The trick in designing hyperlinks is to put yourself in the shoes of your visitor and make hyperlinks as helpful and as easy to follow as possible. In this session, you will explore three basic types of hyperlinks:

❖ Hyperlinks *within* a single Web page—these links are called "bookmarks"

❖ Hyperlinks *between pages* in your Web site

❖ Hyperlinks between your site and the World Wide Web

The basic elements in all hyperlinks are similar: an object—either text (called *hypertext* when it's used with more than one page) or an image (called a *hotspot*) that is the starting point of the hyperlink—and a Web site or a part of that site that is the ending point of the hyperlink.

A Few Notes on Building Your Web Site from Here

Up to now, you've had plenty of opportunity to create a Web site of your own. If you've already started, keep at it! After each session, remember your checklist:

❖ Always have FrontPage Explorer running when you work on Web pages.

❖ Always open Web pages from FrontPage Explorer (by double-clicking the file in the Summary or Hyperlinks View).

❖ Save *all* pages in FrontPage Editor before you exit.

These three steps ensure that your work is saved, and more than that, that the hyperlinks within your Web site are kept up to date. As you save pages in FrontPage Editor or exit Explorer, FrontPage prompts you to import files or save changes to them. That is FrontPage's job.

Using Bookmarks

Bookmarks are a form of hyperlink that connect to a place *within* a Web page. The term *bookmark* is a metaphor for those handy placeholders you use to mark a page in a book. When you place a bookmark in a long book, you can go right to that spot whenever you wish. Bookmarks in a Web page permit your visitors to jump right to a selected spot. If your page has more information on it than can be viewed in one screen, bookmarks are especially helpful. They allow your visitors to jump from one area to another on the same page. Creating bookmark hyperlinks involves two steps:

1. Assigning the bookmark
2. Defining the hyperlink

A hyperlink is hypertext or a graphic that is linked to the bookmark. Clicking on the hyperlink jumps to the bookmark.

At this point, you should have a Web site open. Make sure you have a page open that contains text or graphics—so that you have something to hyperlink.

Assigning Bookmarks

The first step in creating bookmark hyperlinks is to assign bookmarks to selected text in your page. You can assign bookmarks to text only—you cannot make a graphic image a bookmark. You can change a bookmark name or remove an assignment as a bookmark from text. To assign a bookmark to text:

1. Click and drag to select text you want to use as a bookmark.

2. Select Edit, Bookmark, as shown in Figure 4.1.

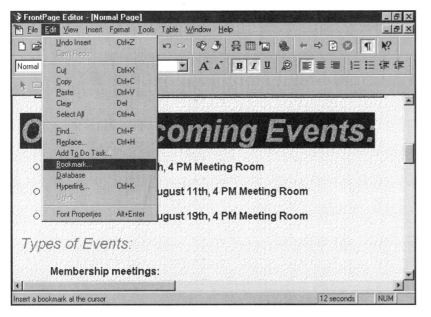

Figure 4.1

Assigning a bookmark
to selected text

3. Enter an easy-to-remember bookmark name in the Bookmark Name area of the Bookmark dialog box, as shown in Figure 4.2.

Figure 4.2

Naming your bookmark

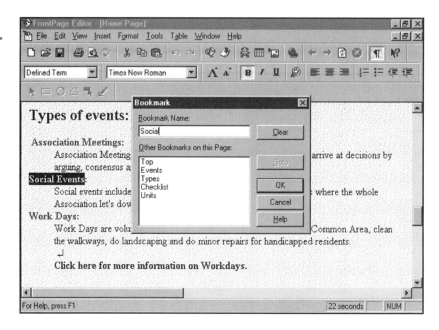

TIP

I find it reduces snags and bugs if I don't include spaces in my bookmark names.

4. Click OK in the Bookmark dialog box. A dotted line appears beneath the bookmark text.

TIP

Assigning a bookmark to text at the top of the page lets your visitors jump to the beginning of the page. Try something like the bookmark shown in Figure 4.3.

You can insert a bookmark without selecting text—for instance, at the top of a page as in the previous example. When you do, a small flag appears in FrontPage Editor to mark the bookmark spot, as shown in Figure 4.4. This flag doesn't show up when visitors see your Web site in their browsers.

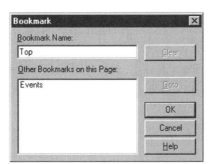

Figure 4.3

This bookmark will let visitors jump back to the top of the page.

Figure 4.4

A bookmark indicated by a flag

To change bookmark properties:

1. Right-click the bookmark text and select Bookmark Properties from the shortcut menu.

2. Enter a new bookmark name in the Bookmark Name text box, as shown in Figure 4.5.

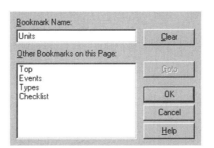

Figure 4.5

Renaming a bookmark

To clear bookmark properties:

1. Right-click the bookmark text and select Bookmark Properties from the shortcut menu.

2. Click the Clear button in the Bookmark dialog box to clear all bookmark connections.

Defining Hyperlinks to Bookmarks

After you're satisfied with your assigned bookmarks, you are ready to assign them hyperlinks. Often Web sites have a group of hyperlinks—either hypertext or graphics—at the top of each page so that visitors can jump to the area of their interest. Figure 4.6 shows a page with text at the top, ready to have hyperlinks assigned to bookmarks.

Figure 4.6

Bookmark text—ready for linking

Bookmark hyperlinks also can be used to let visitors who have viewed one section of a Web page jump to a related area, or back to the top of a page, as shown in Figure 4.7.

 TIP   Today's modern Web pages don't usually use "Click here." Instead, sophisticated and Web-wise visitors know that when they see underlined text in blue, the text is hyperlinked.

To define text hyperlinks to a bookmark:

1. Select the text that will be linked to the bookmark.

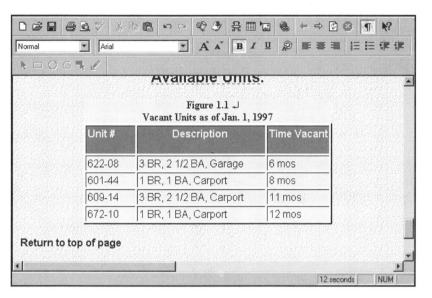

Figure 4.7

A bookmark to take visitors back to the top of the page

2. With the text selected, click the Create or Edit Hyperlink button in the FrontPage Editor toolbar, as shown in Figure 4.8.

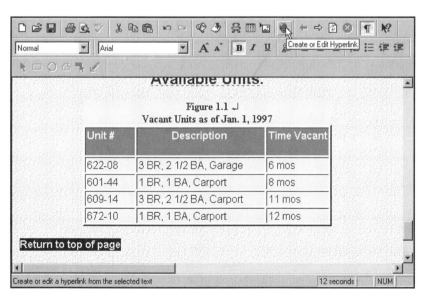

Figure 4.8

Selected text—ready to hyperlink to a bookmark

3. Select the Open Pages tab in the Create Hyperlink dialog box and click the page to which the bookmark will be assigned. If you only have one page open, that page will already be selected.

4. Pull down the Bookmark list and select the bookmark to which the text will be linked, as shown in Figure 4.9.

Figure 4.9

Matching a bookmark to a hyperlink

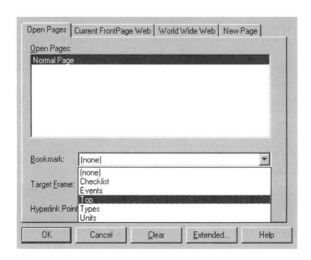

5. Click OK in the Create Hyperlink dialog box.

To clear or edit bookmark hyperlinks:

1. Click anywhere in the hypertext you have assigned to hyperlink to a bookmark.

2. Click the Create or Edit Hyperlink button in the FrontPage Editor toolbar.

3. Pull down the list of bookmarks to change the assigned hyperlink.

4. Click the Clear button in the Hyperlinks dialog box to clear a hyperlink to a bookmark, as shown in Figure 4.10.

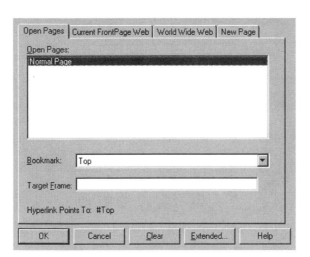

Figure 4.10

Clearing a bookmark hyperlink

Checking Out Your Bookmark Hyperlinks

If your page is longer than one screen, bookmarks help your visitors find what they want. Well-designed Web sites are full of handy bookmarks that anticipate where a visitor wants to go. Put yourself in the shoes of someone who has come to your Web site looking for information on something, and add bookmarks to help them quickly and easily find what you think they want. You can work through your Web site, testing it, right in FrontPage Editor. When you move your cursor over a hyperlink, the linked bookmark displays in the status bar with a "#" symbol in front, as shown in Figure 4.11.

Bookmark hyperlinks can be tested in FrontPage Editor without using a browser. To test bookmark hyperlinks:

1. Hold down the ⌈CTRL⌋ key on your keyboard while you place your cursor over the hypertext.

2. An arrow appears over the linked text (see Figure 4.12), and the linked bookmark displays with a "#" sign in front of it in the status bar of FrontPage Editor.

Figure 4.11

Bookmark link indicated in the status bar

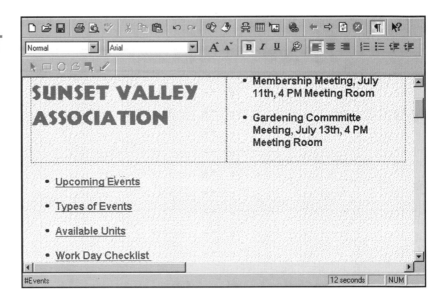

Figure 4.12

Testing a hyperlink to a bookmark

- Upcoming Events

3. With the [CTRL] key pressed, click the hypertext to follow the hyperlink to the bookmark.

 NOTE Later in this session, you'll explore hyperlinks to other pages in the Web site.

Creating Hyperlinks to Pages in Your Web Site

Up until now, you've just been working with a single page in your Web site. You added additional files—graphic images. Now it's time to stretch and weave your Web a bit larger. Because I haven't discussed working with more than one page in a Web site yet, you'll start there. Usually, pages in Web sites are hyperlinked so that visitors can jump from one to another.

As you are creating a Web site, often you will decide that some of your information should go in a separate Web page. When that happens, you can create that separate Web page "on the fly" as you create a hyperlink to the new page.

After you create a new page and a hyperlink at the same time, you'll also explore the process of creating hyperlinks between existing pages in a Web site. When you've seen both of these options, you'll be in position to spin your Web pages together like a pro. Why not just put all the information you have to offer on a single Web page? It's not a bad question. If all the news fits on one page, no problem. Because you've learned to help visitors navigate with bookmarks, the sheer size of a page shouldn't be a problem.

There are many situations where organizing your Web site into many pages is a big help. Sometimes it's easier to maintain a Web site if the information is broken up into separate pages. For example, a visitor may not know that there's more information on a page.

You might want to keep information that is updated frequently on a separate Web page. You could have a price sheet that changes every day linked to a product list that stays the same for weeks or months. Another example is providing hyperlinks from your home page to late-breaking news. An organization could put a "latest meeting minutes" reference on one page, with hyperlinks to a page with the minutes of the meeting. In short, one important function of breaking up information onto separate Web pages is to make it easier for you to update and maintain the Web site.

Creating Hyperlinks to New Pages

FrontPage Explorer, working quietly in the background, keeps track of and maintains all the hyperlinks you define in your Web site—you only need to keep it open while you work.

Remember that the checklist of steps to ensure the integrity of your page still applies. Always open Explorer before you work on a page. Always open pages from Explorer or create new pages from within FrontPage Editor, and remember to save each page in Editor before you end an editing session.

You're using FrontPage Editor to create new pages and define hyperlinks between them. You are counting on the whole package to mesh when someone visits your site. Explorer is backing you up the whole way and making sure this will happen.

You can create a hyperlink to a page that doesn't exist—yet. Sometimes the process of designing your Web site works that way. You're creating and adding text and graphics to your Web page, and you decide that some information should be better placed in a separate, linked page. No problem. You can create a new page directly from the Create and Edit Hyperlinks dialog box. Here's how that works. To create a hyperlink as you create a new page:

1. Select the text you wish to hyperlink to a new page.

2. Click the Create or Edit Hyperlink button in the FrontPage Editor toolbar.

3. Click the New Page tab in the Create Hyperlink dialog box. FrontPage suggests a *title* for the page, using the selected text.

4. Accept the FrontPage suggested title or enter a new title.

 NOTE   Remember that the page *title* is just an internal name in FrontPage. Every FrontPage file must also have a URL filename.

5. Accept FrontPage's suggestion for URL filename (or change it), as shown in Figure 4.13. The URL filename is required.

6. Select the Edit New Page Immediately radio button.

 TIP   You'll explore the To Do List in the Sunday Evening session of this book.

7. Click OK in the Create Hyperlink dialog box.

8. Select a Normal template for your new page.

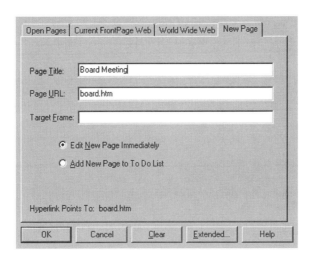

Figure 4.13

Defining a new page

TIP At this stage of the game, you're avoiding the more complex templates and wizards. You'll dive into them when you are more comfortable creating pages from scratch.

9. Click OK in the New Page dialog box.

10. Create your new page, as shown in Figure 4.14.

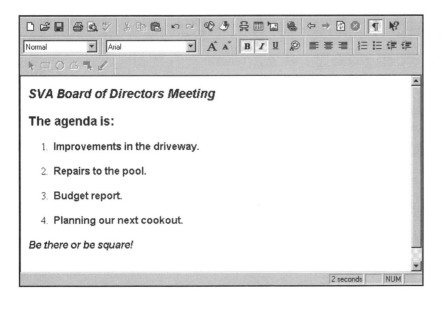

Figure 4.14

Editing your new Web page

11. Remember to save your work on the new page. It already has a title and name, so you can just click the Save button in the FrontPage Editor toolbar.

TIP

You can confirm the link between your home page and your new page in FrontPage Explorer, as shown in Figure 4.15.

Figure 4.15

A new page—hyper-linked to a home page

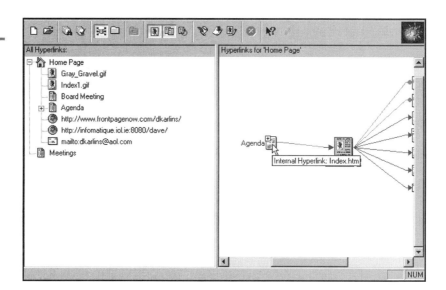

Creating Hyperlinks to Existing Pages

If you have already created and saved a page as part of your Web site, you can create hyperlinks to that page. You can also import existing pages into your Web site.

Say, for example, that you created a long document in a word processor that you wish to use as a Web page. More and more word processors have the ability to save a page as an HTML (Hypertext Markup Language), which is the format required to add text to your Web site, or there are many utilities that do this. You can attach this file to your Web site using FrontPage Explorer, and then use FrontPage Editor to create hyperlinks to it. You can use the following procedure to import an HTML file into a Web site. To import an HTML file into a Web site:

1. Start by switching to FrontPage Explorer.

2. Select File, Import, and click the Add File button in the Import File to FrontPage Web dialog box.

3. From the Files Of Type list, select HTML pages.

4. Navigate to the folder on your drive or CD where the file is located and double-click the file you wish to import.

 TIP There's an HTML file called "Minutes" on the CD. You can import that file for practice.

5. Click the OK button in the Import File to Web dialog box.

6. Close the Import File to Web dialog box, and notice the file in the Folder View of FrontPage Explorer.

 NOTE A look at the Hyperlinks View of FrontPage Explorer confirms that the new, imported page is not yet linked to the Index.htm page in the Web site.

To create a hyperlink to an existing page:

1. Select the text that is to serve as the hyperlink to an existing Web page.

2. Click the Create or Edit Hyperlink button in the FrontPage Editor toolbar.

3. Select the Current FrontPage Web tab in the Edit Hyperlink dialog box.

4. Click the Browse button to see a list of all the pages that are part of the current Web site.

5. Click the target page for the hyperlink, as shown in Figure 4.16.

Figure 4.16

Selecting a target page for a hyperlink

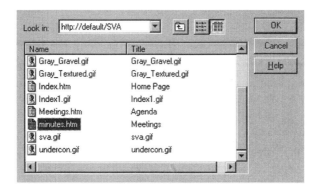

6. Click OK in the Current Web dialog box.

7. Click OK in the Create Hyperlink dialog box.

Navigating Between Pages in FrontPage

Now that you've got more than one page to manage, it would be nice to know how to get from one to the other. One page uses FrontPage Explorer and two use FrontPage Editor. To switch between pages using FrontPage Explorer:

1. Click the Show FrontPage Explorer button, shown in Figure 4.17

Figure 4.17

Show FrontPage Explorer

2. Double-click the page you wish to switch to in the Hyperlink or Folder View.

To switch between open pages using FrontPage Editor:

❖ Select <u>W</u>indow and select the page

    or

❖ You can use the Back navigation button in the FrontPage Editor toolbar to go to the last page you worked on, or return forward by clicking the Forward navigation button. The Back button is shown in Figure 4.18.

Figure 4.18

The Back navigation button

Creating Hyperlinks to Bookmarked Pages in the Web

Creating a hyperlink to another page is nice. But to really send a visitor directly to where he or she wants to go, you can create hyperlinks that go to a specific bookmark on another page on the Web. To create hyperlinks to bookmarks on pages in the Web:

1. Select the text that is to serve as the hyperlink to a bookmark on an existing Web page.

2. Click the Create or Edit Hyperlink button in the FrontPage Editor toolbar.

3. Select the Current FrontPage Web tab in the Create Hyperlink dialog box.

 TIP   If the page to which you are linking is open in FrontPage Editor, you can select the Open Pages.

4. Select the page and bookmark to which you are linking, as shown in Figure 4.19.

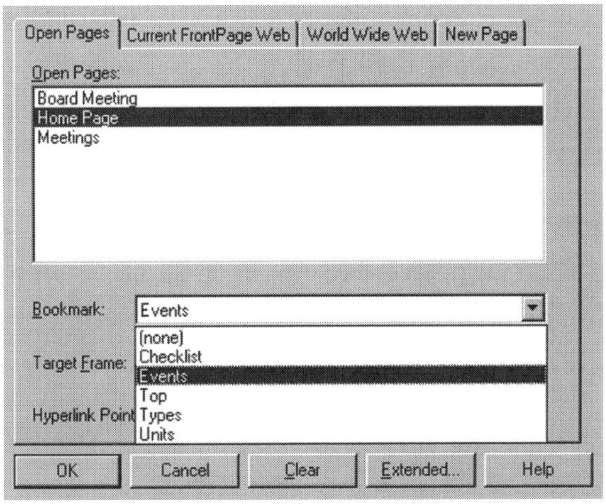

Figure 4.19

Selecting a page and bookmark target for a hyperlink

5. Click OK in the Create Hyperlink dialog box.

 TIP You can use CTRL +click to test the hyperlink to a bookmark on another Web page.

6. As always, save your work on each page of FrontPage Editor before you exit your editing session.

Linking to the World Wide Web

One of my favorite ways to enhance a Web site is to hyperlink to a jazzy World Wide Web (WWW) site. Hyperlinks to other Web sites can connect your site to other sites with similar information, and can provide additional research resources, or even support systems for your visitors.

Of course, it's great to get other sites to hyperlink to your Web. Linking Web sites is a form of business or educational networking. How do you do that? One way is to just ask. Occasionally, I will visit a Web site and think that the people who visit this site might like to know about my Web site—and vice versa. I then just e-mail the Web sponsor and propose a trade: I'll let you put a link on my site if you let me put a link on yours. There are also businesses that arrange these trades. If your site stays on the World Wide Web more than a month or two, you'll be approached by one of the commercial services that arranges these mutual links. Commercial services usually want you to host two hyperlinks to other sites in exchange for placing a link to your site on one other Web site. Somehow they parlay that uneven deal into a profit—don't ask me exactly how. I've never taken them up on their offers. I think you can make arrangements on your own to share links with compatible Web sites.

World Wide Web sites are identified by their address, which is technically called their URL (Uniform Resource Locator). You need to know the URL for a Web site to create a hyperlink to it. As you surf the Net, note the addresses that would make a good addition to your own site. To create a hyperlink to a World Wide Web site:

1. Select the text you wish to use as hypertext, just as you did for other types of hyperlinks.

2. Click the Create or Edit Hyperlink button in the FrontPage Editor toolbar.

3. Click the World Wide Web tab in the Create Hyperlink dialog box.

4. Enter a World Wide Web URL (address) in the <u>U</u>RL area of the Create Hyperlink dialog box, as shown in Figure 4.20.

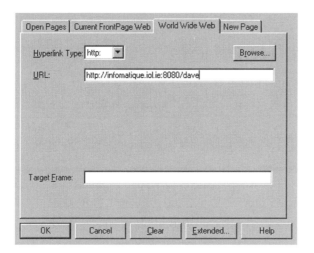

Figure 4.20

Linking to my Web site

5. Click OK in the Create Hyperlink dialog box.

6. You cannot test hyperlinks to World Wide Web sites unless you are logged onto the Internet with your service provider and using an Internet server. However, World Wide Web hyperlinks display in the status bar when you place your cursor over the hypertext.

Using Graphics as Hyperlinks

In the ever-escalating battle to create more intuitive and friendly Web sites, everything is going graphical. In the previous session, you saw how attractive images and tasteful backgrounds can add to the impact of a site.

Many designers are using graphical hyperlinks to enable visitors to visually and intuitively navigate around a Web site. A graphic of a big question mark can zip the visitor to help. A picture of a person can be a hyperlink to that person's biography. Click a product and see a description of the product. You get the picture (excuse the pun).

Creating graphic hyperlinks involves concepts and procedures you have already learned. In the previous session, you imported graphics into a page. Earlier in this session, you created hyperlinks. Now you need to explore some design approaches, get the hang of assigning graphic hotspot hyperlinks, and then have some fun. One approach to using graphic hyperlinks is to create icon-type pictures or artistic text images at the top of a home page.

Assigning Graphic Hotspots

If you have created bookmarks on your page, or if you have other pages to hyperlink a graphic to, you're halfway to creating a linked image. Another option is to use a graphic hyperlinked to another World Wide Web site. If you have graphics on your page to use as hyperlink objects, you're ready to assign graphic hotspots that hyperlink all or part of a graphic to a bookmark or Web page.

In the next example, I insert the Microsoft Internet Explorer icon that comes with the collection of FrontPage Clip Art, and I hyperlink that graphic image to Microsoft's Web site so that visitors (who don't have the latest version of Internet Explorer) can download it directly from my Web site. To make a graphic image a hyperlink:

1. Click the graphic image that serves as a hyperlink.

2. Click the Create or Edit Hyperlink button in the FrontPage toolbar.

3. Select or enter a hyperlink target, as shown in Figure 4.21.

4. Click OK on the Create Hyperlink dialog box.

 TIP When you move your cursor over the hyperlinked graphic image, the hyperlink target address shows in the status bar (see Figure 4.22).

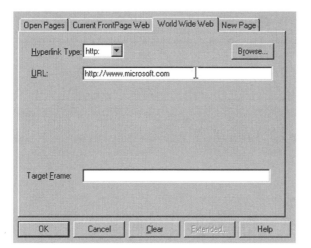

Figure 4.21

Defining a hyperlink target for an image

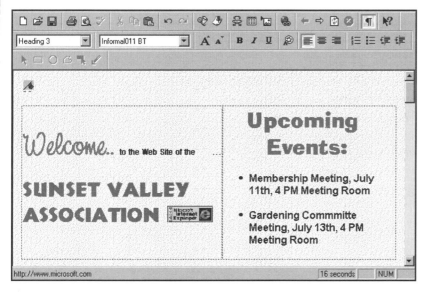

Figure 4.22

The image hyperlink shows in the status bar

Many Web sites include *site maps*—graphic images with *several* hotspots, or hyperlinks, within them. Site maps can be button bars with several buttons, each with its own hyperlink. If you include graphic site maps *and* text hyperlinks, you can be assured that *any* visitor to your site can find their way around—even if their browser has trouble with your site map graphic, or the visitor doesn't feel like waiting for it to materialize.

If you have defined image maps on your own—without FrontPage—you'll be pleasantly surprised that there's no need to deal with map files. FrontPage handles all files and links for you. It's as easy as drawing circles and rectangles, as you shall see. When you select a graphic in FrontPage Editor, the Image toolbar becomes active, as shown in Figure 4.23.

Figure 4.23

FrontPage Editor's image toolbar

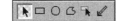

The image toolbar includes six buttons:

Button	Function
Select	Allows you to select (and delete or edit) an already created hotspot
Rectangle	Allows you to draw a rectangular hotspot
Circle	Allows you to create a circular hotspot
Polygon	Allows you to create odd-shaped hotspots
Highlight	Highlights hotspots
Make Transparent	Makes GIF images transparent

You'll experiment with creating, editing, and testing graphic hotspots. To assign a rectangular graphic hotspot:

1. Click the graphic image that contains the picture to launch the hyperlink, causing the Images toolbar to become active.

 TIP A graphic hotspot can be the entire image or a part of the image.

2. Click the Rectangular Hotspot tool and draw a rectangle around the hotspot area, as shown in Figure 4.24. Don't worry if the rectangle isn't perfect—you can adjust the size of the hotspot later.

Figure 4.24

Defining a rectangular hotspot

3. As soon as you release your mouse button, the Create Hyperlink dialog box appears. Select a Web page (and bookmark if you wish) or World Wide Web address with which to hyperlink the graphic hotspot.

 TIP When you move your cursor over an assigned hotspot, the filename of the hyperlink displays in the FrontPage Editor status bar.

4. Click OK in the Create Hyperlink dialog box.

 TIP You can test hotspot hyperlinks the same way you tested text hyper-links—by holding down the CTRL key while you click the hotspot.

To assign a circular graphic hotspot:

1. Click the image that is to become a hyperlink, and the Images toolbar becomes active.

2. Click the Circular Hotspot tool and draw a circle *starting from the middle* of the hotspot area, as shown in Figure 4.25.

3. As soon as you release your mouse button, the Create Hyperlink dialog box appears. Select a Web page (and bookmark if you wish) with which to hyper-link the circular hotspot.

4. Click OK in the Create Hyperlink dialog box

The Polygon button in the Images toolbar enables you to outline odd-shaped objects. This feature allows you to create fun hotspots out of objects, such as stars, shapes, icons, or other irregularly-shaped objects. To assign an irregular graphic hotspot:

1. Click a graphic image to activate the Images toolbar and click the Polygon button, as shown in Figure 4.26.

Figure 4.25

Defining a circular hotspot

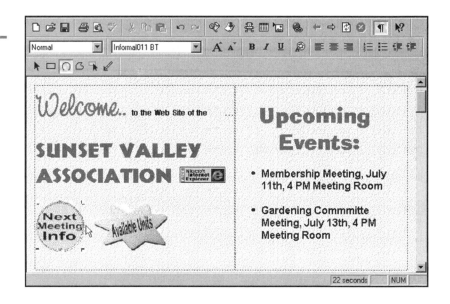

Figure 4.26

Selecting the polygon hotspot tool

2. Point the pencil-cursor at one corner of the hotspot and click.

3. Click again at the next nodal point in the polygon, as shown in Figure 4.27.

4. Continue to click at each nodal point until you have completed a polygon around the hotspot.

Figure 4.27

Outlining a polygon-
shaped hotspot

5. When you have completed the polygon, double-click.

6. As soon as you release your mouse button, the Create Hyperlink dialog box
appears. Select a Web page (and bookmark if you wish) with which to hyperlink the polygon hotspot.

7. Click OK in the Create Hyperlink dialog box.

Editing a Graphic Hotspot

You can edit hotspot sizes and shapes. To edit hotspot properties, double-click the
hotspot, the same way you edit text hyperlinks. To edit a graphic hotspot:

1. Sometimes it's easier to identify hotspots if you can see them without the
image in the background. You can view your hotspots by clicking the
Highlight Hotspots button in the Images toolbar, as shown in Figure 4.28.

Figure 4.28

Highlighted hotspot

2. Deselect the Highlight Hotspots button to edit the hotspot size and shape.

3. Click the Select button to select a hotspot to edit.

4. Click and drag on the small rectangular handles around the hotspot to resize it, as shown in Figure 4.29 with the "Events" hotspot.

Figure 4.29

Resizing a hotspot

Creating E-mail Hyperlinks

In this session, you have created hyperlinks to bookmarks within your Web page, to other pages in your Web site, and even to other sites within the World Wide Web. What a tangled Web we weave! There's a very useful type of hyperlink that you haven't yet explored—e-mail hyperlinks.

In your Sunday sessions, you'll explore various ways to collect feedback from visitors to your Web site. One of the easiest ways is to provide a hyperlink to your e-mail address. The process is similar to the one you used to create Web hyperlinks. As long as your visitors' browsers have e-mail capability (such as Microsoft Internet Explorer and Netscape Navigator), they can click a hyperlink (text or graphic) and send you e-mail. You could put your e-mail address on your site and let them use their e-mail accounts to contact you, but this is much more convenient. If it's feedback you want, convenience is what you provide. To create an e-mail hyperlink:

1. Select the text (or graphic hotspot) you wish to hyperlink to your e-mail address.

2. Click the Create or Edit Hyperlink button in the toolbar.

TIP If you are creating a hyperlink from a graphic hotspot, the Create Hyperlink dialog box opens automatically.

3. Select the World Wide Web tab in the Create Hyperlink dialog box.

4. Pull down the Hyperlink Type list in the Create Hyperlink dialog box, and select "mailto:," as shown in Figure 4.30.

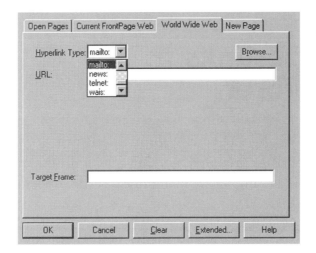

Figure 4.30

Defining an e-mail hyperlink

5. Enter your e-mail address in the URL area of the Create Hyperlink dialog box, after "mailto:," as shown in Figure 4.31. (This example is using my e-mail address).

6. Click OK in the Create Hyperlink dialog box.

Figure 4.31

Linking my e-mail address

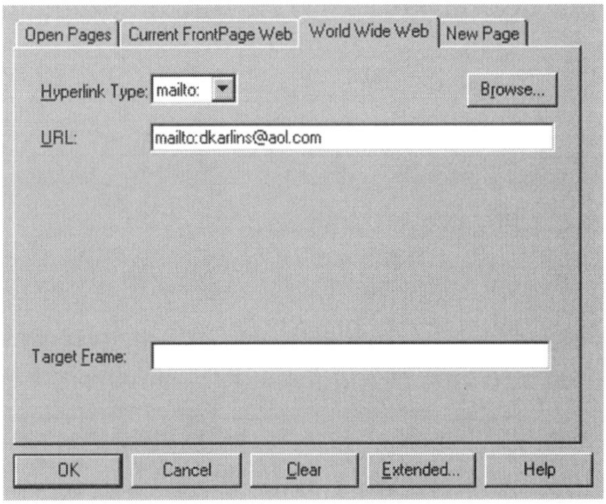

NOTE You need to have your Web site placed on the Internet to test this hyperlink. I cover that process in the Sunday sessions.

Examining Hyperlinks in FrontPage Explorer

Throughout this book, I emphasize that as long as you start FrontPage Explorer first, and save changes to pages or new pages to your Web, you don't need to worry about the hyperlinks you create. FrontPage Explorer, working quietly in the background, makes sure that all the files you are linking are maintained in the proper directories.

To copy your Web site to an Internet Service Provider (and I go over that in the Sunday sessions), use the Copy Web command in the FrontPage Explorer menu. Your entire site, with all its complex directories of files, are copied. FrontPage Explorer maintains proper directories and makes sure all the files needed to run your Web site make it to your provider. Still, it's useful to visit FrontPage Explorer periodically and note the files and hyperlinks you've created. Files are viewed in Summary View. Site hyperlinks are best viewed in Hyperlinks View. To view files in Summary View in FrontPage Explorer:

   1. In FrontPage Editor, click the FrontPage Explorer button in the toolbar, as shown in Figure 4.32.

Figure 4.32

Viewing FrontPage Explorer

   2. In FrontPage Explorer, click the Folder View button in the toolbar or pull down the View menu and select Folder View, as shown in Figure 4.33.

TIP The Folder View in FrontPage Explorer shows file sizes, file modification time and date, filename, and title.

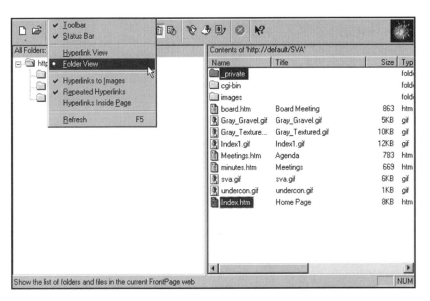

Figure 4.33

Switching to Folder
View

To examine hyperlinks in FrontPage Explorer:

1. In FrontPage Editor, click the FrontPage Explorer button in the toolbar.

2. Select View, Hyperlink View to examine Web hyperlinks.

> **TIP** You can drag the split bar between the Outline View and the Hyperlink View to see more of your hyperlinks, as shown in Figure 4.34.

3. Select Hyperlinks Inside Page in the View menu to see all the hyperlinks within a page (bookmarks). You can see details on a link by moving your cursor over it, as shown in Figure 4.35. Deselect Hyperlinks Inside Page if you want a less-cluttered view of your site.

> **TIP** You can display (or hide) images by clicking the Hyperlinks to Images button in the FrontPage Explorer toolbar, as shown in figure 4.36.

Figure 4.34

Show those hyperlinks

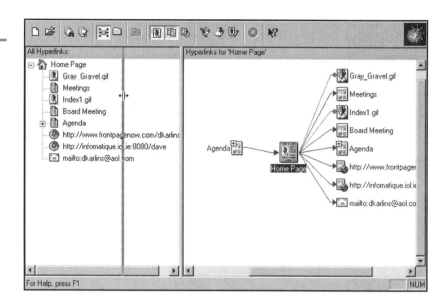

Figure 4.35

Viewing hyperlinks
within a page

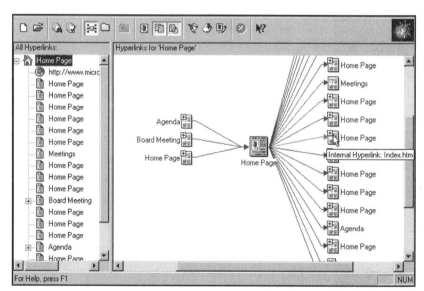

What's Next!

Your Web site is starting to hum. Not only does it look good, but you have explored
the process of creating hyperlinks within, and from, your site. You could certainly
skip ahead at this point to the final session on Sunday, upload your Web site to a
friendly Web site provider, and get online with a nice Web site.

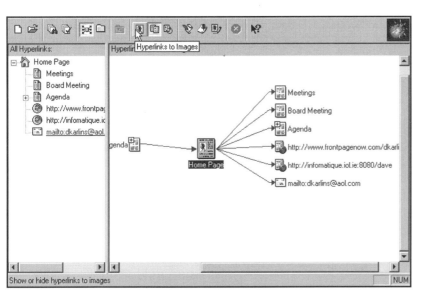

Figure 4.36

Viewing image hyperlinks

Still, there's more to add to the site in order to maximize the impact and functionality of your Web site. For example, there's the whole process of creating forms and getting input. In this session, you began that process by allowing visitors to e-mail you directly from your site. FrontPage enables you to do much more—from creating forms to collecting user input to offering different formats to collect that data. Start brainstorming about how you can use forms. Perhaps you can collect mailing lists from your visitors, survey who's visiting, sell your product—even collect credit card information and take orders for products.

Microsoft FrontPage also enables you to create a number of features that make your site even easier to visit. In the Sunday sessions, you'll explore FrontPage's robots, or "bots," for short. Bots enable you to create tables of contents, page headers and footers, attach scheduled files, and to make other handy additions to your Web sites.

So, pat yourself on the back, you've accomplished quite a bit. Start thinking about how you'll take advantage of the features you'll be adding to your Web site on Sunday!

CHAPTER 5

Sunday Morning:

Letting Visitors Plug In with Forms

n earlier sessions, you created an attractive Web site. You formatted text, customized the site background, and inserted images. In the previous session, you created links that tied your site together and spun it into the World Wide Web. Now you can create a site that is friendly and useful.

You next need to make your site a two-way street. Wouldn't you like to hear from your visitors? They can make suggestions on how you can improve your Web site, place orders, tell you about themselves, get on your mailing list—the possibilities are endless. The way to collect all this information from your visitors is to place input forms on your Web site. The process of designing an input form involves three main steps:

1. Place the input forms that enable you to collect information. You'll walk through the whole process in just a bit.

2. Add Submit (and Reset) buttons so that visitors can send you their input (or to bail out without sending the information).

3. Define the input target (the file for storing the information collected from your Web site).

So, if you've had a healthy breakfast, a refreshing swim, a quick jog—or maybe just a couple of cups of strong black coffee—you should be ready to start this session.

I know I keep reminding you about the routine for opening or creating a Web site, but if you remember the basic principles, you'll never experience the annoyance of losing pages or links in your Web site.

For a review: Start in the Explorer and open pages by double-clicking the page in the Folder or Hyperlink views. That way your Web site stays intact and will be ready to copy to a Web site provider when the time comes (and it will come soon).

Forms Your Visitors Can Use to Give You Information

Internet browsers that interpret HTML can handle a variety of input forms. Remember those tests that required fill-in circles with number 2 pencils? Those circles are available—only now they're called radio buttons, and a pencil isn't required. You can also allow visitors to write freestyle verse. In short, FrontPage offers so many ways to get information from visitors that you should be able to find out just about anything you want to know, in any format you wish. When you collect information, you'll do it in one of the available forms:

* ❖ Check boxes
* ❖ Radio buttons
* ❖ Drop-down menus
* ❖ One-line text boxes
* ❖ Scrolling text boxes

You'll explore each of these formats for collecting visitor input. The input area in Figure 5.1 shows a Web site that uses each type of input form.

Figure 5.1

Five types of input

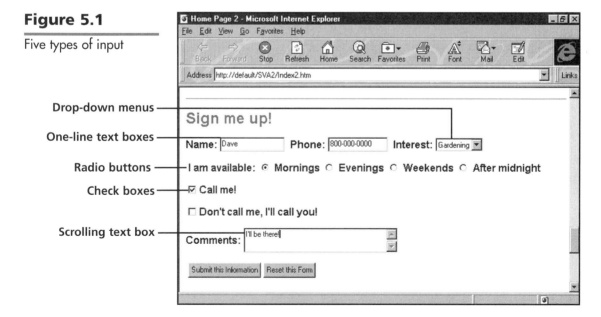

Using Check Boxes

A check box can be one of two things—checked, or unchecked. There's no room here for "maybe" or "sort of." Sometimes that's a fine way to collect information from your visitors. Do they want to be on your mailing list? Do they want to buy a product? Are they volunteering to work on the garden project this weekend? Basic questions like this are appropriate for check box input. Can you have more than one check box on your Web page? Sure. You can have as many as you want. But each check box will give the visitor only two options—to check it, or to leave it unchecked.

If a check box is appropriate, placing one in a Web site is pretty simple. You pose an option, decide whether the check box should appear checked or empty (depending on which answer you want to suggest), and put the check box on the page. For example, if you want to let a visitor select from a list of products they are interested in, check boxes allow your visitors select one, many, or no items from the list. To place a check box:

1. Place your cursor on the spot in the page where you want the Check Box button to appear.

2. Select <u>V</u>iew and click the Forms toolbar to display the Forms toolbar if it is not visible. The Forms toolbar is shown in Figure 5.2.

Figure 5.2

The Forms toolbar

3. Click the Check Box button in the Forms toolbar, as shown in Figure 5.3.

Figure 5.3

The Check Box button

4. Type a prompt to your visitor next to the check box—something like "Send me information" or "Sign me up!"

5. Right-click the new check box and select Form Field Properties from the shortcut menu. In the Check Box Properties dialog box that appears, you must give three elements to the information—a name, the value, and the initial state of the check box.

TIP   The name and value fields define information that only you see. When you read the results of visitor input, a report displays the field name and value. For example, if a check box field name is "Send me a catalog" and the value is set to "On," your report states: **Send Me a Catalog—On**. You'll know that this person wants a catalog. What your visitor sees is simply the text you type on the page next to the check box.

6. Enter a name in the Name area of the Check Box Properties dialog box that is easy to interpret when input is posted to a file.

7. Enter a value in the Value area that appears in the results file if the user selects the check box. "ON" is usually a nice choice.

8. Select an Initial State of Checked or Not Checked. This is where you get to suggest a response. You must set the default to either checked not checked. The simple check box is not subtle in its method of collecting information.

9. When you have entered a Name and a Value and decided on an initial state for the check box, click OK in the Check Box Properties dialog box, as shown in Figure 5.4.

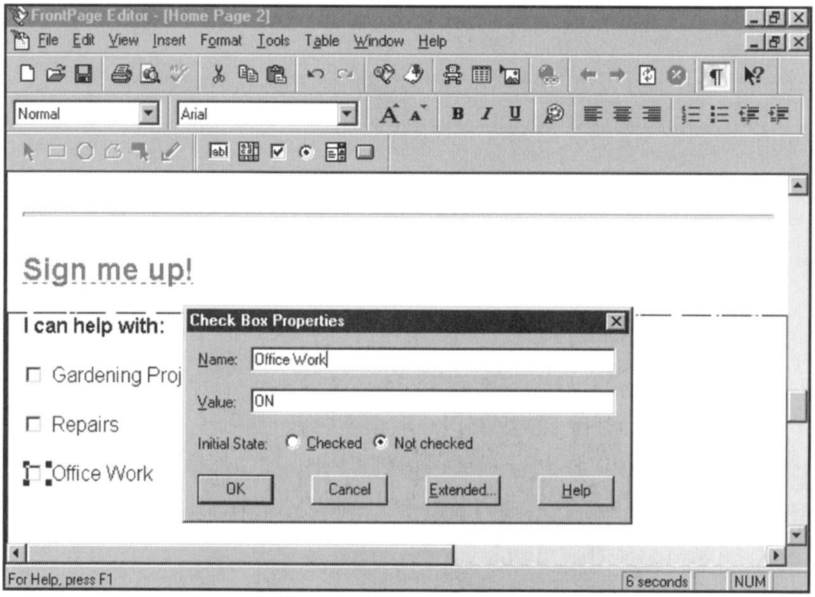

Figure 5.4

Defining a check box

![FrontPage Editor screen showing the Check Box Properties dialog box with Name field "Office Work", Value field "ON", and Initial State set to Not checked. The page shows "Sign me up!" with "I can help with:" and checkboxes for Gardening Proj, Repairs, and Office Work.]

> **TIP**
> When you create a check box or any other input form, horizontal lines appear defining the form area. These lines are not visible to your visitors, but they identify the form. You'll examine how this works later in this session when you assign a target for the input and add Submit and Clear buttons.

Using Radio Buttons—Shades of the Old SAT

I'm sorry. Maybe it's because I was a round peg in a square hole in college, but there's an ominous connotation to me when I see a form that has those buttons that look like they came straight from a college entrance exam.

Okay, putting my discomfort and prejudices aside, radio buttons are a fine way to collect information if you're administering personality tests, letting people choose colors for a car interior, or having visitors decide whether to pay using VISA, MasterCard, or Discover. The really intriguing thing about radio buttons is that you can create a set of radio buttons, where *only one button can be selected*. Therefore, radio buttons typically are put together in groups.

Remember: A group of radio buttons that shares the same Group Name can have only one radio button selected by the visitor. It might be helpful to jot down the Group Name on a Post-It note, because you'll be assigning other radio buttons to the same group. I have my own trick for keeping radio button groups organized, which I show you as you walk through this. To collect information with radio buttons:

1. Click the spot on your page where the first of your radio buttons is to appear.

2. Click the Radio Button option in the toolbar, as shown in Figure 5.5.

Figure 5.5

Inserting a radio button

3. Type a user prompt for the radio button. The final graphic result is shown in Figure 5.6.

Figure 5.6

The result from entering
your user prompt

I am available:

○ **Mornings**

4. Right-click the radio button and select Form Field Properties. Then enter a group name in the Group Name area of the Radio Button Properties dialog box, and a value in the Value area, as shown in Figure 5.7

Figure 5.7

Defining a radio button

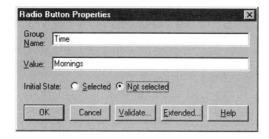

TIP

Here's my trick for remembering the group name for radio buttons—I just create one radio button, copy it as many times as needed, and change the values, but not the group name.

5. Decide an initial state for the radio button, but remember only one button in the group can have an initial state of being selected.

6. Click OK in the Radio Button Properties dialog box.

7. Add additional radio buttons with the same group name, but with different value names. You will need to type new text prompts so that your visitors know what it is they're choosing. Try my trick of using copy and paste, and changing the values for the different radio buttons, as shown in Figure 5.8

Using One-Line Text Boxes

If the type of information you want to collect (for example, your visitor's e-mail address) is a little too complex to fit into a check box or radio button, the one-line text box may be a better choice.

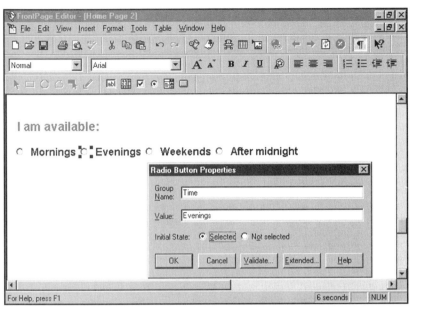

Figure 5.8

A group of radio buttons

Examples of one-line input include phone numbers, names, addresses, city, state, ZIP code, and so on. (Don't worry. If you want to give your visitors a lot of space to pontificate, scrolling text boxes are next). A little later, you will save one-line input to a file with a field name and the input, so you need to name the field something that will make sense when you try to sort through a file that collected everyone's responses. For example, you can call the phone field "phone." Call the address field "address." You get the pattern. To create a one-line text box:

1. Place your cursor on the page where the input form should appear. Click the One-Line Text Box button in the Forms toolbar, as shown in Figure 5.9.

Figure 5.9

Creating a one-line text box

2. Type a text prompt for your text box, as shown in Figure 5.10.

Figure 5.10

Name: ☐

Adding a prompt for a
text box

3. Right-click the text box and select Form Field Properties from the shortcut
menu. Enter a name for the field in the <u>N</u>ame box in the Text Box Properties
dialog box that appears. This field name does not display for visitors. The
purpose is to help you remember the information you're collecting when you
review it in the target file (see Figure 5.11).

Figure 5.11

<u>N</u>ame: Name

Naming the text box
field

4. Enter an initial value in the Initial <u>V</u>alue area only if you want to prompt
your visitor to enter certain information. If you wanted to do that, wouldn't
you be using a check box field? Not necessarily—you might want to suggest
input, but not require it.

5. Define limits for the display of width in the <u>W</u>idth in characters field and
the maximum number of characters in the <u>M</u>aximum character field.

6. You can elect to have this field be a *password field* (which means that the visitor must supply a password) or not, by selecting one of the radio buttons.

TIP

Defining passwords is beyond the scope of this session, but there is an
advantage to selecting this feature even if you're not defining a password. Password fields display as asterisks on the input screen. If you're
asking a visitor to enter sensitive information, such as a credit card number, you can select the <u>Y</u>es radio button.

7. When you've at least defined a field <u>N</u>ame (and that is the only required element of a text box), click OK in the Text Box Properties dialog box.

Drop-Down Menus

Your visitor can pick from a list of choices from the drop-down menus. Drop-down menus are more flexible than radio buttons, because you allow the visitor to choose only one option, or more than one option.

You can use CTRL +click to choose more than one option. If visitors can choose more than one of the drop-down menu items, give them a hint in some other text that they should use CTRL +click to do that, with a helpful bit of text like, "Use Ctrl + click to select more than one choice." Drop-down menus do not allow visitors to enter text— only to choose from a list you prepare. To create a drop-down menu:

1. Start creating a drop-down menu by clicking your page at the spot where the form is to appear.

2. Click the Drop-Down Menu button in the Forms toolbar, as shown in Figure 5.12.

Figure 5.12

Inserting a drop-down menu

3. Right-click in the Drop-Down Menu box and select Form Field Properties.

4. In the Name area of the Drop-Down Menu Properties dialog box that appears, enter the field name to identify this input in the target file.

5. Click the Add button in the Drop-Down Menu Properties dialog box.

6. Enter a choice in the Choice area of the Add Choice dialog box that appears.

7. In the Initial State area of the Add Choice dialog box, choose either Selected or Not Selected to determine if the initial state of the choice will be selected when the visitor pulls down the list.

TIP Remember, you can allow more than one selected choice—and you can define the initial state of more than one menu selection "Selected."

8. Use the Specify Value area if you want different information to appear in your target file—for example, if the visitor chooses, "I just want to bug you," from the menu, you can display that information as "bugging" in the results file.

8. When you have defined a menu choice, click OK in the Add Choice dialog box.

9. Use the Add button in the Drop-Down Menu Properties dialog box to add more choices to the menu, as shown in Figure 5.13.

Figure 5.13

Four choices added to the drop-down menu

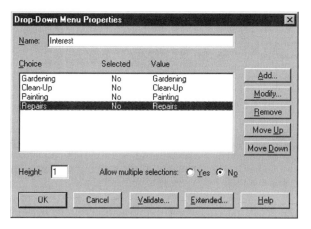

10. When you've defined the drop-down menu, click OK in the Drop-Down Menu Properties dialog box.

> You can change drop-down menu properties by double-clicking the menu in FrontPage Editor.

Using Freeform Input

If it's poetry you're soliciting, or maybe just general comments, the scrolling text box is the best choice. They call these forms "scrolling" because the box scrolls from left to right, or up and down, just like a little window on the page with its own vertical and horizontal scroll bars. scrolling text box input is also attached to a field name, so when you read it in the target file, you can tell what it's about. To gather input in a scrolling text box:

1. Place your cursor where the text box is to appear (this might be just past some helpful text like "Comments?") and click the Scrolling Text Box button in the Forms toolbar, as shown in Figure 5.14.

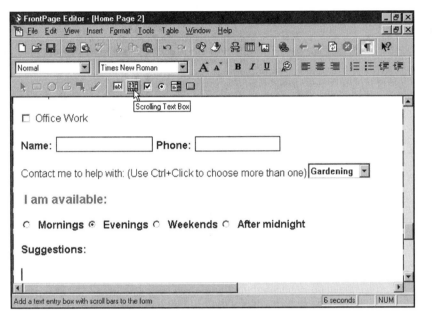

Figure 5.14

Inserting a scrolling text box

2. Right-click in the scrolling text box and select Form Field Properties from the shortcut menu.

3. Enter a field name in the <u>N</u>ame area of the Scrolling Text Properties dialog box, as shown in Figure 5.15.

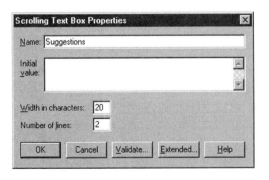

Figure 5.15

Naming a scrolling text box field

You need to enter something in the Initial value area *only* if you want to prompt your visitor with some suggested text.

The Width in characters and Number of lines fields do not constrain the amount of text that can be entered—they only define the form size. You'll learn a better way to adjust that in a minute.

4. Click OK in the Scrolling Text Box Properties dialog box when you've at least defined a name for the field.

Adjust Form Size

You can change the size of scrolling text boxes, one-line text boxes, and drop-down menus. You didn't pay too much attention to the options for assigning form size in the dialog boxes because it's easier to do this right on the FrontPage Editor page. To resize a form:

1. Click anywhere in the form. Handles (small rectangles on the top, bottom, and corners of the form) appear.

2. Click and drag on a handle to resize the form, as shown in Figure 5.16.

Figure 5.16

Resizing an input form

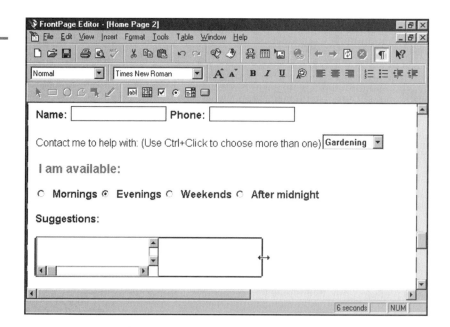

Time for a Break

So far, you've designed some very nice, if eclectic, input forms. You can allow a visitor to enter just about any kind of information. The next step is to assign properties to your forms so that this valuable information gets shuttled down the information highway to a file where you can collect and use it.

Before you move on and do that, it's time for a stretch. Take some time to create and modify input forms, and then be sure to save the page you're working on in FrontPage Editor. Assuming you started the page from FrontPage Explorer, saving your work in Editor ensures the integrity of your Web site. If FrontPage Explorer detects Web pages that are not linked into the site, it prompts you to link them when the pages are saved in Editor.

After you create some input forms, relax for a bit. Think about how you'd like to get the information that is being collected. In a text file? Something you can import into a database easily? Or perhaps in an HTML file that can be viewed using FrontPage Editor or your Web browser?

Giving the Visitors a Way to Submit Their Input

By now, you are all dressed up with nowhere to go. You've created five different types of input forms—check boxes, radio buttons, drop-down menus, one-line text boxes, and scrolling text boxes. What happens, however, when your visitors interact with your form? So far, not much. They can see their input on their own screens, but as soon as they leave your Web site, the input is gone forever.

Adding Submit and Reset Buttons

The next step in the process of actually collecting data is to create a push button that allows the visitor to submit the information they typed into the form. This Submit button is accompanied by a Reset button that allows the user to say, "Oh, never mind," and either enter new information or just give up. The Submit and Reset buttons are placed by clicking the Push Button option on the Forms toolbar.

Omitting a Reset button can be annoying to your visitors—but omitting a Submit button means you'll never see the information your visitor entered in your form. In short, every form needs a Submit button.

If you've actually been creating a Web, and following along even loosely with this book, you've got some input forms on a Web page in FrontPage Editor. As you work with the forms, you need to know these points:

❖ Input forms are bounded by dashed lines—one above and one below the form.

❖ A form can include just one input object (such as a one-line text box) or a bunch of objects (such as several radio buttons). All the input objects bounded by the dashed lines are part of the same form. Only one Submit button is required per form.

❖ When you right-click within a form (between the dashed lines), a shortcut menu that has Form Properties as one of the options appears, as shown in Figure 5.17.

Figure 5.17

Opening the Form
Properties dialog box

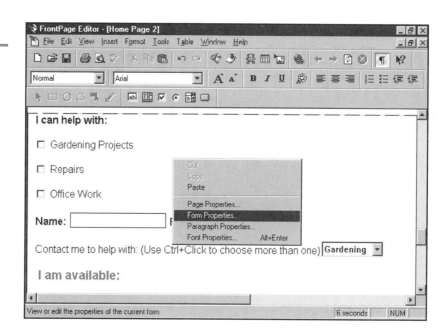

❖ If you right-click elsewhere in a page, you won't see the Form Properties option. Try it and see.

❖ Each form should have one Submit button and one Reset button.

❖ The Reset button is normally on the same line as, and right of, the Submit button.

After you create Submit and Reset buttons in your form, you'll finish the process by defining the destination and format of the information you're collecting. To place a Submit button:

1. Place your cursor after the end of your last input object—a check box, a group of radio buttons, text box, and so on.

2. If you want to place your submit button on a separate line (and most folks do), press ENTER to create a new line for the Submit button.

3. Click the Push Button option on the Forms toolbar, the button shown in Figure 5.18.

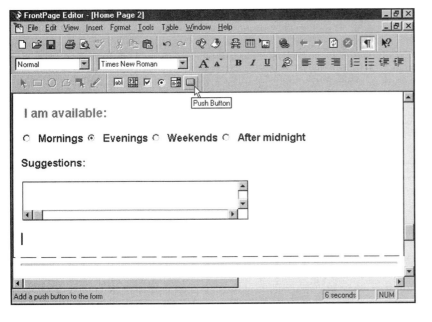

Figure 5.18

Inserting a Push button

Right-click the new Submit button and select Form Field Properties. Because all you are doing is creating a button to submit the contents of a form, a button name isn't necessary.

4. Enter additional text in the <u>V</u>alue/Label box in the Push Button Properties dialog box if you wish to edit the label that appears on the screen, as shown in Figure 5.19.

Figure 5.19

Editing the Submit button label

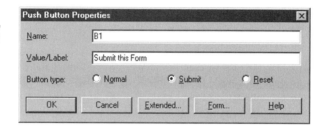

 TIP   Many Net cruisers are used to seeing the word "Submit" on Submit buttons, but you can place any text you wish on the Submit button. Even if you want to get creative, you should keep the word "Submit" somewhere on the button. You can even embellish it with "Submit Response Now," or something similar.

5. When you have edited the text that you wish to appear on your Submit button, make sure the <u>S</u>ubmit radio button is selected and click OK in the Push Button Properties dialog box. A Submit button appears in your form, as shown in Figure 5.20.

To place a Reset button:

1. With your cursor just to the right of your Submit button, click the Push Button option on the Forms toolbar.

2. Right-click the new button and select Form Field Properties from the shortcut menu. When the Push Button Properties dialog box appears, click the <u>R</u>eset radio button, as shown in Figure 5.21.

 TIP   Clicking the <u>R</u>eset radio button automatically places the word "Reset" in the <u>V</u>alue/Label area of the Push Button Properties dialog box.

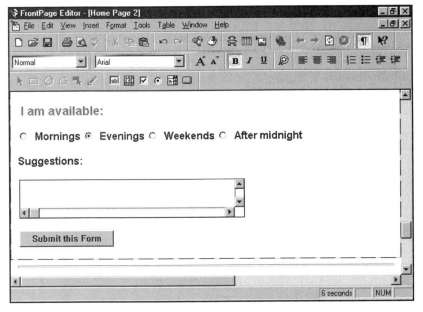

Figure 5.20

Submit this!

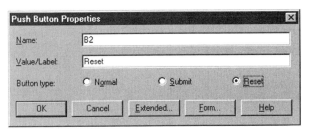

Figure 5.21

Defining a Reset button

3. You can also edit the text in the <u>V</u>alue/Label area.

TIP

There are plenty of opportunities to break new ground in designing a Web site, but this is not one of them. Visitors are likely to look for the word "Reset" if they want to change the form content.

4. Click OK in the Push Button Properties dialog box. A Reset button appears in your form, as shown in Figure 5.22.

Figure 5.22

Two choices: submit or reset

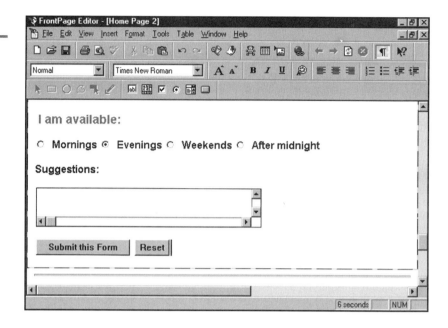

You might want to change the label on a button after you have placed it. Editing the Value/Label on a button is easy. To edit Push Button Properties:

1. Double-click the button for which you wish to edit the properties. (see Figure 5.23)

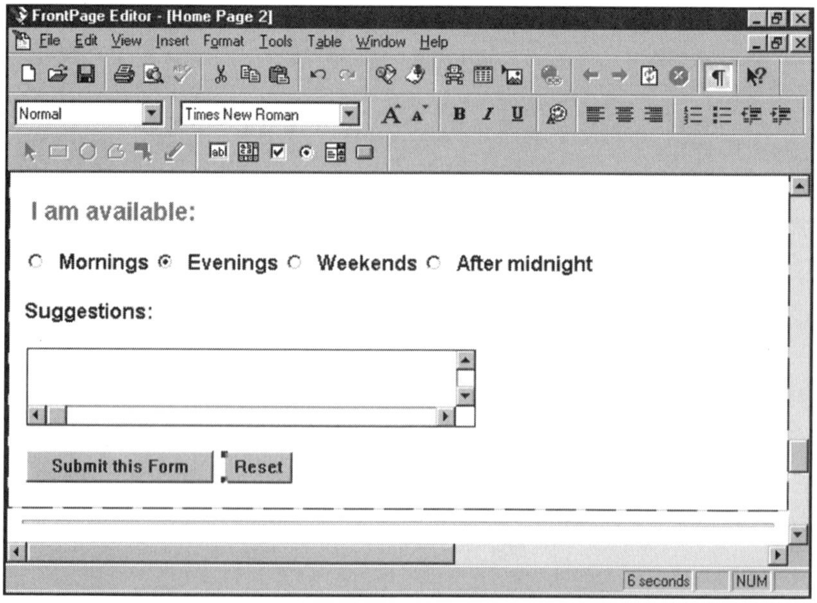

Figure 5.23

Opening the Reset Button Properties dialog box

2. Make changes in the properties assigned to the push button (see Figure 5.24).

3. Click OK in the Push Button Properties dialog box.

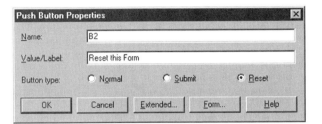

Figure 5.24

Editing the Reset button label

Using More Than One Form Within a Form Outline

You can have many Form objects within a single form outline. An input form that has radio buttons, check boxes, a drop-down menu, and text boxes is shown in Figure 5.25.

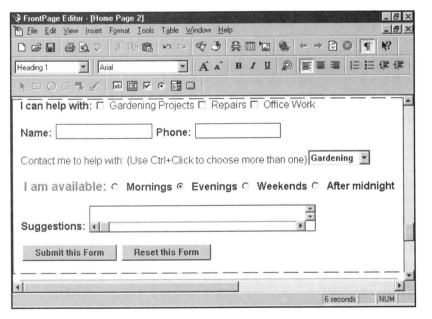

Figure 5.25

So many questions in just one form!

It is possible, and often useful, to organize your input form objects into more than one Form. For example, you might want to collect information about visitors and access that information yourself in a form that enables you to tally it, generate form letters, or just keep it out of view of your visitors. At the same time, you might want to collect information, on the same page, that is accessible to visitors. You can do this by organizing your form objects into more than one form, as shown in Figure 5.26. All of this will make more sense when you actually explore the different forms for collecting input.

Figure 5.26

Two forms—you can tell by the dotted lines around each

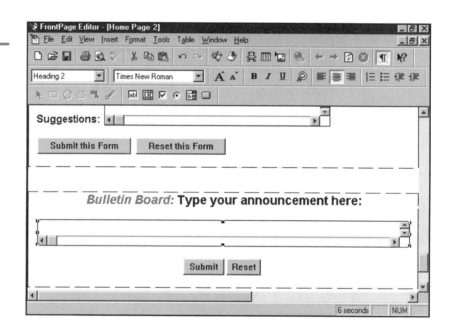

Managing Form Results

After you've defined and refined your form, it's time to decide what should happen when a visitor clicks on the Submit button. In the old days ("BF", Before FrontPage), HTML coders who wanted to collect input in forms had to either create or borrow executable programs written in programming languages, such as Visual Basic or Perl. These batches of programming code were called CGI (Common Gateway Interface) scripts. In fact, what most folks did to create a form was to find pre-fab CGI scripts at Web sites and plug them into their HTML code. Thank goodness that FrontPage lets you move past having to deal with CGIs.

In FrontPage, you can use the Form Handler to determine what happens when a visitor submits input. Although the Form Handler is one of the most important components of FrontPage, it's not the most intuitive. The Form Handler offers five options for handling input:

❖ Custom ISAPI, NSAPI, or CGI Scripts

❖ Internet Database Connector

❖ WebBot Discussion Component

❖ WebBot Registration Component

❖ WebBot Save Result Component

The Custom ISAPI, NSAPI, or CGI scripts option enables you to plug in an existing, custom-coded data collection programming module. The Internet Database Connector option is used with programmed queries for Internet databases. You can use the Internet Database Connector with programs such as Microsoft Access 97 to let users work with online databases through your Web site. That process is beyond the scope of this book, but check out a good reference book on Microsoft Access 97 if this is a feature you need. The other three Form Handler options are different kinds of bots. *Bot* is short for roBot, and it's a term FrontPage uses for automated features that perform functions in Web sites. In the next session, you'll explore many of these handy little guys and the dynamic things they do in your Web site. In this session, you'll be using a bot to handle your form input.

Selecting one of the form options in the Form Handler is easy. The first trick to making sure that the option works is to ignore all the options except for the WebBot Save Results Component. Before you make that choice, take a quick look at the other options.

Custom ISAPI, NSAPI, or CGI Scripts

As a concession to those who would want to do some of their own coding, FrontPage allows form input to be handled by Custom ISAPI, NSAPI, or CGI scripts, which you can write or copy from someone.

ISAPI and NSAPI are both similar to CGI, described earlier. ISAPI stands for Internet Server Application Programming Interface, and NSAPI stands for Netscape Server Application Programming Interface. While these two competing programming languages battle it out for supremacy in the form handler coding universe, ignore them both and simply use the powerful, convenient, and easy-to-use Save Results WebBot that comes with FrontPage.

If you have written a custom script (and you most likely have not!), you can choose this option. If for some reason you feel you need to find a custom CGI script, one source is:

```
http://www.nlc-bnc.ca/pubs/netnotes/notes19.htm
```

But, if you are tempted to use a custom CGI script, hold off until you've explored what FrontPage can do without having to look for custom CGI scripts. If you don't have a custom CGI script, just be thankful that you don't need to write or copy CGI scripts anymore, and move on.

Using the Internet Database Connector

The Internet Database Connector option enables you to create a file that stores queries using the Microsoft Internet Information Server. These queries work with online databases compatible with a universal database format called Open Data Base Connectivity (ODBC). ODBC and Internet database queries are used in customized, sophisticated database applications that are well beyond the scope of this book.

If you want a system that records, stores, and helps organize input from visitors, you can manage that kind of record keeping using the WebBot Save Results Component. That's the approach you'll take here.

WebBot Discussion Components

You can use Discussion Bots to create input forms that interact with a page where other input is posted so that a visitor can read other contributions, and then add comments. That's a great feature of Web sites. However, there is an easier and better way to create a discussion page, and I advise staying away from the Discussion Bot in the Form Handler. The easier way? Use the Discussion Web Wizard if you want a full-fledged, interactive forum with generated tables of contents so that visitors can find discussion areas of interest. You'll explore it when you investigate some of FrontPage's Wizards and Templates at the end of the weekend.

 NOTE You may have noticed that you've been avoiding Wizards and Templates. The problem with jumping into Wizards and Templates right away is that the moment you want to modify them, you are going to need the skills and tools you're picking up by doing things the hard way. I'll hold off with the Wizards and Templates until you master the skills you are now learning here. That way, when you do enter the world of Wizards, you'll be prepared.

The WebBot Registration Component

Another option for handling a form is to create a Registration Bot. This bot allows you to restrict your Web site to users who have been assigned a passcode. If you want to do that, use the FrontPage Registration Page Template. That process is explored in Appendix A of this book.

The WebBot Save Results Component

The Save Results Component in the Form Handler gives you the option of collecting input in eight different formats. I'll show you all of them, but they boil down to variations on two possibilities:

❖ Saving the results to an HTML page

❖ Saving the results to a text file

If you save your results as an HTML file, your visitors can see the input with a Web browser. This is handy for creating bulletin boards and other information that should be shared by all visitors. The bulletin board in Figure 5.27 is a result of input being sent to an HTML that can be accessed by any visitor to the Web site.

Figure 5.27

Input form results displayed on an HTML page

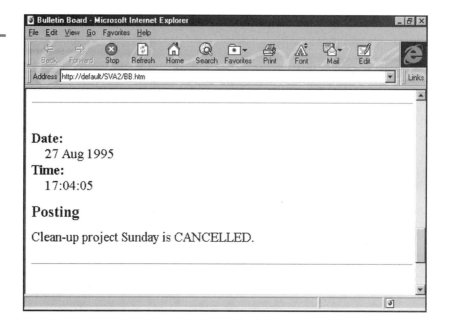

You can restrict visitors to the results page by not publicizing the URL address of the page where the input was saved. You can still view the input because you know the page where it was stored.

FrontPage gives you some variety in formatting HTML target files. Figure 5.28 shows an example of a target page using an HTML definition list with fields formatted as terms, and input formatted as definitions.

Directing input to HTML files opens up many possibilities for sharing input. Not only are your visitors getting information from your page and sending responses, they are contributing to the Web site itself. Which, in an endless loop, contributes to a dynamic Web site.

On the other hand, saving input as text files is loaded with just as much potential as using HTML pages as targets for input. Imagine collecting the names and fax numbers of everyone who visits your site and following up with a fax the next day. You

Figure 5.28

Displaying input results using HTML styles

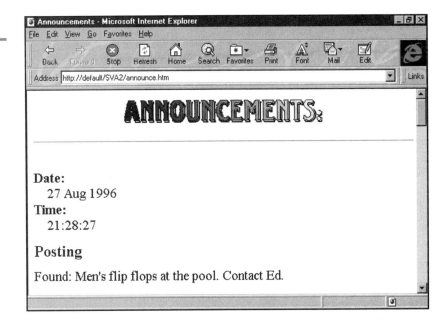

can also sort visitors by the product or topic that they indicate they want information about. The possibilities are as endless as the number of readers of this book—which hopefully is a large number.

FrontPage itself does not come with a text processor or spreadsheet. Microsoft Windows 95 does provide a crude text processor to view text-formatted input. The real fun, in my opinion, comes from dumping that input into a program such as Microsoft Word or Excel and manipulating it. Results opened as a Microsoft Word document can easily be used as data files for mailing lists. When a results document is opened in Excel, it can be edited, organized, even sorted, as shown in Figure 5.29. First, save your form input as an HTML page, and then save the input as a text file.

Figure 5.29

Input form data sent to
Microsoft Excel

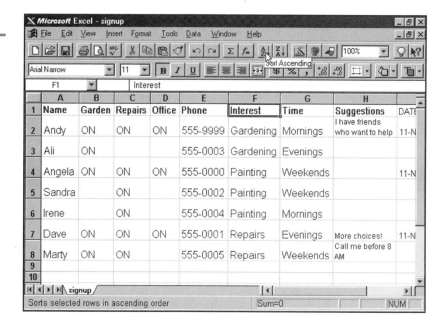

Saving Results as an HTML File

I've touched on some of the usefulness of being able to take input off the Internet and stash it in a file that visitors can view. The most expedient way to do that is to store your data to one of the four HTML formats available in the Form Handler. Those formats are listed in the following table.

In each of the four HTML file options, your visitors' input is placed in an HTML file. You, or your visitors, can go to the URL you assign this page to and see the results. FrontPage 97 places a handy bookmark at the top and bottom (a **Go to Top** hyperlink at the bottom and a **Go to Bottom** hyperlink at the top). The **Go to Bottom** hyperlink is handy—you can use it to zip right to the bottom of the list and see if anyone has contributed new input through your form. Table 5.1 provides four choices for formatting input in an HTML Web page.

Table 5.1	
Format	Results
HTML	The results are stored in an HTML page with a horizontal line separating each new entry.
HTML definition list	The results are saved in definition-list format, with a defined term and an indented definition. This is handy for input forms with two fields, such as Name and Suggestion, where you wish to indent the contents of the second field (see Figure 5.28).
HTML bulleted list	The results display as a bulleted list. This works best with single-field input forms.
Formatted text within HTML	The results go into an HTML Web page, but some formatting features display like extra spacing between fields that are not normally available in HTML.

To save Form Input as an HTML page:

1. Open a page that has a form on it. An ideal form for saving to HTML pages is something like a "Guest Book" or comments form, where visitors can share comments on your site on a topic of discussion or leave you messages. You can then make the results HTML page accessible via a link, or keep it a secret.

2. Right-click within the form to which you are assigning Form Handler properties.

3. Select Form Properties from the same shortcut menu you've seen before.

 TIP If Form Properties is not an option on the shortcut menu, your cursor is not inside a form.

4. Pull down the Form Handler list and select WebBot Save Results Component.

5. Click the Settings button and pull down the File Format list, as shown in Figure 5.30. Note that the eight format options divide into HTML pages and text documents.

Figure 5.30

Selecting a file format for collected data

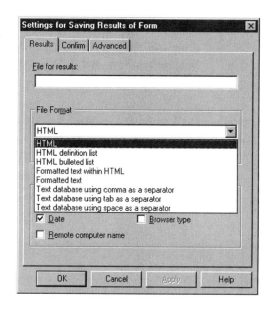

Select one of the HTML formats.

In the File for results area of the Settings for Saving Results of Form dialog box, enter a filename using eight characters or less with the old-fashioned, DOS file-naming rules (no commas, spaces). Use a filename extension of **.HTM**.

8. Select or deselect check boxes in the Results tab of the Settings for Saving Results of Form dialog box to display (or not display) the form field name, time, date, user name, browser type or Remote computer name, as shown in Figure 5.31.

TIP

If your data is being collected in a single field, including the field name in the results page will probably just clutter up the page. The other check box options add data to your results page, and you should use your discretion in filling up the page with information. Will those reading the results (including yourself) be interested in the time and date the input was sent? Often, yes. The other information? You be the judge.

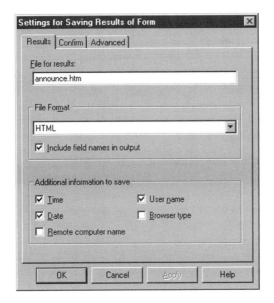

Figure 5.31

Defining a results file for input

9. Even though the URL of the confirmation page is marked "optional," you can create your own confirmation page. Because FrontPage generates a confirmation automatically, the Confirmation URL is also unnecessary.

10. When you have completed the Settings for Saving Results of Form dialog box, click OK.

TIP   The Advanced tab allows you to define a second file to save input results, which can be a different format (and must be a different filename), as shown in Figure 5.32.

11. Save the Web page with the form in FrontPage Editor.

Creating Links to Input Form Results

Because you defined an HTML (also known as HTM) file as the target for your results, you can visit the results file from your Internet browser and see the results right on the Web. That won't be possible when you experiment with saving results to a text file.

Figure 5.32

Defining an alternate results file

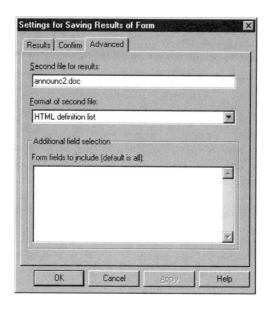

If your results file is something you want to share with your visitors, you'll want to add a convenient link so that visitors can review all the input. Create a link to your results page, and then test the Form. To create a link to a results page:

1. Save your page in FrontPage Editor, with the results for the Form defined.

2. Right-click in the Form area and select Form Properties from the shortcut menu.

3. In the Form Properties dialog box, click the Settings button.

4. Click and drag to select the filename in the File for Results area (or if it is already selected, do nothing).

5. Press CTRL + C to copy the filename to the Clipboard.

6. Cancel the Settings and Form Properties dialog boxes.

7. Type text below the form that is to become a link to the bulletin board, as shown in Figure 5.33.

TIP   You could also use a graphic hotlink here.

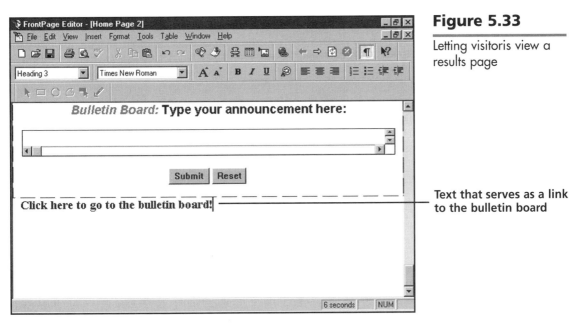

Figure 5.33

Letting visitoris view a
results page

Text that serves as a link
to the bulletin board

8. Select the text and click the Create or Edit Hyperlink button in the
   FrontPage Editor toolbar.

9. Select the Current FrontPage Web tab in the Edit Link dialog box and click
   in the Page area (see Figure 5.34).

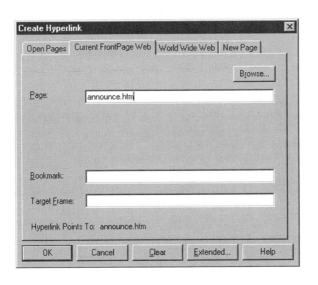

Figure 5.34

Defining a link to your
results page

10. Press CTRL + V to paste the results page filename from the Clipboard.

11. Click OK in the Edit Link dialog box.

 If you did not save your FrontPage Editor file before creating this link, you'll be warned that FrontPage can't find this file. Save the link anyway, and then save the FrontPage Editor file.

Preparing an HTML Page to Receive Form Results

The page that you designate to receive input is just like any other HTML page that you create or edit in FrontPage Editor. You can place headings, links, and edit the background on that page. And perhaps you should, especially if you wish to make the page accessible to others. To edit an HTML results page:

1. Press CTRL +click to follow the link you defined to your results page.

 If your results file does not show up as a file in your Web in FrontPage Editor, switch to FrontPage Explorer and select View, Refresh from the menu.

2. Move your cursor over the text **Form Results Inserted Here** on the results page and note the cursor turns into the little roBot, as shown in Figure 5.35.

 You're using a bot, even though you haven't explored bots yet. In this case, results from the input form get placed where the bot text indicates.

3. Place your cursor before the text **Form Results Inserted Here** and press ENTER to create a line for a heading.

4. Enter a heading for the page, as shown in Figure 5.36

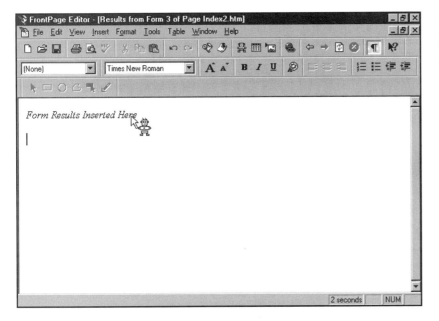

Figure 5.35

Opening the results page

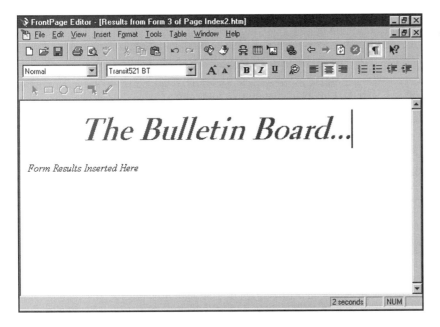

Figure 5.36

Making the results page a friendly place to visit

5. Place your cursor at the end of the text **Form Results Inserted Here** and press ENTER to create a new line.

6. Place an appropriate link back to the home page for your Web site, as shown in Figure 5.37.

Figure 5.37

Don't leave visitors stranded!

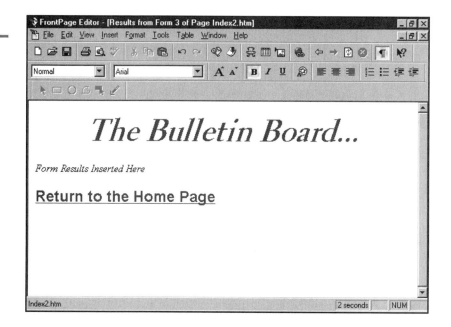

TIP Don't forget to send visitors back to an appropriate bookmark on the home page.

7. Add images and adjust background color as you would with any other page—especially if you'll be welcoming visitors to the page, as shown in Figure 5.38.

8. Save changes to your results file.

Did you save changes to *all* the Web pages you've worked on in FrontPage Editor? Just checking.

Figure 5.38

A results page doesn't have to look dull.

Testing Your Input Form

Now that you have defined a results file, you have completed the most complex part of creating a Web site that you've tried so far. From here on in, it's all easy street—provided that the form you created actually works!

To test your form, use a Web browser. Testing your form ensures that it works and gives you a visitor's perspective so that you can make adjustments, if necessary, to make the form clear and easy to use. To test your form:

1. Open the page with your input form in FrontPage Explorer. Save it.

2. Use the Preview in the Browser button located on the FrontPage Editor toolbar to open your Web page with an input form using your Web browser.

3. Enter, and submit, several messages in your form, as shown in Figure 5.39.

TIP   Each time you submit a form, FrontPage provides a confirmation message and a link back to the Form, as shown in Figure 5.40.

Figure 5.39

Hello? Hello? Can anybody read this?

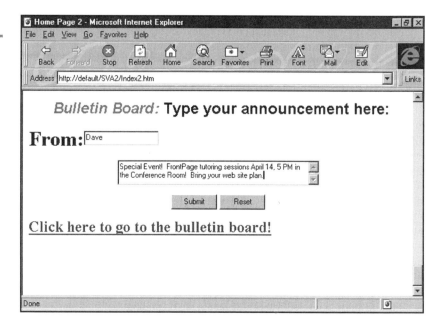

Figure 5.40

Confirmed!

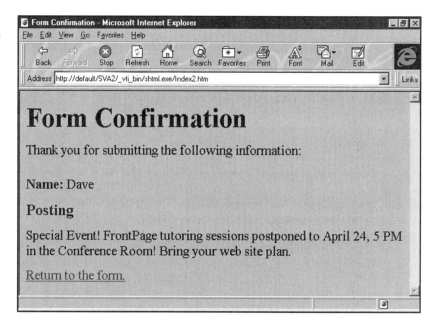

4. When you have submitted a few messages to your form, follow your link to the results page or type the address of your results page in the URL area of your browser, as shown in Figure 5.41.

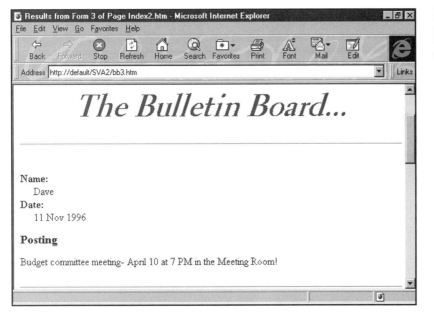

Figure 5.41

Results—posted on a Web page

Maintaining a Bulletin Board

You (or others) may decide that, as Web administrator, it is your responsibility to edit the contents of a visitor-accessible page.

A full discussion and debate of ethics, freedom of speech, and good taste is beyond the scope of my job here. But, *somebody* has to take responsibility for the contents of an accessible Web site and touch it up from time to time. One approach used by many Web site administrators is to delete comments when necessary, but to acknowledge that the page was censored by replacing the offending comment with a message like, **A comment was deleted here for violating the Web site rule against bad grammar**, or something similar. To edit visitor input in a results page:

1. No need to exit your Web browser, you can edit a page even as it is being accessed by visitors.

2. Open the results page in FrontPage Editor.

3. Edit the results file, just as you would any other FrontPage HTML file, by cutting, pasting, or editing text. Site administrators will be tempted to become powermad, as shown in Figure 5.42.

Figure 5.42

Censoring in
FrontPage Editor

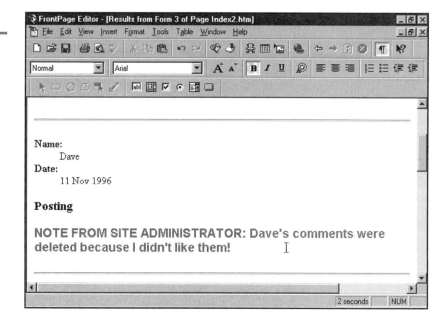

4. After you have edited the results page, save your changes and reload the page in your Internet browser. Edited changes to the page are reflected when you visit your page with your browser, as shown in Figure 5.43.

Figure 5.43

Dave's comments—
censored!

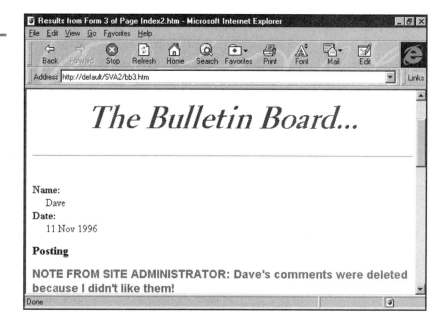

Saving Results as a Text File

I've touched on some of the usefulness of being able to take input off the Internet and stash it in a file that can be used to tabulate a poll, generate form letters, or just print a report. The most expedient way to do that is to store your data to one of the four text formats available in the Form Handler (see Table 5.2).

Table 5.2	
Format	Results
Formatted text	This is the way to save text that you want to be able to read in your word processor.
Text database using comma as a separator	This format saves input and places a comma between fields. If you're using a database or spreadsheet that supports "comma-delimited" text (and many do), try this format.
Text database using tab as a separator	This format works like comma-delimited text (preceding), but it places a tab between fields. This format works nicely for importing data into Microsoft Word or Excel.
Text database using space as a separator	Chances are your database, spreadsheet, or word processor prefers tab or comma-delimited fields to space-delimited fields. Those space-delimited fields can be unreliable given that your input will probably also have spaces. It's an option, but you don't have to use it.

These four text output options are of two main types—formatted text and delimited text. Formatted text is easier to handle if you want free-form word processing. Delimited text is necessary if you'll be dumping the input results into a spreadsheet or database—or even a Microsoft Word file where you want to organize the data in a table.

Using a Formatted Text File as a Target for Input

The main difference between sending input data to an HTML file (as you did earlier) and sending it to a text file is that a text file is not accessible on the Web with your Internet browser. You can probably open an HTML file with any of today's hi-tech word processors, but that's not going to be the most convenient form to edit your input data.

When you save input to a formatted text file, you can open the text file from FrontPage Explorer, which automatically launches your default word processor. You can set the file to launch a word processing program such as Microsoft Word by using an appropriate extension when you assign a target filename, as you shall see. To send input data to a formatted text file:

1. Right-click the Form with the data that is to be sent to a formatted text file.

2. Select Form Properties from the shortcut menu.

3. Select WebBot Save Results Component from the Form Handler list, as shown in Figure 5.44.

Figure 5.44

The WebBot Save Results Component does it all

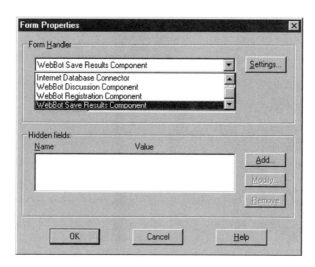

4. Click the Settings button in the Form Properties dialog box.

5. If you have already defined one results file, and you wish to add a second one, click the Advanced tab in the Form Properties dialog box, as shown in Figure 5.45.

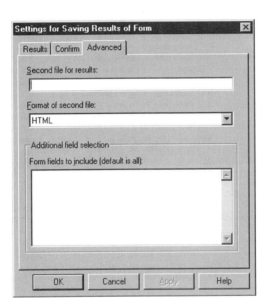

Figure 5.45

Results can go to an HTML page *and* a text file

TIP You have the option of, for example, saving results to a visitor accessible Web Page in HTML format and to a formatted text page as well.

6. Enter a filename for the formatted text file in the appropriate area of the Settings for Saving Results of Forms dialog box. This will be different and depends on whether you are defining just one file in the Results tab, or a second results file in the Advanced tab.

TIP This is one of my favorite tricks: If you attach the filename extension *.doc to your filename, you can open the file in Word directly from FrontPage Explorer (see Figure 5.46).

Figure 5.46

Input results will go to a text file with a *.doc filename extension

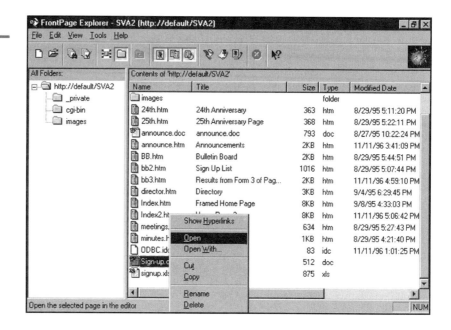

7. Click OK in the Settings for Saving Results of Form dialog box as well as the Form Properties dialog box.

You can then test a form that sends results to a formatted text file using your Internet browser, just as you tested the form that sends results to an HTML page. One difference is that you won't be able to review your results with your browser—you'll need to open the results file from within FrontPage Explorer. To test a form sending input to a formatted text file:

1. Save your page with the defined Form in FrontPage Editor.

2. Open the Web page with the input Form using your Internet browser.

3. Enter data in the form, just as you did earlier with a form that saved input to an HTML page. Fill out and submit several test input forms so that you can give your system a real workout, as shown in Figure 5.47.

NOTE You've done all of this before, and so far the process is the same no matter where the input is going.

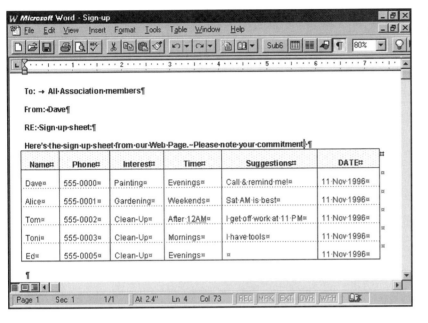

Figure 5.47

Will this data really end up in a text file?

4. Switch to FrontPage Explorer.

> **TIP** If you have not sent input to your formatted text file, the file is not yet showing in the Folder View.

5. Select <u>V</u>iew, <u>R</u>efresh from the FrontPage Explorer menu to update the file list in Folder View.

6. When the FrontPage Explorer Folder View is refreshed, the new text format results file is listed in Folder View. Right-click the file and select Open from the shortcut menu, as shown in Figure 5.48.

7. If you open your results file in your favorite word processor, you can format the text any way you like. Input results can become part of a report, a table, or a memo—the possibilities are endless. One use of input form results is shown in Figure 5.49.

Figure 5.48

Opening the results file in your word processor

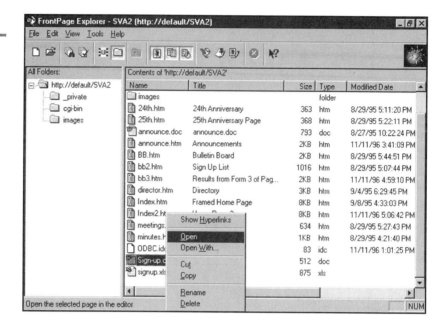

Figure 5.49

From the Internet to your word processor

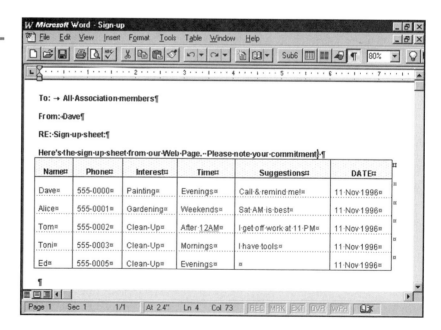

TIP If you wish to define or change the default word processor that opens filenames with a set extension, you can use the Configure Editors tab in the Options dialog box, which is accessed from the tools menu (see Figure 5.50).

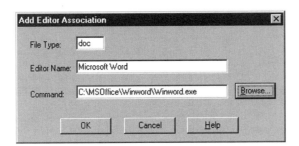

Figure 5.50

Configuring your word processor to mesh with FrontPage

Using a Delimited Text File as a Target for Input

There's no big wall between working with formatted text and delimited text—they both stash input in a text file that is accessible with a text editor. Delimited files do, however, fit nicely into spreadsheets and database files, so they have some unique advantages that are worth exploring in their own right.

Again, my little trick of using a filename extension to launch an application from FrontPage Explorer might come in handy. You can use an ***.xls** filename extension with a delimited text file and jump right into viewing your input in spreadsheet format.

 TIP Each time you get input from visitors, your results file changes. New data gets appended to your results file. If the results are being saved as text, more text gets stuck on at the end. To refresh the text file, don't open the file from your word processor. That will be an old file that doesn't include new results. Instead, open the file and launch your word processor by opening your text file from FrontPage Explorer.

To use delimited text results with a spreadsheet:

1. Right-click a form with fields that work well in a spreadsheet format and select Form Properties.

 TIP A one-field form isn't that useful in a spreadsheet format.

2. Select the Save Results Bot from the Form Handler list.

3. Click the Settings button.

4. Select Text database using a tab as a separator from the File Format list.

 TIP The tab-delimited text format works smoothly with Excel.

5. Enter a filename in the File for Results area, with an *.xls filename extension, as shown in Figure 5.51.

Figure 5.51

Defining a results file with an *.xls filename extension

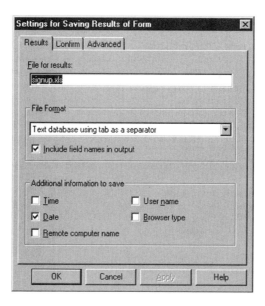

6. Click OK in the Settings and Form Properties dialog boxes.

7. Save your page with the Form in FrontPage Editor.

8. Open the Web page using your Internet browser.

9. Enter data in the form, just as you did earlier with a form that saved input to an HTML page.

> **TIP** Use the Submit button and the Confirmation Form to take you back to the Form.

10. It is not necessary to exit your browser to view or edit the Form results. Switch to FrontPage Explorer and use View, Refresh to update the file list in Summary View.

11. Double-click the new results file in the Summary View of FrontPage Explorer to launch an associated application for your new file.

> **TIP** If you added an ***.xls** extension to the filename, and you have Excel on your computer, you'll see (and be able to format or edit) the results in Excel (see Figure 5.52).

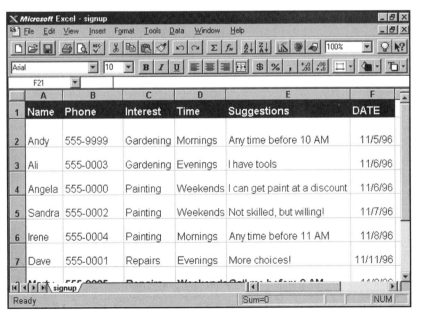

Figure 5.52

Web input results in an Excel spreadsheet

What's Next!

At this point in the process, you've constructed a powerful Web site. The site looks good; you accomplished that early in the game with formatting, graphic images, backgrounds, and tables. It's hyperlinked with easy-to-follow links to bookmarks, other Web pages on your site, and to the Internet.

In this session, you added a whole new dimension to your Web site—the ability to interact with your visitors. You explored methods to collect and save input that made that input accessible to visitors on the Web, as well as diverting that input to forms where you can organize it off the Web and use it any way you wish.

You might conclude that you've got enough tools now to create a really functional Web site—and you do. If you're itching to put the site up on the World Wide Web right now, I can't blame you.

You will, however, find some features in the next session that give your site a more polished look and feel—things such as header and footer files that provide continuity between all the pages in your site, annotations that can only be ready by you (and not your visitors), images or text that go away at a set date, search engines to help visitors find just what they're looking for, generated tables of contents, and more.

In short, stay tuned. In the next session, you'll explore some features that are loosely lumped together under the heading of "Bots," which will put the finishing touches on your site. Finally, at the end of the weekend, you'll walk through the process of copying your site to an Internet Service Provider who can host your page for you. I help you find a friendly one.

So take a break, a real one this time. You have accomplished quite a bit. A truly professional Web site is within sight!

CHAPTER 6

Sunday Afternoon:

Activating FrontPage's
Handy RoBots

s Web cruisers become more sophisticated, the excitement of simply finding information on a Web site begins to wane. Your visitors have seen many Web sites, so you should make your site as pleasant and convenient a place to visit as possible. This helps to draw visitors to, and maintain their interest in, your site.

You've already done much of that. Your site has tastefully formatted text and headings, and included graphic images and plenty of convenient links that allow your visitors to jump here and there (and back). In the last session, you created input forms that allow visitors to interact with the site in a number of ways—from posting an opinion to placing an order. Still, folks have come to expect some features in professional Web sites that you don't have yet. Those features may include:

❖ A table of contents

❖ A search box so that visitors can find items of interest in your site

❖ Footers or headers that are uniform from page to page

❖ Objects that appear (and disappear) on your site according to a set schedule

Your site may not have these features yet, but it will. I promised you that designing forms and assigning form properties would be the most complex thing you'd do. With forms under your belt, you'll find the features you create in this session fun and easy, and after you've explored them all, you'll probably find several to enhance your Web site.

What Are WebBot Components?

WebBot Component is short for roBots. FrontPage's robot metaphor comes from the capability of WebBot Components to interact dynamically with your site. For example, a Timestamp WebBot Component changes whenever your site is updated.

A Table of Contents WebBot Component regenerates a table of contents every time a new page is added to the site. A Replace WebBot Component places information from FrontPage Explorer on a page and changes that information when the data in FrontPage Explorer changes.

In short, WebBot Components are a set of handy, automated functions that FrontPage provides to plug into your Web site. Together, they give you the ability to create a site that interacts with itself, constantly updating, changing, and facilitating visitors' needs.

Types of WebBot Components

The Insert WebBot Component menu lists eight WebBot Components. FrontPage has more—in fact, you've stumbled on at least one already. You used the Save Results WebBot Component that popped up in the Form Handler to send form input to files. Here, you'll focus on seven WebBot Components on the Insert WebBot Component menu list.

You'll also explore comments in this section. Comments work like WebBot Components. In fact, they *are* WebBots. They're just created a little differently than the other WebBots you'll work with. Comments are listed in the Insert menu by themselves, not as part of the Insert WebBot Component list (see Table 6.1).

Table 6.1	
Type of WebBot Component	Description
Comment	Adds text that can be viewed in FrontPage Editor, but is not seen by visitors to the Web site.
Confirmation Field	Part of creating a Registration page that forces visitors to their Web site to sign a Registration Form before entering.
Include	Allows you to place one Web page inside another—ideal for headers and footers.
Scheduled Image	An image appears only during an assigned time period.
Scheduled Include	A file appears only during an assigned time period.

Type of WebBot Component	Description
Search	Puts one of those handy, search dialog boxes on your page.
Substitution	Plugs in information from FrontPage Explorer.
Table of Contents	Generates a table of contents that lists each page in your site that can be updated.
Timestamp	Like the "best used by" stamps on yogurt in the grocery store, it assures your visitors that your site is fresh.

Leaving Yourself Messages with Comment Text

Comments can be viewed in FrontPage Editor, but the text is invisible to visitors to your Web site. One reason to leave these "secret messages" on your site is to remind yourself of tasks that need to be accomplished—as illustrated with the "Remember" text in Figure 6.1.

Figure 6.1

Adding a comment

If you are collaborating with other developers on a Web site, comment text can be a form for communicating with the other Web site authors (see Figure 6.2).

Figure 6.2

Using a comment
to work with
a co-developer

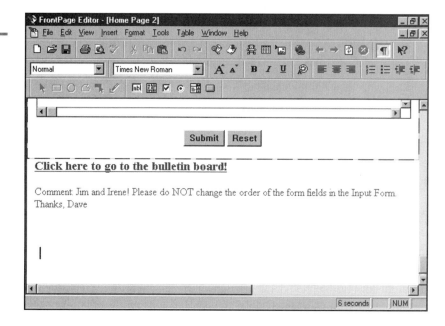

To place a comment:

1. Place your insertion point at the spot in the page where you wish to display the comment.

   TIP Because visitors do not see the comment, your only consideration is a location that is convenient to you and other developers who will read the comment text.

2. Select Insert, Comment.

3. The Insert Comment WebBot Component dialog box appears, as shown in Figure 6.3.

4. Type the comment text in the Comment area of the WebBot Component dialog box, as shown in Figure 6.4.

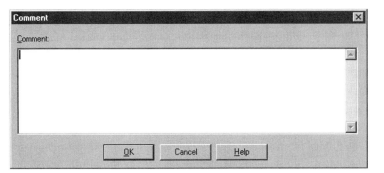

Figure 6.3

Ready for comment text

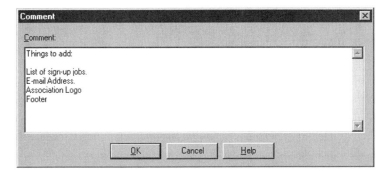

Figure 6.4

Inserting comment text in your Web page

5. After you enter (and edit, if necessary) your comment, click OK in the dialog box.

To edit annotation text:

1. Move your cursor to the comment. The cursor becomes a cute, little roBot, as shown in Figure 6.5.

2. Double-click the comment text with the special roBot cursor.

3. The Comment dialog box appears, and you can edit the text, as shown in Figure 6.6.

 TIP   You can also open the Comment dialog box by right-clicking on the comment and selecting Properties from the shortcut menu.

4. When you finish editing the comment text, click OK in the dialog box.

Figure 6.5

A friendly roBot

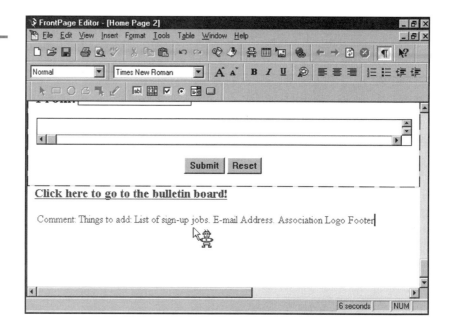

Figure 6.6

Editing a comment

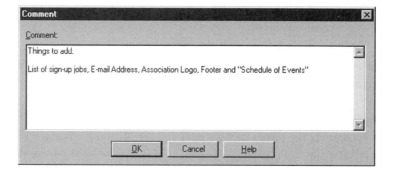

To delete a comment:

1. Right-click the comment.

2. Select Cut from the shortcut menu, as shown in Figure 6.7.

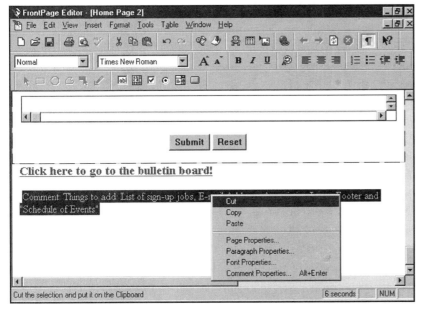

Figure 6.7

Bye bye!

Keeping a To Do List

FrontPage has another way to keep notes on needed changes to a Web site. Annotation text is fine for leaving a note on a single page, but the limitation of comment text can be an awkward way to keep track of those tasks if you have a list of work to be done—including creating new pages.

FrontPage Explorer's To Do List enables you to keep track of tasks as you work. It can mark completed tasks, and even keep a lot of the work you have done on a site (a handy feature if you're lucky enough to be billing for your work). You can keep the To Do List window open while you work in FrontPage Explorer or FrontPage Editor, and use the To Do List window as a pop-up Post-It on the screen to remind you of required work, as shown in Figure 6.8.

If your To Do List gets lengthy, you can sort it by clicking on any of the column headings. For example, if several developers are working on a project, you can click the Assigned To column heading to sort the tasks by developer, as shown in Figure 6.9.

Figure 6.8

The To Do List

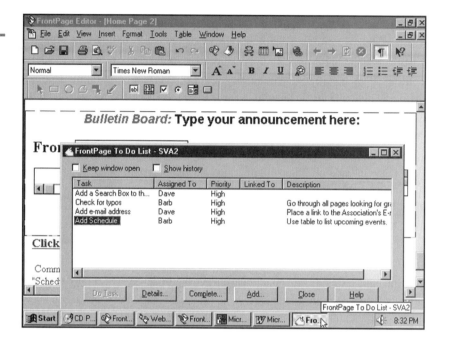

Figure 6.9

Work to do—sorted
by "Assigned To"

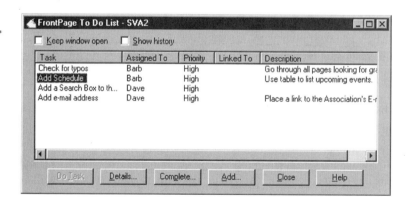

To create a To Do List:

1. Select <u>T</u>ools, Show To <u>D</u>o List from the FrontPage Editor menu bar.

2. Click the <u>K</u>eep Window Open check box in the FrontPage To Do List dialog box if you want the To Do List to remain open in a separate window after you add or edit tasks.

3. Click the <u>A</u>dd button in the To Do List dialog box to add a new task.

4. Enter a short description in the <u>T</u>ask Name area of the Task Details dialog box, as shown in Figure 6.10.

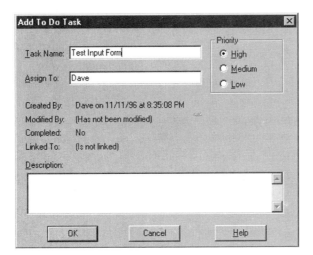

Figure 6.10

Adding a task to the To Do List

5. You can edit the name of the person responsible for the task in the <u>A</u>ssign To area of the Task Details dialog box.

6. You can select a Priority by using the <u>H</u>igh, <u>M</u>edium, or <u>L</u>ow radio buttons.

7. You may type a longer explanation of the task in the <u>D</u>escription area, if necessary.

8. When you have completed the Task Details dialog box, click OK.

To edit a task in the To Do List:

1. Click the task in the To Do List.

2. Click the <u>D</u>etails button.

3. Make any changes to the task details and click OK in the Task Details dialog box.

FrontPage has two ways to remove a task from the To Do List. You can mark it completed, but leave it as part of the list (helpful if you're keeping track of your work on a project), or you can delete it. To remove a task from the To Do List:

1. Click the task in the To Do List.

2. Click the Complete button.

3. If you wish to keep the task on your list, click the Mark This Task As Completed radio button in the Complete Task dialog box, as shown in Figure 6.11. If you want to delete the task, click the Delete This Task radio button.

Figure 6.11

This task is done!

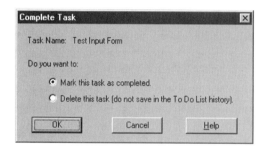

4. Click OK in the Complete Task dialog box.

5. Click the Show History check box in the FrontPage To Do List dialog box to display completed tasks. Completed tasks have the date the task was finished in the Completed column, as shown in Figure 6.12.

Figure 6.12

A To Do List—with completed tasks

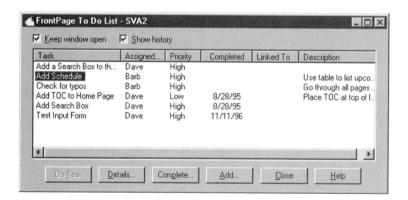

6. If you can't see an element in the dialog box, you can adjust column widths in the To Do List by clicking and dragging on the lines between column names, as shown in Figure 6.13.

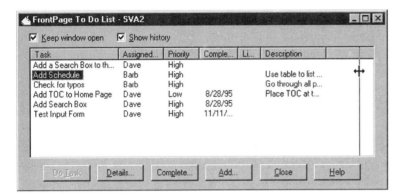

Figure 6.13

Adjusting column width

TIP

The Linked Page element of the To Do List is designed to work *only* when you create a site using FrontPage Templates and Wizards and is not available for individually created lists.

Attaching Headers and Footers with the Include WebBot Component

As your Web site expands, you'll find it handy to create headers and footers. Headers and footers can be separate files that appear on the top and bottom, respectively, of any Web page. They can also have images and links. One user-friendly approach is to have links to pages in the footer so that when your visitors scroll to the end of a page, they can easily jump directly to any page.

With your Copy and Paste skills, you *could* just create some text, or even an image to go at the top of each page, and copy it everywhere in your Web. The advantage of creating a separate header or footer page is that when you edit that page, FrontPage automatically updates the headers and/or footers on each page where the file was inserted. All this is possible through the Include WebBot Component. To create a footer:

1. Create a footer in a new file from FrontPage Editor, something like the one shown in Figure 6.14.

Figure 6.14

Creating a footer page

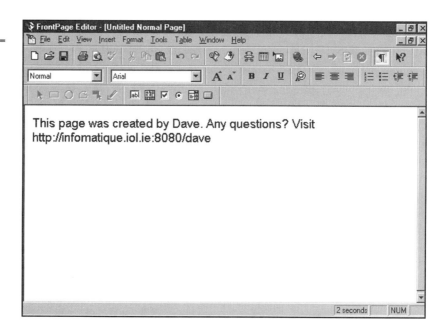

 TIP Don't worry about a background for this page—it will adopt the background of the pages it is inserted in.

2. Add the text for your footer and format it as Heading 6. As you noticed when you first started formatting, this style isn't really a heading at all, but is great for fine print.

3. Insert any graphics or links that you want included in your footer.

4. Traditionally, footers are saved with the filename **Footer.htm**. Try that.

If you have created and saved a **Footer.htm** page, it's time to insert it into other pages on your Web site. To include a page:

1. Open or go to the page on which you will include the footer (or header).

TIP You can move to any open page by pulling down the Window menu, shown in Figure 6.15, and then selecting that page.

Figure 6.15

Switching windows

2. Place your cursor at the bottom of the page if you are inserting a footer (the top for a header).

3. Select Insert, WebBot Component.

4. Double-click Include.

5. In the WebBot Component Include Properties dialog box, click Browse to see a list of saved pages in the Web site (see Figure 6.16).

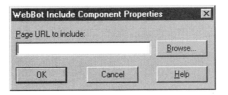

Figure 6.16

Defining an included page

6. Click the page you wish to insert from the list in the Current Web dialog box, as shown in Figure 6.17.

7. Click OK in the Current Web dialog box.

8. Click OK in the WebBot Component Include Properties dialog box.

Figure 6.17

Selecting an included page

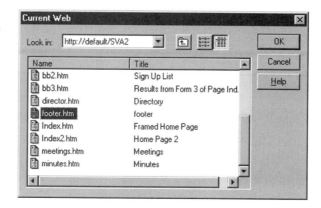

The footer will appear on the page, as shown in Figure 6.18.

Figure 6.18

The footer appears!

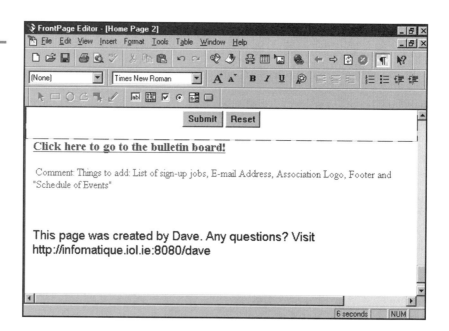

To edit an Included File:

1. Move your cursor over the included file. The cursor becomes a roBot.

2. Right-click the inserted file.

3. Select Open [the filename] from the shortcut menu, as shown in Figure 6.19.

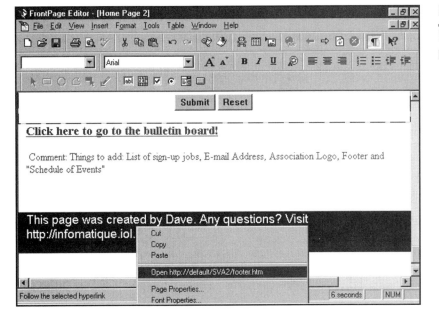

Figure 6.19

Editing an included page

4. Make any editing changes to the included file.

5. Save the included file.

6. Return to the page where the file was inserted. You can use the <u>W</u>indow menu to do this.

7. Select <u>V</u>iew, <u>R</u>efresh. This refreshes all links on the page, and the inserted file updates.

TIP Try including your footer file on several pages, updating it, and examining the changes on each page where the footer is included.

Scheduling Images

You know those late-night infomercials that end their pitch with, "If you call within the next 24 hours," you get the vegi-slicer included at no extra charge? How about print ads with offers like "expires 12/31/95" that come in a box of cereal you purchased in 1996? The purpose of these challenging philosophical questions is not simply to vent against annoying sales pitches. There are times when you want a time-sensitive message to display on your Web site. One of the valuable things about the format of a Web site is that it instantly updates. Yesterday's message is not today's message. This is true even if you are gone during the time that your message should be changing.

Microsoft FrontPage enables you to schedule images that will appear on cue, and then disappear. A picture of a skier racing down the slopes can be replaced by a diver in the swimming pool when summer rolls around. Your "24th Anniversary" logo can switch to the "25th Anniversary" at the appointed time and date, and all this can be preprogrammed.

The process of placing scheduled images involves assigning an image to appear and disappear on set dates. The Scheduled Image WebBot Component includes an option to assign an alternate image to appear the rest of the time. To place a scheduled image:

1. Before you place a Scheduled Image WebBot Component, the image (as well as any replacement image) should be imported into your Web site in FrontPage Explorer.

   TIP You explored the process of importing graphics into FrontPage Explorer in the Saturday Afternoon session of this book. A quick reminder: switch to FrontPage Explorer, select File, Import, click the Add button, and navigate to the file you want to import.

2. Place your cursor at the point where the scheduled image should appear.

3. Select Insert, WebBot Component.

4. Click Scheduled Image and click OK in the dialog box, as shown in Figure 6.20.

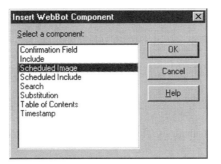

Figure 6.20

Inserting a scheduled image

5. Click the <u>B</u>rowse button in the Scheduled Image WebBot Component Properties dialog box, and double-click the filename of the image to display during the dates you will define.

 TIP   The scheduled image filename appears in the Image to include area of the Scheduled Image WebBot Component Properties dialog box, as shown in Figure 6.21.

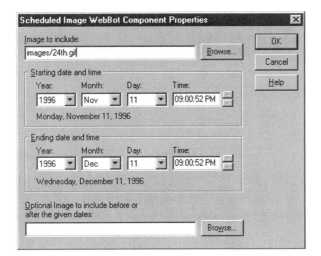

Figure 6.21

Scheduling an image— as easy as program- ming your VCR

6. If you want to define an alternate image that will appear when the scheduled image "isn't scheduled," click in the <u>O</u>ptional Image to Include Before or

After the Given Dates area of the Scheduled Image WebBot Component Properties dialog box, and click the Bro<u>w</u>se button.

7. Double-click the filename of the image to appear when the scheduled image is *not* scheduled to display. The alternate image filename appears in the <u>O</u>ptional Image area of the Scheduled Image WebBot Component Properties dialog box, as shown in Figure 6.22.

Figure 6.22

Selecting an alternate image to appear

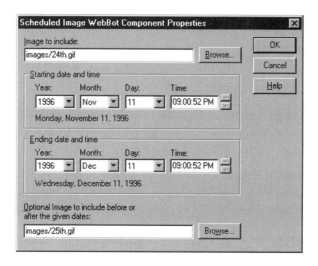

8. Type the date to start the display of the scheduled image in the <u>S</u>tarting Date and Time area of the Scheduled Image WebBot Component Properties dialog box.

 TIP You need to follow the format that the date is currently displayed in— two characters for the day of the month, followed by a three-letter abbreviation for the month, and the time in 24-hour military time.

9. Enter the time and date the scheduled image should "turn off" in the <u>E</u>nding Date and Time area, and click OK in the Scheduled Image WebBot Component Properties dialog box.

10. Save the page with the included scheduled image.

TIP   If you defined an optional image, one or the other of your two images will display.

Scheduling Inserted Pages

Including a page within a page is not a new concept. You already inserted an included footer page. The Insert Scheduled WebBot Component allows you to do that with a twist—you can restrict the inserted page to a defined schedule.

To schedule an inserted page, you need two, maybe three, pages: a page that will host the inserted page, a page to insert, and an alternate page to insert. The process goes much more smoothly if both (or all three) pages are ready to go before you start working with the Scheduled Include WebBot Component. Two different pages that could be used as scheduled included pages are shown in Figure 6.23.

Figure 6.23

Alternate scheduled images

TIP You can view all open pages by selecting Window, Tile.

If your creative juices are stimulated sufficiently by my example, or you have a better idea of a scheduled inserted page, try it. To place a scheduled, inserted page:

1. Create a page to insert—two pages if you'll be assigning an alternate inserted page to display when the scheduled inserted page is "not scheduled."

NOTE When you created footers, you used inserted pages. The difference here is that the inserted page(s) display only on schedule.

2. Make sure that you have saved the page to insert as well as the alternate page, if you are creating one.

3. Place your cursor in the spot in your page where the scheduled inserted page is to appear.

4. Select Insert, WebBot Component and click Scheduled Include.

5. Use the Browse buttons to select a scheduled page file and an alternate page file.

6. Enter dates to turn the scheduled, inserted file "on" and "off."

TIP This part of the process is identical to defining parameters for a scheduled image. Your Scheduled Include WebBot Component Properties dialog box should look something like the one in Figure 6.24.

7. When you have defined the scheduled included file (and, optionally, an alternate file), click OK in the Scheduled Include WebBot Component Properties dialog box. If you scheduled your included file to appear today, it should display on the page as shown in Figure 6.25.

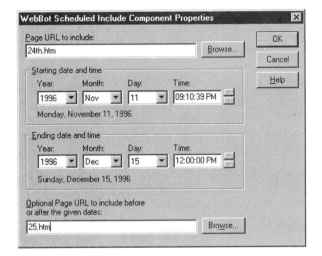

Figure 6.24

Getting ready for the 25th anniversary

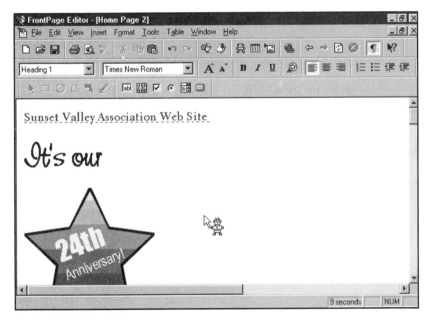

Figure 6.25

The scheduled image will change when the SVA turns 25.

To edit a Scheduled Include WebBot Component:

1. Move your cursor over the Scheduled Include WebBot Component object. The cursor becomes a roBot, as shown in Figure 6.25.

2. Double-click the Scheduled Include WebBot Component object and make changes in the Scheduled Include WebBot Component Properties dialog box.

 TIP   You can change scheduled include dates or the included page(s).

Click OK in the Scheduled Include WebBot Component Properties dialog box when you've completed editing your Include parameters.

Helping Visitors Search Your Site

If your Web site is a short, single page, you don't need a search box to help your visitors find exactly what they're looking for. But, if you have many pages, long pages, or both, it's helpful to provide a search box for visitors.

The search box that FrontPage creates isn't intuitive—it just searches for text. For example, if you have information in your site on pricing, don't expect a visitor to get there by searching for "cost." They must use the same wording that you use, so you must either include some explanation with the search box you create, or try to include text within your page that searchers are likely to look for.

Placing a search box in your Web site is really easy. After you place the search box, you can touch it up with a little explanation, some helpful tips, and a heading.

The final step in creating a search box is to test it. Testing your search box helps you to refine the relationship between anticipated search terms and your text. If you try out your search box and don't find what you hoped to find, the solution is to add text to your pages. To create a search box:

1. Place your cursor where you want to insert the search box.

 TIP   You may want to place the search box (or a link) at the top of your home page.

2. Select <u>I</u>nsert, WebBot Component, and double-click Search.

3. The Search Input Form section of the Search WebBot Component Properties dialog box should look familiar because you are defining a one-line input form with options to rename the Submit and Reset buttons. The defaults of calling the Submit button "Search For," and calling the Reset button "Reset" should work fine (see Figure 6.26).

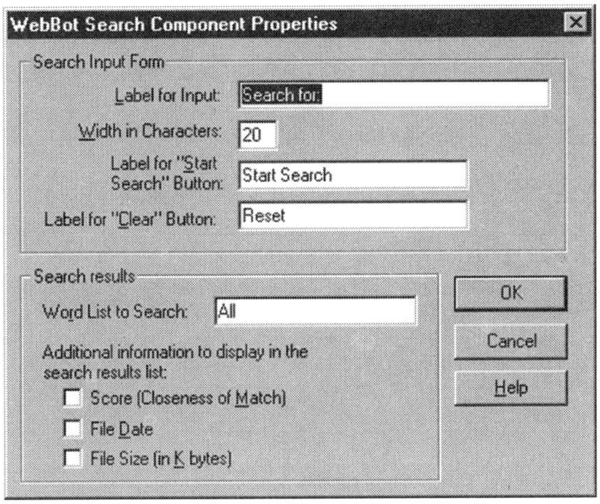

Figure 6.26

Defining a search box for your site

4. Selecting any of the check box options in the Search Results area produces a cluttered-looking results table. If you think a calculated percentage ratio of matched characters, the file creation date, or the file size are going to be of real interest to your visitors, select the check boxes for Score (Closeness of Match), File Date, and File Size (in K bytes). You can try them and change the WebBot Search Component Properties if you end up deciding that they're not that helpful. There's no real reason to tamper with the default suggestion that the Word List to Search include "All" pages.

5. When you've looked at and edited the Search WebBot Component properties, click OK in the WebBot Search Component Properties dialog box as shown in Figure 6.27.

6. You might want to add some helpful text above the search box, as shown in Figure 6.28.

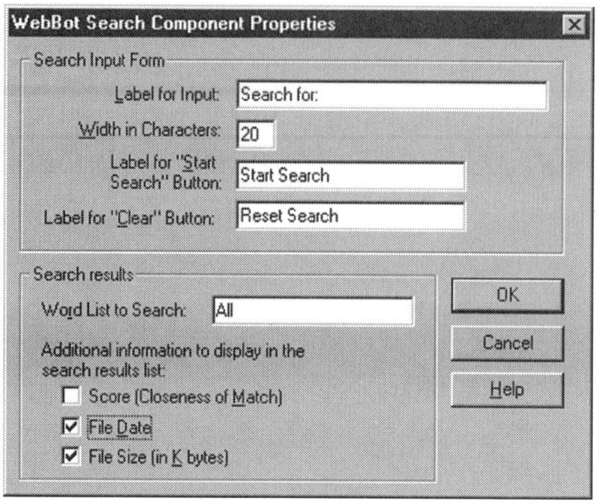

Figure 6.27

File date and size included in search results

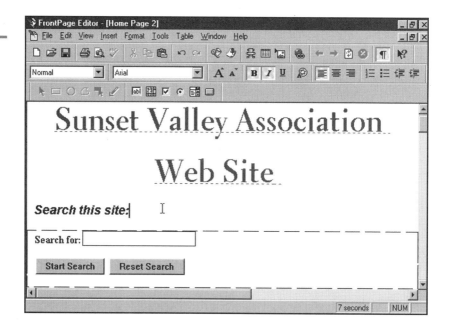

Figure 6.28

Visitors can search your site

7. Save your page to update your Web.

To edit WebBot Search Component Properties:

1. Double-click the Search WebBot Component object.

2. Edit the properties and click OK in the Search WebBot Component Properties dialog box.

3. Remember to re-save your page.

To test your search box:

1. Launch your Web browser and go to the page with the search box.

2. Try entering some text in your search box, and then click the Start Search button, as shown in Figure 6.29.

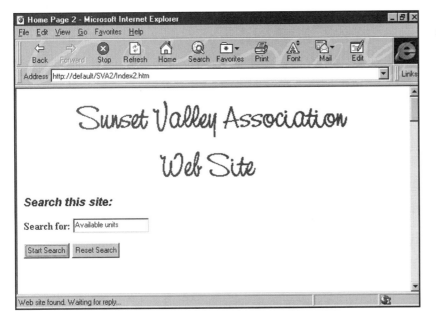

Figure 6.29

Try searching for available units

3. Examine the results of the search. A table with files that contain matching text will display with the filenames linked to the pages with matching text. If you selected the relevant check boxes, file size, date, and closeness of match will appear. In Figure 6.30, the search table shows page name, date the file was last modified, and file size.

4. Try following the links from the list created by the search.

Figure 6.30

Search results

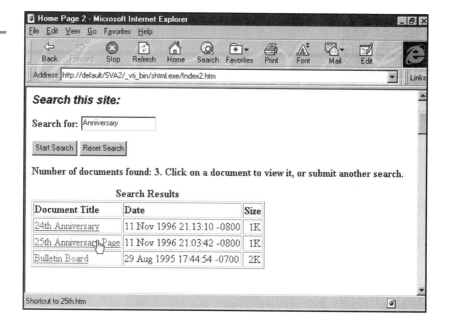

 TIP After testing your search box, you can add text to pages back in FrontPage Editor so that they are linked to search text. You can save changes in FrontPage Editor and retest your search using your Web browser—all in a nearly endless quest to provide a functional search box.

Substituting

In order to appreciate what the Substitute WebBot Component can contribute to your site, check FrontPage Explorer and see some of the Web properties it has been quietly storing. To edit file properties:

1. Switch to FrontPage Explorer.

2. Right-click a file in Folder View and select Properties from the shortcut menu. The resulting dialog box is shown in Figure 6.31.

3. Click the Summary tab of the Properties dialog box.

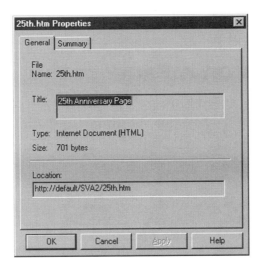

Figure 6.31

Page properties

4. Enter a comment in the Comments area of the Properties dialog box describing the page, as shown in Figure 6.32.

NOTE You cannot edit the Created date, Created by field, and modification information, but you can edit the Comments area of the Properties dialog box.

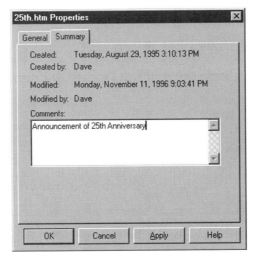

Figure 6.32

Defining page comments

5. Click OK in the Properties dialog box.

Placing Properties on a Page

Now that you've examined and created some page properties, you can plug this information into the Web page using the WebBot Substitute Component. A Substitution WebBot Component is an object that can display any of the information in Table 6.2 from the Page Properties dialog box:

Table 6.2	
Substitution Component	What It Does
Author	This is the person who created the page; listed in the Created by field of the page's Properties dialog box in FrontPage Explorer.
Modified By	This is the person who last modified the page; listed in the Modified by field of the page's Properties dialog box in FrontPage Explorer.
Description	The Description WebBot Component is replaced by whatever you typed in the Comments field Properties dialog box in FrontPage Explorer.
Page-URL	If you select this Substitution WebBot Component, the URL of the page will display.

To place a WebBot Substitution Component:

1. With the page you are editing open in the FrontPage Editor, place your cursor in the spot where the WebBot Substitution Component should go.

2. Select Insert, WebBot Component and click Substitution.

3. Click OK in the Insert WebBot Component dialog box.

4. Pull down the Substitute With list in the Substitution WebBot Component Properties dialog box.

5. Select one of the Substitution options. In Figure 6.33, I select the Description.

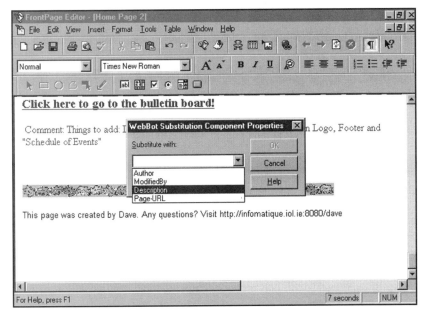

Figure 6.33

Inserting the page description

6. Save the page with the Substitution WebBot Component.

To edit a Substitution WebBot Component: You can select a *different* Substitution WebBot Component by double-clicking with the roBot cursor on the WebBot Component, as shown in Figure 6.34.

You can't edit a Description in FrontPage Editor unless you go back to FrontPage Explorer and edit the file properties.

Creating a Dynamic Table of Contents

You've already explored at least two ways to help visitors find their way around your site from your home page. You can place useful linked text and images at the top of the page, and/or you can provide a search box. A list or collection of images or text hyperlinks is what most visitors expect to find as a functioning table of contents.

Figure 6.34

Inserting Page-URL

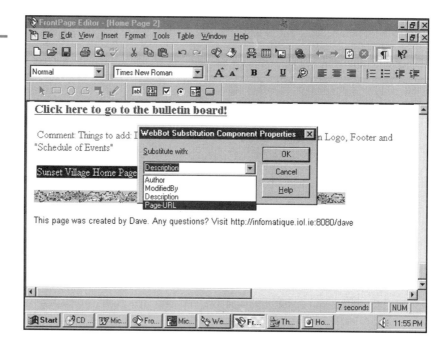

Generated tables of contents are most useful in running discussion Web sites. That's a topic to explore for those who will work with the Discussion WebBot Component in the Appendix section of this book.

Another function of a generated table of contents is to provide something like an index of all pages for your visitors. Because you're about to generate that list, rename Web pages that have default names that are not descriptive. Your visitors can then go to a page called "Bulletin Board" instead of one called "Results of Index 1," or some other equally unhelpful page title. To change a page title:

1. In FrontPage Editor, right-click and select Page Properties from the shortcut menu.

2. Along with other properties, such as page background, you can edit a Page title in the Title area of the Page Properties dialog box. Here's a title that won't be very helpful to my visitors when they see it in a table of contents— "Results from Form 3 of Page Index2.htm" (see Figure 6.35).

3. Edit the page title in the Title area, as shown in Figure 6.36.

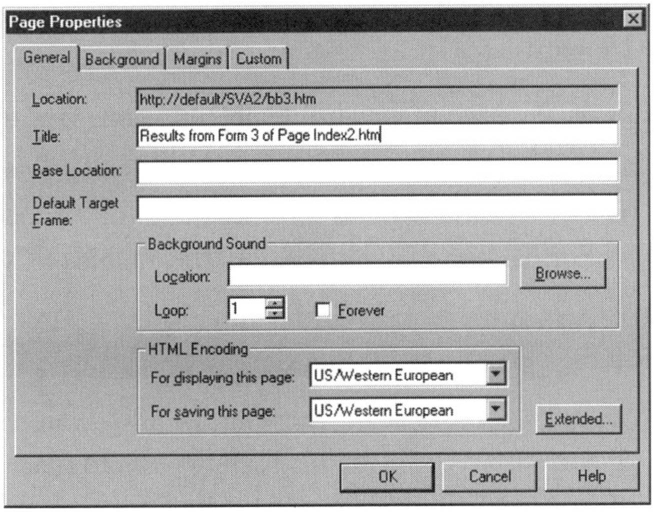

Figure 6.35

This page title doesn't tell visitors much.

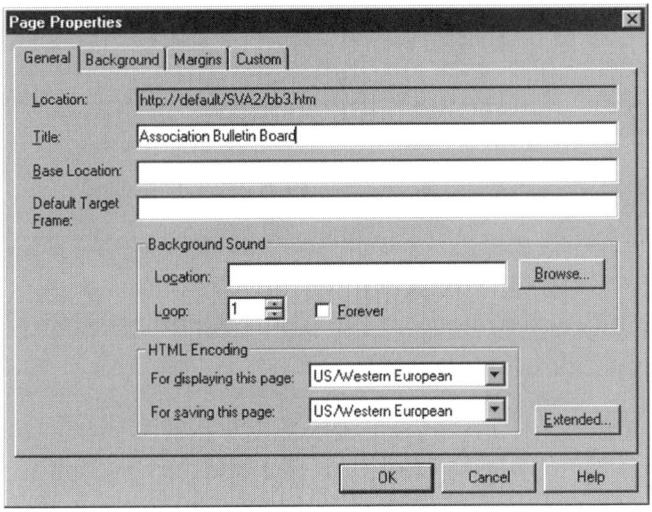

Figure 6.36

A friendlier page title

4. Click OK in the Page Properties dialog box and save the page. Now, when you generate a table of contents, the page titles will be useful and descriptive.

To generate a table of contents:

1. Place your cursor on the page in which the table of contents is to appear. You can type a heading such as "Site Contents" if you think that might help your visitors.

2. Select Insert, WebBot Component, and double-click Table of Contents.

   The default entry is your home page (**index.htm**). This ensures that all pages are listed in the table of contents.

3. The Heading Size area of the Table of Contents WebBot Component Properties dialog box, shown in Figure 6.37, allows you to make one basic decision—do you want the Home Page displayed as a title? If you want to create your own title, select "none" from the drop-down menu. If you do want to display the home page as a title, select a size for the text.

4. Click the Show each page only once check box to make sure that pages with multiple links don't end up in the table of contents multiple times.

5. Click the Show pages with no incoming links check box if you want to display pages that are a part of your Web site, but to which you have not defined links. One example might be results files from user input Forms. If you want those files accessible from the table of contents (which *will* create a link), select this check box.

6. Click the Recompute Table Of Contents When Any Other Page Is Edited check box if you want your table of contents updated each time you edit the Web and create (or delete, or rename) Web pages. This is one of the best things about letting FrontPage generate a table of contents. Normally you will want to enable this, as shown in Figure 6.37.

7. When you've completed the Table of Contents WebBot Component Properties dialog box, click OK.

8. Feel free to add your own title to the "Table of Contents"—especially if you selected "none" as your heading style in the WebBot Table of Contents Component Properties dialog box. One example of a title is shown in Figure 6.38.

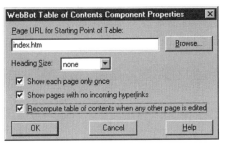

Figure 6.37

Defining a table
of contents

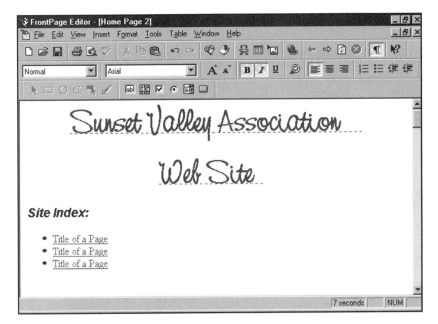

Figure 6.38

The table of contents
doesn't tell you much in
FrontPage Editor.

To test your Table of Contents WebBot Component:

1. Save the page with the Table of Contents WebBot Component.

2. Use the Preview in Browser button on your Web browser and go to the page in your Web site with the generated table of contents.

3. Test the links in the generated table, as shown in Figure 6.39.

Figure 6.39

Table of contents—
viewed with a browser

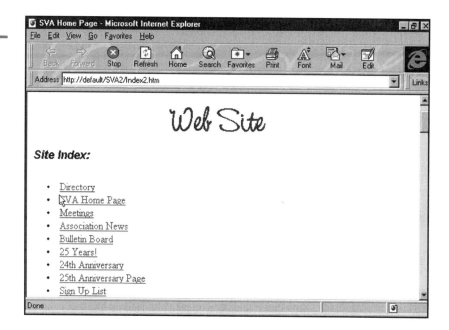

TIP

You can modify your generated table of contents by:

❖ Adding new pages and saving them

❖ Deleting pages

❖ Editing page titles and saving the edited pages

❖ Reload the page with your table of contents in your browser and watch it update

Timestamping Your Page

The finishing touch on your Web site is to place a timestamp on a page. Time-stamping is like those freshness dates you find on food at the grocery store—the ones that say "Best Used by December, 2999." One of my friends insists that this is only a "suggested" date and emphasizes that the message doesn't say you *have* to eat the food by the year 2999; it's just that the food is "best" if used by that date.

Nevertheless, many people tend to throw out items with obsolete dates stamped on them. The same goes for Web site visitors. They're looking for fresh stuff, and one way to show them you've got it is to timestamp your page.

A message indicating that your page was updated as of yesterday indicates to visitors that there's something new to see. Of course, you need to actually update the page, but FrontPage allows you to inform visitors that the page was changed even if the only change was something automatic such as a visitor adding a comment to the site or a scheduled image changing. To place a timestamp:

1. Enter the text to precede the timestamp into the page. You can use text such as, "This page was last updated."

2. Place your cursor in the position where you want the timestamp to appear.

3. Select Insert, WebBot Component and double-click Timestamp.

4. Pull down the Date Format list and select a format to display the date, as shown in Figure 6.40.

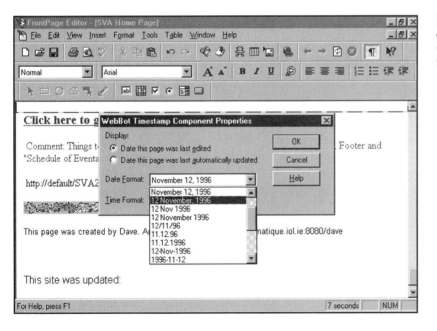

Figure 6.40

Selecting a timestamp format

5. Click the Date This Page Was Last Edited radio button to display the date you last made changes to a page and saved them.

6. Click the Date This Page Was Last Automatically Updated to display the date the page was last changed—whether by you editing it or any other saved change to the page.

7. You can select a Time Format from the list, or select "none" to display only the date.

8. Click OK in the Timestamp WebBot Component Properties dialog box and note the date displayed on your page (see Figure 6.41).

Figure 6.41

This page is fresh as of November 12.

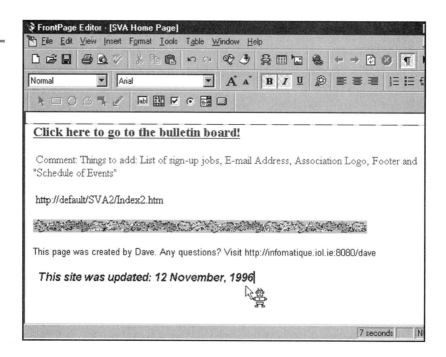

What's Next!

By now you've explored all the main features of FrontPage, and you've digested enough features to create a sophisticated Web site. What remains is to actually post your Web site. You may feel that you're ready to do that now, or you might want to deviate from the plan and experiment a bit before you finalize your site for posting.

If you've been working along with me through this book, you've had a chance to find out which features you like and which ones you won't need in your Web site.

In a sense, I've covered everything there is to learn, but in another sense, the learning and the work is just beginning because you are discovering many things as you actually do the work of creating and maintaining your own Web site.

One possibility, now that you've mastered the fundamental elements of creating Web sites in FrontPage, is to use the Wizards and Templates. They can save you some of the grunt work of manufacturing a site and allow you to edit a site to your taste and needs. Since the Wizards and Templates you are interested in will vary, depending on the type of site you're creating, I address these approaches to Web site building in appendixes. Another "scenic route" detour at this point is to browse through the appendixes and see if the Wizards, Templates, or Registration WebBot Component covered in them are things you might want to use in building your site.

After your site is created, it's time to publish it from the default Web you created on your own computer to the Internet. I've mainly been aiming this book at readers who are creating a Web site on their own PCs, and who will be copying that site to a Web they rent from an Internet Service Provider (ISP). A growing number of ISPs have configured their Web sites to work very smoothly with FrontPage. I've used many of them, and I share some advice in the next section of this book on how to find a good one, and how to shop for a good deal. I also walk you through the process of finding an Internet Service Provider, copying your Web site to the World Wide Web, and maintaining your site.

If you have been working with a site on the Internet already and posted it, you can skip through the beginning of the next session and pick up where I discuss maintaining an existing site. If your Web site is part of an intranet, you'll need to find out from your network administrator how to copy your FrontPage Web site to the local intranet server.

Of course, after you copy your Web site to the Internet, the process of improving, monitoring, and maintaining that site is ongoing, and I discuss that too. The light is shining at the end of the tunnel—you're about to get on the Net!

Sunday Evening:

Publishing Your Site on the World Wide Web

I've covered techniques that enable you to create a sophisticated, powerful, and attractive Web site. You can do more than that. The process is endless, and you will refine your Web design skills in an ongoing way as you get feedback from your site. Now it's time to publish your Web site on the World Wide Web.

You may decide to explore some of the templates and wizards in the appendixes to this book before you make your Web site available. Those appendixes address features that not everyone wants or needs in their Web site. And, after all, you are trying to get your site posted on the World Wide Web *in a weekend*! But, if you do want to include any of the following listed features, take a detour to the appropriate appendix and come back here when your site is finished. Here's a quick outline of what's covered in the appendixes:

❖ Registration forms for visitors to sign in (see Appendix A)

❖ A nice shortcut for a customer support site (see Appendix A)

❖ Dividing your Web site into independent frames (see Appendix B)

❖ Password protection to restrict entry to your Web site (see Appendix C)

❖ Including audio (background sounds) or video in your Web site (see Appendix D)

How do you get your Web site from your own computer's practice Web site to the real World Wide Web? You need:

1. A FrontPage Web site. You've been working on one all weekend.

2. An Internet Service Provider, such as The Microsoft Network, that will let you access the Internet from your computer's modem.

3. A Web site provider who will sell you space to put your FrontPage site on the World Wide Web.

Dozens of companies provide you with easy-to-access space on the World Wide Web. Publishing your site to the space they rent you is pretty simple. The hard part is doing comparison shopping to figure out what is the best deal.

I will give you some information to help you shop for a Web site provider. Web site providers offer a range of pricing, from stripped-down models to sites with some extras. I show you how to contact and bargain with these providers through e-mail, and I give you some tips on what to look for in your site provider.

After you make a deal with a site provider, FrontPage makes it easy to publish your site on the Web. Most of the providers I recommend can sign you up via e-mail and get you started immediately. Finally, in this chapter, I also discuss strategies for attracting visitors to your site.

Selecting an Internet Service Provider

In order for you to copy your FrontPage Web from the Personal Web Server on your own computer to the World Wide Web, you must be connected to the Internet. Up until now, it was possible to test your site on your own computer. Not any more. That awesome Web site of yours is ready to publish on the World Wide Web, and to do that, you'll need an Internet connection.

The folks who provide access to the Internet are called *Internet Service Providers*, or ISPs, for short. ISPs handle the process of physically connecting your computer to the Internet. They purchase Internet connections and sell you access to those connections.

It may be that you have an ISP. Gee, who doesn't these days? How could you live without e-mail? But, will your current Internet Service Provider be sufficient to publish your FrontPage Web site on the World Wide Web? Not necessarily.

Not every Internet Service Provider handles transmitting FrontPage Web sites to site providers on the Web. For example, an America Online connection does not handle this process. If you are using America Online as your Internet Service Provider (ISP), you are going to need to contract with another ISP to send your FrontPage site to the World Wide Web.

To publish your FrontPage Site on the Web, you may need to sign up with The Microsoft Network (MSN). If you have an ISP other than The Microsoft Network, try it. If there are snags in publishing your site, you probably will sign up with MSN because Microsoft made sure that MSN and FrontPage 97 would work well together.

If you are accessing the Internet with a Service Provider who will not support publishing of your FrontPage Web, you can sign up with The Microsoft Network at its Web site:

```
http://www.msn.com
```

Shopping for a Web Site Provider

Contracting for space for your Web site is a little like renting a post office box from the U.S. Postal Service. Just as the cost for renting a postal box is determined by its size, the cost for publishing your Web site is usually linked in some way to the amount of space you need for your site. The point is not to keep your Web site so small it isn't useful. But, if you know how much space you need for your Web site, you can shop around and get a good deal.

The main factors are deciding whether you want a domain name, figuring out the size of your Web site, and connecting to The Microsoft Network (or other ISP) so that you can copy your sites without problems. First, I discuss the factors involved in selecting someone to host your site.

What Features Do I Look For in a Web Site Provider?

Don't be intimidated by the prospects of selecting a Web site provider. Use this list to decide which features you need:

❖ **Reliability.**   In my experience, every Web site provider I've worked with has been pretty reliable. When I have had difficulties, I've been able to get a quick response to my e-mail questions.

❖ **Free trial usage.**   Testing how well a Web site provider handles your site before you buy can save you a lot of grief.

❖ **Technical support.**   Nearly every provider offers some type of technical support. Often, a quick way to judge the support an IPS gives is to send them a question before you commit yourself to renting a Web site from them. See how quick, useful, and friendly the response is. In general, I think you'll be happy. It isn't like shopping for a used car—the folks who provide ISP's tend to be people who really enjoy seeing your site get on the World Wide Web, and they want to help.

❖ **Speed of service.**   Some Web sites provide faster service than others, but it's difficult to determine this without testing them. Many sites provide demo pages, or other ways to test your site, before you purchase space. This will tell you more than the claims they make about their bandwidth capabilities. (*Bandwidth* is the amount of data a site provider can transfer per second, and it depends on a number of factors. However, a busy site with a faster bandwidth might end up being slower than a less busy site with a slower bandwidth— hence the need to test them out).

❖ **Acceptance of passcodes.**   If you plan to use a passcode (see the appendix on passcodes), you'll want to make sure your provider can handle that—not all of them want to.

❖ **Acceptance of e-mail.**   If you plan to use an e-mail address in a Form Handler, a feature you explored when you learned to create forms, you might want to verify it with the site provider.

❖ **Some Internet Service Providers have options for free Web sites.** Usually, the amount of space an ISP provides is too small to support a site created in FrontPage. Free space that is provided as part of other packages (for instance, by your Internet access provider) usually doesn't support FrontPage extensions, so important features of your site, such as Forms, won't work. America Online, for example, provides 10MB in space free to AOL subscribers, but it doesn't support FrontPage extensions.

After you've selected a Web site provider, they should give you the following information:

❖ The URL for your Web site

❖ The name of your domain or directory on the site

❖ A password that gives you access to your directory

Domain Names

No matter how low budget your Web site provider is, they are going to give you a URL (Uniform Resource Locator) address for your Web site. It might not be pretty. Mine, provided by my site provider, Infomatique, is

```
http://Infomatique.iol.ie:8080/dave
```

It's not fancy, but it works. What if you want an address that is really flashy? Like

```
http://IamNumber1.com?
```

To get one, you need to contract with your Web site provider for a domain name. Domain names are the "vanity plates" of Web sites. Is having "IM NO 1" on your car license plate a top priority? An easy-to-remember site license name can make it easier for people to remember your URL (site address), and it can also increase traffic to your site.

How much more traffic? If you'll be attracting visitors with a freeway billboard listing your URL (your site address), having a site name that is easy to remember is a big plus. Don't laugh. More and more companies are doing just that. A domain name is something like **DaveK.com**. The kinds of names you get at no additional cost with your Web site look like mine:

```
http://Infomatique.iol.ie:8080/dave
```

Is it worth it to get a domain name? You be the judge. Two points to consider in deciding the importance of a domain name:

❖ When someone visits your site and likes it, you can encourage them to add the site to the list of favorites that are stored by their Web browser. After they do that, they never need to remember your site address again.

❖ If visitors will be coming to your site via links with other sites (more on this later), it really doesn't matter what your site name is.

One intriguing feature that many site providers offer is a fake domain name site. Basically, the fake domain site allows you to rent space from a Web site provider without purchasing an expensive domain name, and your site gives out something that looks like a domain name to your visitors. Usually these fake domain names are cheaper than a real domain name, but more expensive than just a plain old URL like mine. One advantage of real domain names is that if you switch your Web site provider, you can take a real domain name with you.

As you'll see in the table comparing Web site cost in the "Shopping at Dave's Web Site Provider CyberMall" section of this chapter, many providers arrange for a custom domain name either at "cost," or for a fee, or both. "Cost" is usually about $200 to register a name for two years. Then, most sites charge *more* to let you *use* the domain name when you rent space from them.

Web Size and Cost

When you do comparison shopping for a Web site, it helps to know how much space you need to rent. Most ISPs have different pricing, depending primarily on how big your site is.

Unfortunately, FrontPage doesn't yet have a quick, easy way to determine the size of your site. If that feature shows up in a later version, give me some credit; I've suggested it to Microsoft many times.

Why can't you just get out your calculator and total the size of the files listed in Summary View in FrontPage Explorer? Many files associated with your Web site are not listed in the Summary View; for example, files that help handle forms.

Your "work-around" solution is to find the size of the directory holding all your files in Windows Explorer (not FrontPage Explorer, but the one that comes with Windows). Finding the directory with your Web site in FrontPage Explorer isn't easy. To estimate the size of your Web:

1. Right-click the Start button in the Windows 95 taskbar and select <u>F</u>ind, as shown in Figure 7.1.

Figure 7.1

Finding your Web site on your computer

2. Enter the name of your Web site in the <u>L</u>ook In list in the Find dialog box, and select the drive to search, as shown in Figure 7.2.

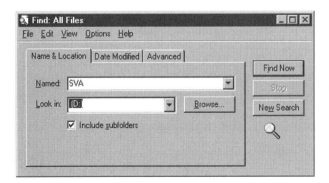

Figure 7.2

I know that Web site is here somewhere!

TIP If you're not sure which drive you installed FrontPage on, select My Computer from the Look in, drop-down list.

3. Click the Find Now button in the Find dialog box.

NOTE When the results appear, you can maximize the Find window to see the filenames more easily.

4. Scroll through the long list of files that match your search criteria until you come to a folder with the name of your Web site, as shown in Figure 7.3.

Figure 7.3

Found it!

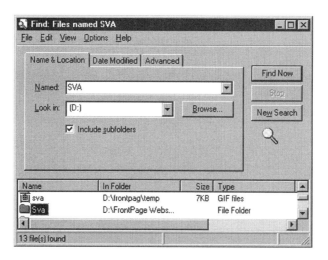

5. Right-click the file folder that has the name of your Web site in the Find dialog box, and select Properties from the shortcut menu.

6. Note the number of files in the folder, the number of directories, and the total file size, as shown in Figure 7.4.

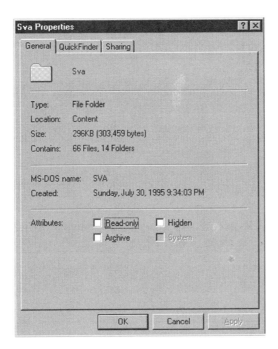

Figure 7.4

Estimating Web site size

This information may be helpful as you shop for a site provider. Being able to tell the provider, "I'm shopping for space for a site with 50 files, 14 folders (or directories), and I need 246KB of space" will, a) really impress them; b) help them give you an accurate estimate of your monthly cost to rent a site; and c) let you brag to your friends about the size of your Web site—if that's important to them. If your Web site provider is friendly, he or she will factor in additional space for discussion postings, new pages you might want to add, and so on. But knowing the current size of your Web site should be enough information for a Web site provider to give you a price.

7. Exit the Find dialog box when you copy the folder size and contents onto a large scrap of paper and stick it on your wall for future reference.

Shopping at Dave's Web Site Provider CyberMall

You can compare pricing, select a Web site provider, and in many cases publish your Web site to the World Wide Web—all in an evening. That's because you can do your shopping from your computer. Many Web site providers allow you to upload your site on a "try now, pay later" basis, or they take credit cards. After you know the size of your site and whether you have extraordinary support demands (like a password or e-mail forms), it is time to go shopping.

Not so long ago, however, finding a Web site provider who was tuned into Microsoft FrontPage was a real hassle. You are lucky that those days are gone! The following list of providers in Table 7.1, who now support FrontPage-created Web sites, is long. I've surveyed and/or tested most of the Web site providers registered with Microsoft as supporting FrontPage. If you stick with a provider on this list, you'll have no problem publishing your site to the World Wide Web. You will need to check with them to verify the pricing.

Table 7.1		
ISP Name, URL, and Contact	Selected Rates	Special Features
The ACT Group Info@ACTGroup.com 100MB—$100/mo.	Setup: $150.00 50 pages—$50/mo.	
Akorn URL: www.akorn.net e-mail: Fpsales@ akorn.net	Rates are by bandwidth utilized —contact Akorn for details.	Copy from FrontPage Free test period, Free help with design, and search listings.
AIS URL: aisnetwork.net e-mail: ais@aisnetwork.net	One-time setup fee: $200 25MB—$300/quarter	Tech support $100/hr. Domain registration for 2 years—$150
AT&T Easy World Wide Web e-mail: hotinfo@attmail.com	Rates not available via the Internet.	

ISP Name, URL, and Contact	Selected Rates	Special Features
BitShop `frontpage.bitshop.com`	No setup charge 25MB—$25/mo. 50MB—$45/mo.	Pricing includes virtual server name `(http://www.[your name]` + $25 processing fee for domain name.
Buckeye Internet Services URL: `buckeyeWeb.com` e-mail: Webslingers@buckeyeWeb.com	50MB—$75/mo. 100MB—$100/mo. 400MB—$200/mo.	Free setup, free e-mail tech support, 2 free phone support calls, and domain name registration is $100 for 2 years.
Cerfnet Call 1-800-876-2373	50MB—$20/mo. + $20 setup 100MB—$99/mo. + $99 setup	
ComCity URL: `Comcity.com` e-mail: Webmaster@comcity.com	20MB— $200 setup, $99.95/mo.	Free test period, free submission to search engines, and specializes in mortgage professionals.
TCSN	5MB—$19.95/mo. + $25.00 setup fee	
Coron URL: `www.coron.com` e-mail: bob@coron.com Call 1-800-626-6727 for more info	5MB—$50/mo.	
CrWeb URL: `www.crWeb.com/` `Webhost.html` e-mail: ron@crWeb.com	Std: 3MB—$10/mo., $4/each add'l MB. Professional: 10MB $30 + $50 setup fee.	Professional site includes use of domain name— plus $100 domain registration for 2 years.

continued

ISP Name, URL, and Contact	Selected Rates	Special Features
CSD Internetworks Professionals e-mail: CSDI@kenton.com		Discounts to non-profit organizations. Reserves the right to review con tent for illegal content. Free test period, limited tech support, and spe- cializes in international Webs. Web design available
CYFI e-mail: nleggett@cfyi.com		Training and support.
Digiserve URL: www.digiserve.com e-mail: sales@digiserve.com	5MB—$29.50/mo. Each 5MB add'l $2.50/mo.	7 days support and online support forum.
Digital Publishing Resources e-mail: Webmaster@digipub.com Call 713-948-2626 for rates		
FrontPage Now URL: frontpagenow.com e-mail: sales@frontpagenow.com	5MB—$14.95/mo. 10MB—$29.95/mo. 20MB—$50/mo.	$50 rate includes domain name. $150 for 2 years of domain name registration.
HiWay Technologies URL: www.hway.net/frontpage e-mail: sales@hway.net	20MB—$24.95. 50MB—$49.95 + $99 setup fee	Tech support via e-mail and prices include domain name use.
Homecom URL: hosting.homecom.com e-mail: hosting@homecom.com	15MB—$24.95/mo. 30MB—$49.95/mo. $50 setup fee	Search engine assistance, 24-hour emergency help, and automated sign-up.
IMVI Internet e-mail: Webmaster@imvi.com	Post your site for free, and then get an estimate.	Free trial negotiable.

ISP Name, URL, and Contact	Selected Rates	Special Features
Infomatique! URL: Iol.ie e-mail: Williamm@infomatique.iol.ie	Personal pages: free to $10/mo. Small Business: $10–$25/mo. Large organizations: $15–$150/mo. Flexible Web rates commission based on sales. Sponsorships are available. Non-commercial accounts should inquire.	Technical support via e-mail, free trial period, language translation services, search and directory available for Infomatique sites, and Web-related software is available.
Instant Technologies e-mail: sales@instantech.com		Commercial and personal sites available. Domain names available.
Internet Web Service Corp URL: www.iwsc.com e-mail: sales@mysite.com	50MB—$99/mo. Mention the title of this book and get a discount from Bryan.	Free demo test area. Tech support: Mon–Sat 8 AM – 8 PM. Reseller program for entrepreneurs.
Internet Presence Providers e-mail: sales@ipp.com Call 800-566-0131 for rates		Online sign-up.
Judd's Online e-mail: online@judds.com Call 800-368-3492 ext. 623 for rates		Specializes in online publishing.
The Vantage Program URL: www.m3cnet.com	Personal sites: $10/MB Corporate sites: $15/MB	Instant sign-up available with check or credit card. 30-day, money-back guarantee.

continued

ISP Name, URL, and Contact	Selected Rates	Special Features
MindSpring	10MB—$75/mo. + $225 startup 20MB—$125/mo. + $275 startup 50MB—$175/mo. + $325 startup 100MB—$275/mo. + $375 startup	Startup fee includes domain name for 2 years—use and registration. 30-day, money-back guarantee.
Nkn Call 214-880-0764	10MB—$50/mo.	
Realacom URL: www.realacom.com e-mail: realacom@ www.realacom.com		Test page open to public.
Shore.net e-mail: sales@shore.net		WebPhone specialists.
Superb Internet e-mail: Info@SUPERB.NET	10 MB—$35/mo + $45 setup Add'l 10MB—$5/mo.	"Fake domain name" simulates domain name.
Virtual Marketing Taskforce URL: www.thevmtbuilding.com e-mail: systems@ thevmtbuilding.com	N/A	N/A
Vivid Net URL: fp.calamistrum. com/frontpage e-mail: frontpage@vivid.net	Personal Site: $50/mo. Full Corporate Site: $150/mo.	Domain name use $50 a year. Demo sites online and database integration. $200/$250 setup fee. Quick e-mail support and training packages available. Free phone support. Assistance with search listings.

Notes on features listed in the table:

Free test period.   The site providers give you a period to try the site out before billing you. These are my kind of sites. Some sites don't advertise this feature, but they may let you try them out for a week if you ask. I would. In one week, you'll know for sure if you like the service you are getting.

All the sites listed support all FrontPage extensions.   All features covered in this book work on their site.

All the sites listed say they allow you to create password-restricted pages— as described in Appendix C, "Creating a Password-Protected Site."

Domain Names—look for two prices here. **Domain name registration** is the cost to register your domain name (usually for two years). **Domain name use** is the price of *using* that domain name with your site. Normally you need to pay for *both*, unless you already have a registered domain name.

Double-check all of this with your Web site provider before you make a final commitment.

Publishing Your Site to a Web Site Provider

When you've shopped around and found a good deal for a Web site provider, you are ready to publish your FrontPage site on the World Wide Web. Remember, the site provider should have given you:

- ❖ A URL
- ❖ A login name
- ❖ A passcode

If you don't have these three things, contact your site provider again and get this information. To publish your FrontPage Web to your World Wide Web site:

1. You must log on the Internet through your Internet Service Provider. Although I would like to be impartial, in my experience, the Microsoft

Internet Explorer using The Microsoft Network is the most reliable conduit to copying Web sites from FrontPage.

2. Open the Web site to publish in FrontPage Explorer.

3. Select File, Publish FrontPage Web from the FrontPage Explorer menu.

4. In the Destination Web Server... area of the dialog box, enter the URL provided to you by your Web site provider.

NOTE   Too many initials? URL is your Web site address (Uniform Resource Locator).

5. In the Name of Destination of FrontPage Web area of the dialog box, enter the directory name provided to you by your ISP.

TIP   If your site provider told you your site

    http://fp.dev-com/dkarlins

for example, the Server is

    http://fp.dev-com

and the Web Name is dkarlins.

6. In the Options area of the dialog box, select the Add to existing Web Check Box.

TIP   Normally, your Web site provider creates a Web for you, and you then copy your site to this "existing Web." If your Web site provider specifically tells you not to select this check box, follow their advice.

7. When your Publish FrontPage Web dialog box looks something like the one in Figure 7.5 (with a different Web addresses typed in), you can click OK in the dialog box.

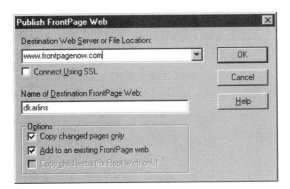

Figure 7.5

Ready to publish!

8. Enter the login name you received from your Web site provider in the Name area of the Name and Password Required dialog box.

9. Enter the password provided by your Web site provider in the Password area of the Name and Password Required dialog box, as shown in Figure 7.6.

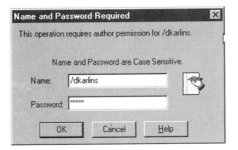

Figure 7.6

You need a user name and password

TIP

Passwords are case-sensitive! If your password is "secret," you cannot type "Secret." If the Name and Password are rejected, contact your service provider to make certain you were given a correct login name and password.

Publishing your Web site to the World Wide Web takes awhile. Take a break, help wash the dishes, and come back in five minutes. The status bar in FrontPage Explorer updates you as to the percentage of your Web site that has been published.

Maintaining Your Web Site

You've uploaded your Web site to your contracted Web service provider, but your work isn't over. All the dynamic features you added will come to life. If you created input forms, you will be having visitors to your site who will be leaving messages, which you will want to pick up. As you visit your site yourself and get feedback from other visitors, you will want to edit the site contents.

Each time you edit your site or open results files created by Form input, you need to log on your site, using the password provided by your Web site provider. After you log on your site, you can read input files and also edit the site online.

Editing Your Site

As soon as you copy your Web site to your new home on the World Wide Web, you have two copies of that site. One copy is on your hard drive and the other copy now resides on a server somewhere in New Jersey, Seoul, Minneapolis, or wherever. That might be obvious, but there's a useful point here. Editing your site online requires that you spend a lot of time logged onto the Internet. Depending on the deal you have with your Internet Service Provider, you might be paying for that time, and you're definitely tying up your phone line while you edit online. Another consideration is that editing a site online is slower than when you were editing using the FrontPage Personal Web Server.

One option is to do all your editing using the *copy* of your site that remains assigned to the Personal Web Server. You can make changes to your site *before* you log on to the Internet, and then *recopy* your site to your Web site provider using the same steps you just walked through.

The limitations of recopying your site are that pages that have been changed by visitors—such as pages created by input Forms—get replaced when you copy an entire site to your site provider. If your site has input Forms that are linked to other pages on the site, recopying is not a good option for editing your site.

The other option is to log on the Internet using your Internet access provider (for example, The Microsoft Network), and then reopen your site in FrontPage Explorer.

You can keep your online time down by making a careful list of what changes you want to make *before* you start editing. Usually, my technique is to go to my site using my Internet browser, make careful notes on what needs to be changed, and crank up FrontPage and make those changes. To edit your site on the Net:

1. Log on the Internet using the Microsoft Internet Explorer or another Internet browser.

2. Select File, Open FrontPage Web from the FrontPage Explorer menu.

3. Pull down the Web Server list in the Open FrontPage Web dialog box and select the Web on which your site is located.

4. Click the List Webs button in the Open Web dialog box and select your Web site.

5. Click OK in the dialog box.

 TIP You'll be prompted for an access name and password. You need to be sure the access name is the correct one for your Web site.

6. Enter the domain name and password for your site, as shown in Figure 7.7, and click OK on the Name and Password Required dialog box.

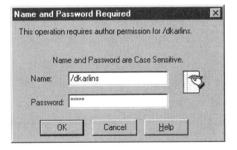

Figure 7.7

Logging on to edit your site

7. Sit and wait awhile. Keep waiting. And waiting. Almost there…. Opening a site on the Web is slower than opening one on your own computer.

8. Edit any of your pages, just as you have been doing throughout this book.

9. When you have finished editing a page, remember to save it.

> **TIP** Saving pages takes longer than when you were just saving to the Personal Web Server.

10. When you have finished making changes to your site (or reading pages that were created or edited by Form results), remember to exit your Internet access provider so that you don't rack up your monthly charge.

Getting Listed

You are now on the Net. You visit your site each hour, looking to see if anyone has responded to your input Forms. Hmm. Where is everybody???

Well, so far, nobody but you, your kids, parents, cat, and your significant other knows that you've even got a Web site. How do you attract visitors? One element of attracting visitors is to tell everyone about your site by putting it on your business card, include it in your ads, and so on.

Still, much of your target audience is to be found on the Web. After all, people already surfing the Net have to have Internet access. How do they find you? Options include:

❖ Your Web site provider may have programs set up that register you with search engines. If not, or if you want to supplement those efforts, register yourself when you use search engines.

❖ Exchange links with others.

❖ Get listed in site directories.

Explore these gateways to attracting visitors. To get listed on search engines:

1. Access a search engine. Your Internet access provider will give you access to one.

2. Enter a search topic where you should be listed, as shown in Figure 7.8.

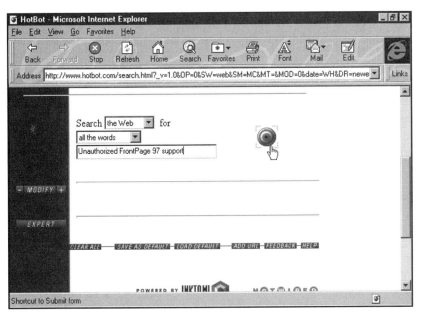

Figure 7.8

Searching for your site

3. Click the Search button, or whatever button begins the search in your Web browser.

4. When your site doesn't show up as one of the 11,994 sites that match the search criteria you entered, scroll to the bottom of the page where you normally find a link to a page that allows you to add a new URL to the search engine, such as the one in Figure 7.9.

Figure 7.9

Adding your site to a search engine

Each Search Engine is different, but they all allow the addition of your site to their list somewhere, as shown in Figure 7.10.

Make a habit of adding your URL to every search engine you come across, even though most search engines warn you that it takes weeks to get listed.

After a few months of adding your URL to search engines, your site will start to pop up when folks go looking for what you have to offer. It took me a year or so to get my site to come up when people look for unauthorized FrontPage support listings, even though I had the advantage of not having much competition, as shown in Figure 7.11.

Figure 7.10

Put my site in your list!

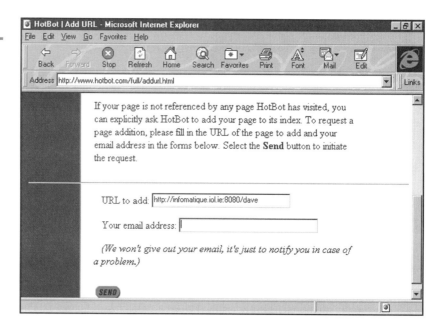

Figure 7.11

Search and Find

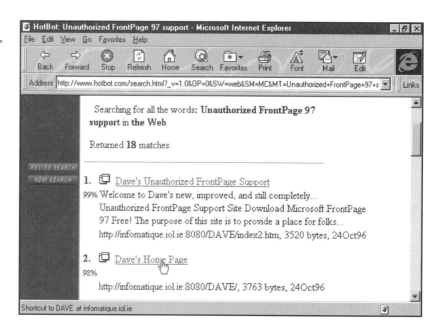

TIP   There are services that will submit your Web site to many search engines. One is called Submit-it, at:

`http://www.submit-it.com/`

To exchange links with others:

One of the most common ways visitors find their way to your site is via links from pages they already visited. Is there a home page for a professional association you belong to? A client who likes your work? Ask if a link to your site can be included on their site, and, in return, you should offer to provide a link from your site to theirs.

To get listed in site directories:

Many Internet Service Providers have directories of all the sites on their Web. That gives you exposure to everyone visiting the Web site provider, which will be quite a few people.

I get many visitors to my Web site who find out about it from Infomatique, my European site provider's home page. Infomatique lists all the sites they host, which is a nice way to network with other Web sites, as shown in Figure 7.12.

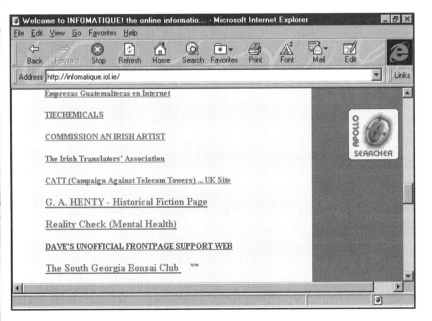

Figure 7.12

Listed and ready for visitors

Ongoing Support

I promised a wild weekend, and at the very least, it probably turned out interesting. You started from pretty much nowhere, and ended up creating and posting sophisticated Web sites. If you got detoured along the way, stretch the weekend out a bit.

As you continue to develop and maintain your Web site, you'll want to share experiences, joys, frustration, and tips. Here are a few resources:

❖ Microsoft's FrontPage support Web is found at

    http://www.microsoft.com/FrontPageSupport/

Don't expect personal attention, but they have a large knowledge base of ready-to-go information.

❖ You can get live phone support from Microsoft by calling 206-882-8080 between 7 A.M. and 5:30 P.M. Pacific Time, Monday through Friday. If you are having trouble installing FrontPage or getting it started, these are the people to call. Have the serial number on your disk handy when you call Microsoft.

❖ I maintain Dave's Unauthorized FrontPage Support Web at

    http://Infomatique.iol.ie:8080/dave

Feel free to drop in at my site anytime. My unauthorized support Web includes a forum where I help you solve vexing FrontPage problems, often with help from the technical wizards at Infomatique.

If you're interested in starting a user group in your area, let me know, and I'll try to put you in touch with others looking for some FrontPage reinforcements.

And, of course, I want to visit your site! Leave your address in the feedback area of my site or send it to my e-mail address:

dkarlins@aol.com

Most of all, have a good time using Microsoft FrontPage!

Appendix A
Taking a Shortcut with Templates

The FrontPage prefabricated templates simplify the process of creating Web pages or even entire Web sites. As you add pages to your site or even develop an entire site from templates, you'll create pages with features you already know how to use.

The Employee Directory template, for example, creates a page with a listing of employees at the top and hyperlinks to information about them below a horizontal line. Whoever knew how to create this page template was a genius! They used a Heading 1 title at the top of the page, so they must have known how to assign styles to text. They created horizontal lines. They created hyperlinks between hypertext at the top of the page and bookmarks lower on the page, and they inserted graphic images. These features are incredibly difficult to manipulate. With the Employee Directory template, it's possible to create a Web page like the one in Figure A.1.

Wait a minute, you know how to do all that stuff. It means you can let FrontPage do some of the grunt work, if you wish, and then you'll know exactly what's going on, and you'll be able to edit the page to fit your specific needs.

Could you have just jumped over all the rest of the things I've covered and started with templates? You could have, but as soon as you start to edit the template-generated page, you need to know what you're working with and how to change it. In sum, templates are a good way to save time, but they don't replace a knowledge of the basic skills you've acquired. In fact, you'll need those skills to use the templates.

Figure A.1

A Web site from a template—haven't you done this?

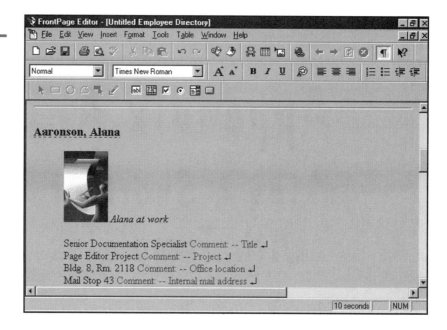

Surveying the Templates

FrontPage has two basic types of templates—templates that create an entire Web site and templates that create a page in a Web site. Templates that create an entire Web site are opened from FrontPage Explorer. Templates that create a single page are initiated from FrontPage Editor. I start with templates for single pages.

FrontPage comes with templates for over 20 types of pages. The New Page dialog box, which you'll explore, lists other things besides templates. Several wizards are also available from this dialog box, and you'll look at them in Appendix B, "Making Frames with a Wizard." Table A.1 lists templates that create Web pages and describes the effect.

Table A.1

Template	Effect
Normal Page	This isn't really a template at all, it just creates a blank page. A shortcut is to click the New button in the FrontPage toolbar.

Template	Effect
Bibliography	Creates book entries in alphabetical order, each with an assigned bookmark. You can create hyperlinks to any particular book from any page in your Web site.
Confirmation Form	Creates a page that acknowledges user input handled by a Discussion, Save Results, or Registration Bot. Because this form creates automatically by the Save Results Bot, you are not likely to need it.
Directory of Press Releases	Creates a page that lists press releases chronologically. You link each listing to a Web page and update the whole list by copying old press releases to another section of the page.
Employee Directory	I discussed this one earlier. It creates a listing of employees with hyperlinks to bookmarks in the body of the page. You have to enter the employee names and information.
Employment Opportunities	Here's one that saves personnel departments some time. It lets you plug in available positions and comes with a form to collect information from respondents.
Feedback Form	A quick way to attach a page to your site to solicit constructive criticism.
Frequently Asked Questions	As long as you stick to the page format, you can quickly put together a list of six questions linked to answers on the page.
Glossary of Terms	Somewhat like a hyper-dictionary with bookmarks from each letter: A, B, C, and so on.
Guest Book	This is nice and handy and gives you a headstart on creating a form for visitors to sign into your Web site.
Hot List	This template creates a page with hyperlinks to other pages.

continues

Table A.1

Template	Effect
HyperDocument Page	This is much like an outlined document and is suitable for hyper-publishing hyper-information hyperbolically. In other words, it's a Web page with hyperlinks.
Lecture Abstract	You are addressing the United Nations on the topic of world peace, and they want a short summary of your lecture to link to their Web site. Start with this template and save yourself a few minutes. The template provides a structure for a lecture. Now all you need is the content! Good luck.
Meeting Agenda	A memo template that has space for the topics of the meeting and names of those who should attend.
Office Directory	Visitors can click their state, province, or country to obtain information on how to contact your nearest office. Ideal for clients in Belize who are trying to figure out if the Costa Rica or Wyoming office would be most convenient. I saw this page used at the Microsoft Web site.
Press Release	Perfect for creating a quick press release to go on your Web site, especially if you're not sure what information a press release is supposed to contain.
Product Description	Includes space for a description of the product, unique features, and its benefits.
Product or Event Registration	These registration templates can save you a lot of time, but you do need to change the Form attributes. I walk you through the process in this appendix.
Search Page	Creates a page where your visitors can search your Web site for matching words.
Seminar Schedule	Plug this into your Lecture Abstract, and you've created a cyberconference. Book

Table A.1	
Template	Effect
	some real speakers, and you've got an event going on.
Software Data Sheet	Legend has it that Bill Gates used this format to sell MS-DOS to IBM. It's useful to describe new software.
Survey Form	Another handy form, but remember to change the Form Handler properties.
Table of Contents	Similar to what you did with the Table of Contents Bot, except that it places the TOC on a separate Web page.
What's New	A chronological list of new pages on your site.

What about the other things in the list? I skip the User Registration template because it requires Web site access that you may not be able to get from your Web site provider. FrontPage also lets you create a new page using wizards, and you'll explore them in Appendix B.

Using a Template

Creating new pages using templates can save you quite a bit of time. Some template pages require more editing than others, however, and some of that editing is more intuitive than the changes that need to be made to template-generated forms.

After you create and edit a Web page using a template, you need to link it to your site via hyperlinks to and from other pages. Remember, without a link *to* your new page, nobody will get there from your home page. You'll probably also want to link the page back to your home page.

You can further integrate your page into your Web site by inserting the same footers and/or headers that you use throughout your site. You can blend the whole site aesthetically by using the same page background you use on your home page for your new page. Just to keep it simple, I use the example of an employee directory first.

Then I test the specific now to walk through the basics. To create a new page with a template:

1. Open an existing Web site or start a new one in FrontPage Explorer.

2. Switch to FrontPage Editor and select File, New.

3. Click the template you wish to use. In Figure A.2, I select the Employee Directory.

Figure A.2

Choosing a template

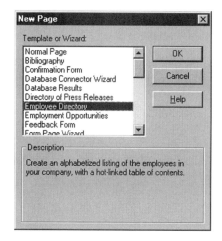

4. Click OK in the New Page dialog box.

5. Read the advice in the Comment at the top of the new page. The Comment text is in purple, and when you move your cursor over it, the RoBot icon appears, as shown in Figure A.3.

6. Many templates come with generic graphic images, but you can also insert your own image. First, delete the phony ones using the shortcut menu, as shown in Figure A.4.

7. Examine hyperlinks in the page before you start editing. Those hyperlinks are your clue to how the template-generated page is organized. In this case, listings at the top of the page are linked to bookmarks later in the page. Placing your cursor over hypertext reveals hyperlinks in the status bar at the bottom of the page, as shown in Figure A.5.

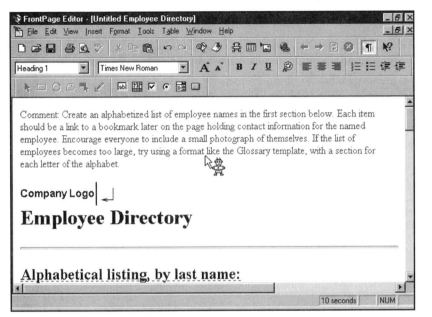

Figure A.3

The RoBot appears

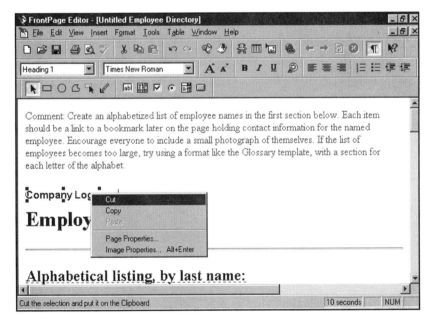

Figure A.4

Get rid of the generic images

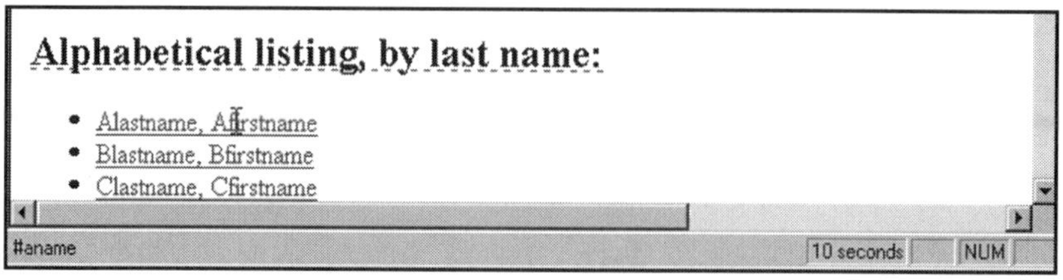

Figure A.5

Checking out template
hyperlinks

Alphabetical listing, by last name:

- Alastname, Afirstname
- Blastname, Bfirstname
- Clastname, Cfirstname

#aname   10 seconds   NUM

8. Use CTRL +click to follow hyperlinks from hypertext. Templates link generic items to other generic items. If the template links will work for the page you are designing, they can save you time. And sometimes the hyperlinks provide good models for how to organize your site. By following the existing links in the template, you will eventually be able to figure out how the template page is organized. In the case of the Employee Directory template, a page was generated that hyperlinks listings at the top to descriptions below.

9. Continue to delete and replace the generic images on the page.

10. Change the generic bookmark and link text, but be careful not to delete the bookmark or link properties. If you simply delete the existing text and type new information, you will likely erase the defined hyperlinks. My trick is to type the new information *inside* the existing text, as shown in Figure A.6.

11. After you have entered new bookmark text, you can delete the old, as shown in Figure A.7.

12. You will probably want to create new bookmarks as you enter employee names, as shown in Figure A.8.

13. You must change link properties, so right-click hyperlinks, select Properties from the shortcut menu, and enter correct link information, as shown in Figure A.9.

14. Go over the page carefully, checking to make sure that you changed all the generic text and images and corrected all hyperlinks.

At this point, you may be asking yourself just how much time was saved by using the template to generate the page. That varies depending on the complexity of the page.

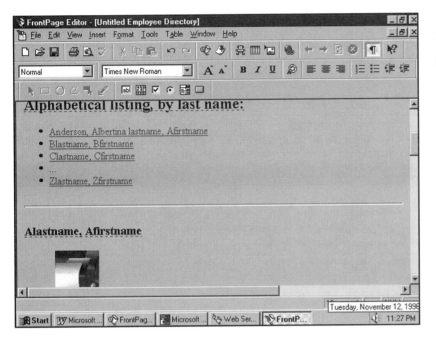

Figure A.6

Inserting text in the middle of a hyperlink

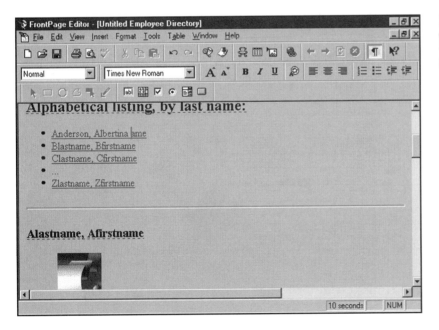

Figure A.7

Deleting text in the middle of a hyperlink

Of course, you will have to spend some time carefully going over your page before you can use it.

Figure A.8

Creating bookmarks

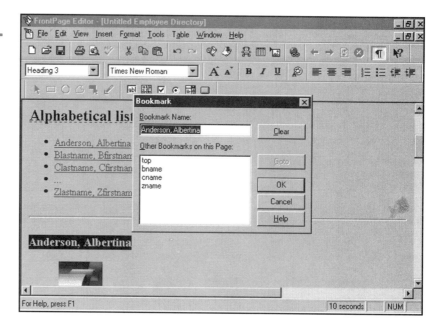

Figure A.9

Change hyperlinks—
unless you have an
employee named
"Bname"

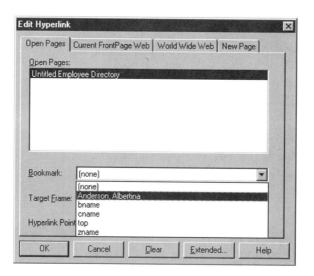

Don't forget that you still need to make the new page match existing Web pages. Integrating your new Web page into your site involves inserting footers and/or headers, matching page background, and creating hyperlinks to and from the home page.

You must then save your new page and give it a title and filename. To match your new page to your Web site:

1. Use the Include Bot to include header and/or footer pages in your newly generated page, as shown in Figure A.10.

Figure A.10

Making your pages mesh with an included footer

2. Match the background to that of the index (home) page by right-clicking the page, selecting Page Properties from the shortcut menu, and linking the page background to the index page, as shown in Figure A.11.

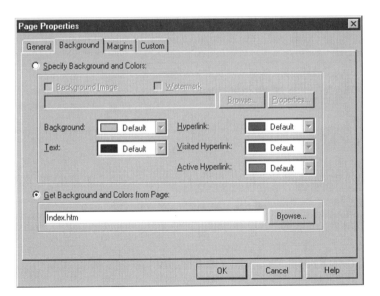

Figure A.11

Matching backgrounds for a color-coordinated Web site

3. Create convenient hyperlinks to the home page, as shown in Figure A.12.

Figure A.12

Give visitors a way
to go home

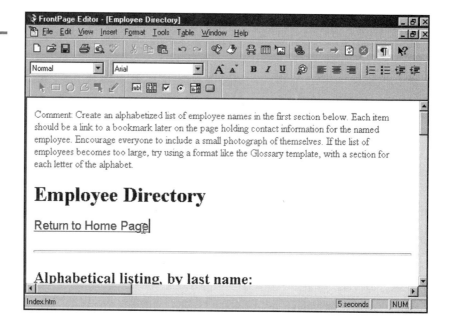

4. Save the new page with an appropriate title (you can let FrontPage figure out the URL), as shown in Figure A.13.

Figure A.13

Template pages must be
saved to your Web site

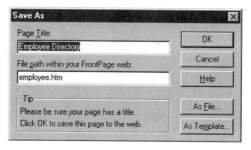

5. Create a graphic and/or text hyperlink from your home page to the new page—perhaps not quite as big as the one shown in Figure A.14.

6. Save your home page with the new link defined.

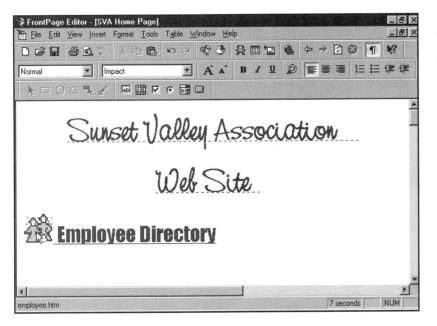

Figure A.14

Add graphics to
a template page

Using Templates to Create Forms

Because forms take time to create, templates are especially helpful in generating pages with a lot of forms. For example, the Registration Form template creates a page for visitors to register for an event or after purchasing a product. This page creates a form with over 20 input objects, all neatly lined up. You can delete them if you wish. Furthermore, how creative does one need to be with a registration form? It might work fine to just use the one FrontPage generates.

You will, however, have to define Form properties. Where will the form output go? Of course, you'll want to edit the specific questions being asked by the form. You can explore this process by creating a registration form using the Registration Form template. To create a registration form:

1. Open an exiting Web site or start a new one in FrontPage Explorer.

2. Switch to FrontPage Editor and select File, New.

3. Click the template you wish to use. In Figure A.15, I select the Product or Event Registration Form.

Figure A.15

Selecting the product or event registration template

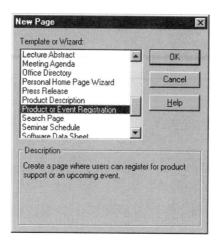

4. Click OK in the New Page dialog box.

5. Edit text that goes with the form objects. In Figure A.16, I change "State" to "Province" and use the ⏎ key to realign the text box.

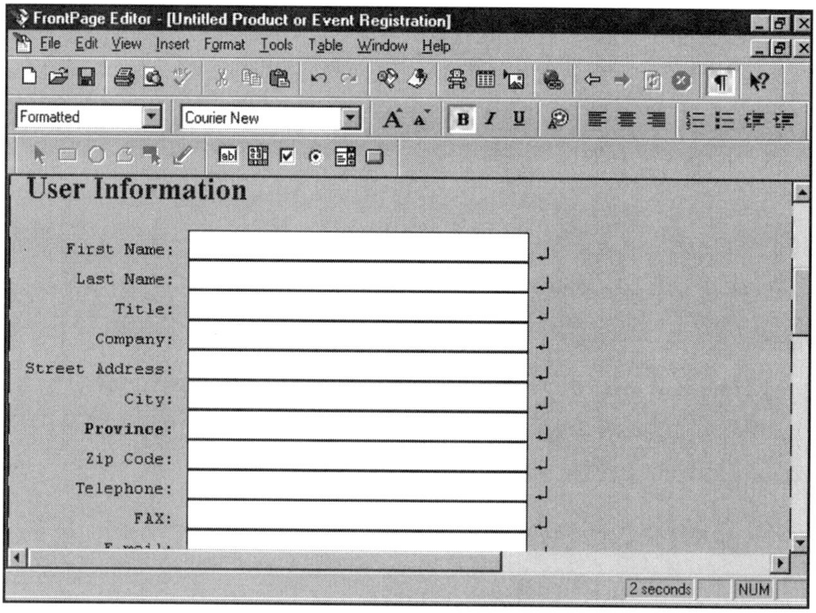

Figure A.16

Editing the template form text label

6. Double-click a form object to edit the properties. In the example in Figure A.17, I change the field name of the old "State" field to "Province."

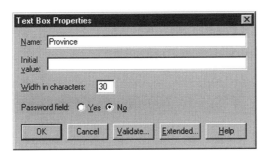

Figure A.17

Changing a field name

TIP

Changing the field name makes it easier to interpret the data in the results file.

7. You can edit the labels or contents of any Form object. In Figure A.18, I change the drop-down menu to allow for different options.

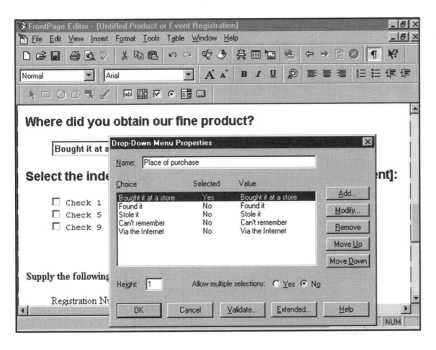

Figure A.18

Editing a template drop-down menu

TIP You can always delete large chunks of input objects if you don't want them.

8. After you have edited the Form contents, right-click within the form and select Form Properties from the shortcut menu.

9. Select the Save Results Bot from the Form Handler list. You might want to refer back to Chapter 5, "Sunday Morning—Letting Visitors Plug In with Forms."

10. Click the Settings button, choose a results filename and format, and deselect any of the check boxes you do not want to be part of your results file, as shown in Figure A.19.

Figure A.19

Choosing input form results

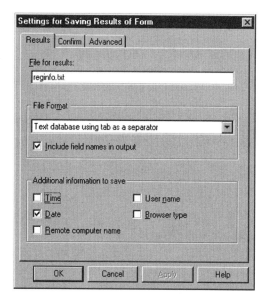

TIP Make a note of the filename you assign the results to.

11. Click OK in the Settings for Saving Results of Form dialog box, and click OK in the Form Properties dialog box.

12. Save the new page with a title and filename.

13. Use the steps discussed earlier in this session to link and integrate this new page into your Web site.

Using Templates to Create Web Sites

Up to now, you've investigated two typical templates for creating Web pages from FrontPage Editor. For those who really want to save time, you can create an entire "proto" Web site quickly using the templates in FrontPage Explorer. You can use the New Web templates in Explorer to add a Web to an existing site, but you're more likely to use one of these templates to create a new Web site from scratch.

Surveying Web Site Templates

The New Web dialog box includes a couple of Wizards, which is a topic for Appendix B. Table A.2 is a list of the Templates.

Table A.2

Templates	Description
Normal Web	You've used this template. It creates a Web site with a single empty Web page.
Customer Support Web	I like this one. It has all the pages you need to provide an instant, online support for your clients.
Empty Web	This template creates a completely empty Web that is different from the Normal Web that starts you out with a page and an image.
Learning FrontPage	This template isn't used to create real Web sites—it's part of the tutorial that comes with FrontPage.

continues

Table A.2	
Templates	Description
Personal Web	This template generates a simple one-page site with sections for personal, professional, and contact information.
Project Web	A little more esoteric, this template helps you organize a project and assign and keep track of tasks.

Not counting the Empty and Normal templates and the Learning FrontPage template that is used only with the tutorial, you're left with three useful templates for creating Web sites from scratch.

The Project Web is pretty specialized. If you're into project management, this Web template is the perfect match for your Gantt Tables in Microsoft Project. One of the pages that comes with this Web is a scheduling page, shown in Figure A.20.

Figure A.20

Using the Project Web Site Template to create a schedule

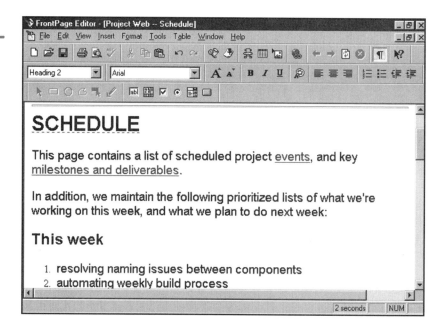

Project management is really a topic for another book, and for now, the folks who are interested can dive into this template on their own. The Personal Web and Customer Support Webs are both handy. You can experiment with the Personal Web on your own. You are familiar with most of the things in it. The page generated by the Personal Web template is shown in Figure A.21.

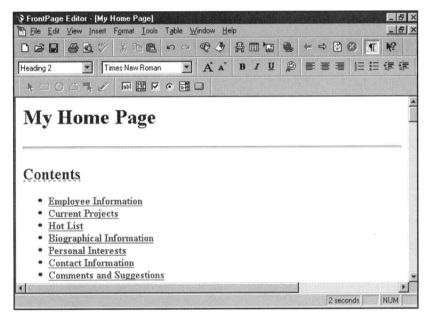

Figure A.21

Getting personal with a FrontPage template

Because the Personal Web generates a one-page site, all you need to do is add text and edit the hyperlinks. Just be sure you do edit all the hyperlinks, or folks who want to find out about your personal interests will end up at a bogus bookmark, and they will think your personal interests are those listed in Figure A.22.

The Customer Support Web

This is the template that makes using a Web template worthwhile. If you are looking for a way to make your clients, friends, creditors, or customers feel wanted and cared for, this could be the solution. I used it as the basis for my Web site. Visit me at

```
http://infomatique.iol.ie:8080/dave
```

and take a look.

Figure A.22

Don't forget to replace generic interests

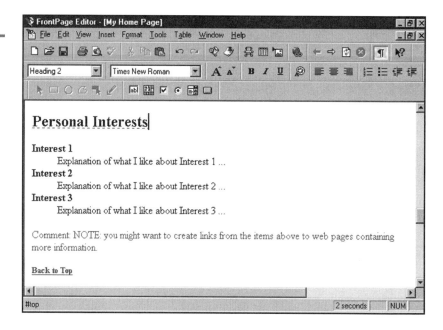

The Customer Support template generates a Web site with pages for visitors to be welcomed (a home page), find out what's new, get answers to Frequently Asked Questions (a.k.a. "FAQs"), report bugs, make suggestions, join a discussion page (similar to the bulletin board you created), and search for information they need. To create a Customer Support Web with a template:

1. Open FrontPage Explorer. If any Web sites are open, close them.

NOTE It *is* possible that you will want to attach this site to an existing Web. In that case, ignore Step 1. I think you'll be happier, however, with creating this as a single Web site.

2. Select File, New, FrontPage Web and click the Customer Support Web in the Template or Wizard list, as shown in Figure A.23.

3. Click OK in the New Web dialog box.

4. Select the Web server to which you will be assigning this Web site.

Figure A.23

Starting a Customer
Support Web using
the template

TIP

You can create the site using the Personal Web Server (default) and copy
it to a Web service provider, as you explored in Chapter 7, "Sunday
Evening—Publishing Your Site on the World Wide Web."

5. Enter a name for your new site in the Web Name area of the Customer
Support Web Template dialog box.

6. Click OK on the New Web… dialog box. Examine the new Web site in the
Hyperlink View of FrontPage Explorer. The "Customer Support—Welcome"
page is the home page. You can see that footer and header files have been created, as well as a Bug Reports and Suggestions from Customers page (see
Figure A.24).

7. Double-click the Customer Support and the Welcome page in the Hyperlink
View of FrontPage Explorer to launch FrontPage Editor to view this page.

8. Edit the home page, and save changes.

9. Follow the link to the What's New page and edit it, as shown in Figure A.25.

10. Save changes to each page as you edit them.

11. You can edit the header by right-clicking the included header file and selecting **Open header.htm** from the shortcut menu, as shown in Figure A.26.

Figure A.24

A Customer Support
site—hyperlinked

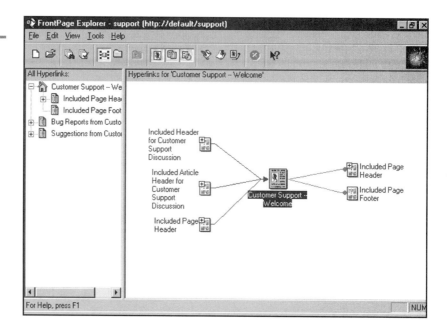

Figure A.25

What's new?

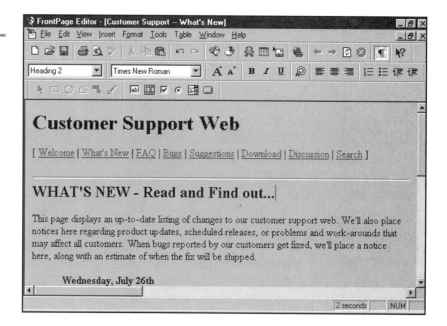

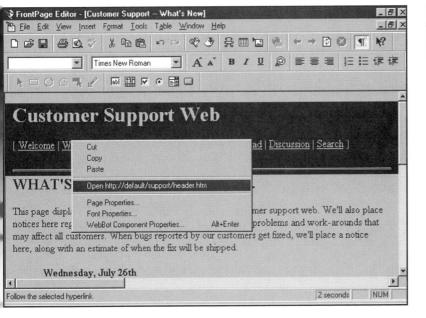

12. Follow hyperlinks to the Bugs, Suggestions, Discussion, FAQ, and Search pages. You are familiar with everything here.

    I discuss the Download page after you finish these steps, and you might decide you don't want it. If you don't, you can delete the hyperlinks to that page and delete the page itself from the Web in FrontPage Explorer.

13. When you've finished editing your site, save all pages in FrontPage Editor.

14. Test your new site using your Web browser and make needed changes.

Downloadable FTP Pages

Once upon a time, and it was not a very long time ago, there already was an Internet (but not what is now called the World Wide Web). Folks visited each other from high atop university libraries and from deep within corporate research departments. They transferred files to and from each other in a very crude way. Their files could not be read on sight, and they didn't have formatted text, images, and hyperlinks. In short, they weren't HTML files, and they definitely weren't created using FrontPage. These files were in a different file protocol called FTP, or "File Transfer Protocol." FTP files are not recognized or interpreted by Web browsers.

The Download page generated by the Customer Support Web template comes with hyperlinks to FTP files. If you have some good reason to provide such a link, edit the hyperlinks on that page to the address of your FTP files. These files are not created with FrontPage.

Today, the terms "World Wide Web," "Web," and "Internet" are often synonymous. Technically, however, FTP files are on the Internet, but not on the Web. Will this file format continue to be used, or will it whither away like the dinosaurs? Only time will tell.

Templates—Reconsidered

There is a time and place to use a template. If you're creating a form to register people for a conference, it may save time to borrow some ideas from the folks who designed FrontPage. If creativity is essential, you have to remember that 20 million other FrontPage users all have the same templates you do.

The nice thing is that the skills you honed over the course of working through this book enable you to examine, use, reject, and/or edit any of the templates FrontPage provides. In short, if you're designing a page where you can use a template, use it. If you're designing the Web site for an online abstract art gallery, start from scratch.

Appendix B
Making Frames with a Wizard

Frames enable visitors to view your Web site in "windows." You can let your visitors view and scroll through more than one "page" at a time by placing each page in a "frame" on the page. In this appendix, you'll explore the Frame Wizard in FrontPage Editor that allows you to create Web sites with frames.

Wizards—Ones You Already Know, Plus a Special One

As you traveled through FrontPage, you may have noticed that occasionally, menu options include wizards. Wizards are different from templates, because they are automated programs within FrontPage that walk you though their particular process. FrontPage Explorer, for example, has two wizards in the New FrontPage Web dialog box. One creates a Discussion Web, and one creates a Corporate Presence Web. These wizards prompt you to select items you want in your Web site, as shown in Figure B.1.

Based on selections you make using radio buttons and filling in blanks, these wizards create an entire Web site for you. You still need to edit the pages the wizard generates, therefore you still need to know how to use FrontPage.

In the File, New menu, FrontPage Editor has a couple wizards that also lead you, step by step, through the process of creating a Web page. Feel free to experiment. You can use these wizards to create and edit quick pages. In this way, wizards are similar to using templates to get a head start on creating pages. FrontPage has one wizard that's special—the Frames Wizard.

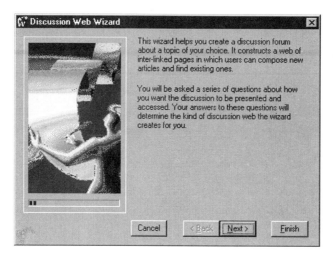

Figure B.1

The Discussion Web Wizard

What Are Frames?

If you're familiar with working with Microsoft Windows, think of each frame as a window. The Web site in Figure B.2 has two frames.

If a frame has more information than will fit in the viewer's frame, a frame-friendly browser displays the frame with scroll bars so that the viewer can move through each frame independently. In the example in Figure B.3, a user is scrolling down the frame on the right, while the frame on the left stays put.

Creating a frame involves at least three pages (actually four, but I get to the fourth page in a minute). The basic elements of a page with frames are:

❖ A page to "hold" the embedded pages. The Frames Wizard creates it.

❖ At least two embedded pages. These are created in FrontPage Editor, the old-fashioned way.

That mysterious fourth element is a backup page. This alternative page is created so that visitors who are using a browser that doesn't recognize frames can view your site. The frame feature is supported by many Web browsers, but Microsoft Internet Explorer 2.0 isn't one of them. Because not all browsers recognize frames, it's best to have a backup page so that those visitors won't get a message telling them the page cannot be loaded into their browser. (Internet Explorer 3.0 and later versions do support frames, as well as Netscape Navigator 2.0 and 3.0).

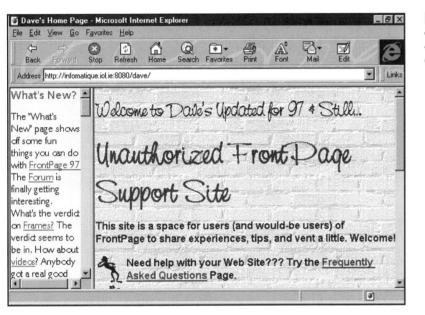

Figure B.2

A Web site with right and left side frames

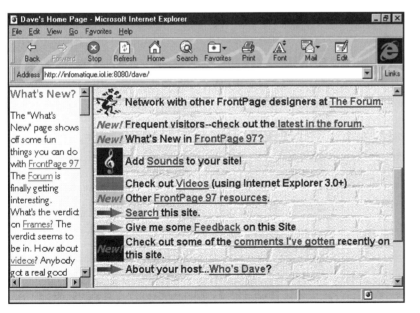

Figure B.3

Scrolling frames

Before you embark on using FrontPage's Frames Wizard, you'll create two pages to be framed together on the frame page, and a backup page for those who visit your site with a browser that doesn't support frame viewing.

Couldn't you just take a couple pages from your existing Web site and stick them together on a frame page? Yes, technically you could, but the main problem is aesthetic. If you placed information on a Web page side by side in tables, the page would create a cluttered look when placed side by side with another page in a framed page. Or, if you are framing two pages with the same inserted header file on a page, two headers will appear next to each other on top of the frame page, and that won't look good. In short, creating framed pages is a process with its own unique design laws. One of those laws is to keep each page that is placed on a frame page simple.

Getting Ready to Frame

It is helpful to get your three pages done before you start to run the Frames Wizard. There are many approaches to designing frames, but one approach is to create a two-column page, with one frame on the left and one on the right. That way, users can scroll down one side of the page, while leaving the other side in place.

The approach I walk you through here involves one frame on the left side of a page that takes up about a quarter of the user's screen, and one frame on the right of the frame page that takes about three-fourths of the screen. The user can scroll down either side. For viewers who don't have a browser that supports frames, you will create a page that puts the same information on one page.

All this has to be thought through before initiating the Frames Wizard. Then, if things don't fall into place, you can go back into the Frames Wizard and make adjustments. To create pages for a frame page:

1. Create a new Web site in FrontPage Explorer. You can use the Empty Web. The Empty Web is better than the Normal Page because the Normal Page names a file **Index.htm**. You don't want an index file yet because you're saving that for a frame page.

2. Switch to FrontPage Editor and create a Web page that will end up on the right three-fourths of a frame page—something like the one in Figure B.4. You can adjust the page later after you see how it looks in a frame.

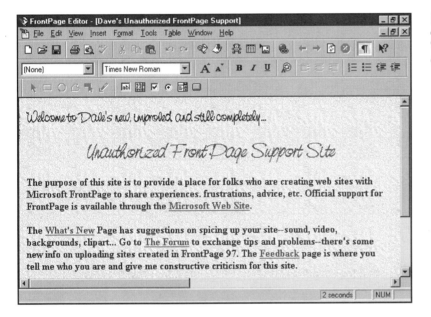

Figure B.4

Creating one page for a frame

3. Save the first Web page with a name and title, but don't use **Index.htm**. You'll save that name for the filename of the frame page you will create later.

4. Create a second Web page that will end up on the left quarter of the frame page—something like the one in Figure B.5.

You can include all the fun things you learned to place on any Web page, such as images, included files, page backgrounds, font colors, and so on.

5. Save the second page with a page title and filename, but avoid **Index.htm**.

6. Create a Web page that can be used as an alternative for viewers who are not armed with frames-friendly browsers. (One difference between organizing a page into tables versus frames is that each frame has its own scroll bar, but a page with tables doesn't have a scroll bar.) One option is to simply use your larger home page frame as the alternate home page. Visitors without a frame-friendly browser will then only miss your auxiliary frame.

Figure B.5

Page to use in the left frame

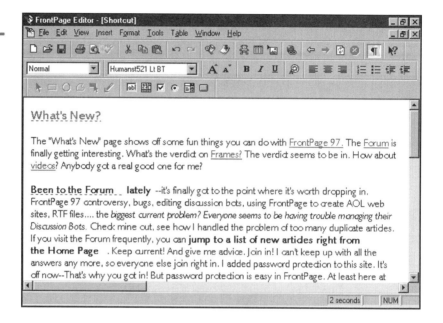

TIP You can copy and paste from your frame pages to create a non-frame alternative page.

7. Save the page you created as a frame-free alternative. You might consider a helpful title such as, "Home Page, No Frames."

Generating a Frame Page with the Frames Wizard

After you save both the pages to include in your framed page and the backup page for frame-free Web browsers, you are ready to generate your frame page with the Frames Wizard.

It isn't necessary to note the names of your files unless you don't think you'll recognize them when you see them in a list. The Frames Wizard allows you to browse through your Web site to find pages to include in the frame page. To create a frame page:

1. Select File, New in FrontPage Editor.

2. Select Frames Wizard in the New Page dialog box, as shown in Figure B.6.

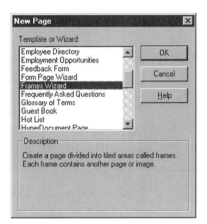

Figure B.6

Choosing the Frames Wizard

3. Click OK in the New Page dialog box. Can you believe it? Templates within wizards! You can experiment with the templates later, after you've mastered the technique of creating a frame page yourself.

4. Click the Make a Custom Grid radio button in the Frames Wizard from the Choose Technique dialog box, as shown in Figure B.7.

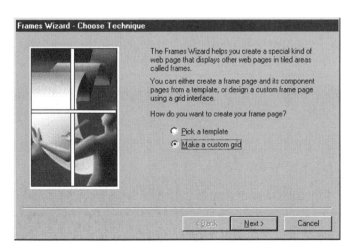

Figure B.7

Choosing a custom grid

5. Click the Next button.

6. In the next Frames Wizard dialog box, select "1" row from the Rows drop-down list, as shown in Figure B.8.

Figure B.8

Selecting a 1 row frame

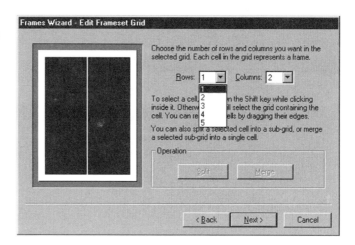

7. Leave the Columns setting at "2."

Even years from now, after you've created a thousand Web sites with frames, you're likely to be selecting "1" row and "2" column settings. Note the appearance of other frame pages you visit. Complex frame pages with more than two columns and/or more than one row are distracting.

8. Click the Next button in the Frames Wizard from the Edit Frameset Grid dialog box.

9. Click the left frame in the Frames Wizard, Edit Frame Attributes dialog, as shown in Figure B.9.

10. Click the Browse button in the Source URL area, and double-click the page that is to appear on the left side of the frame page.

11. Enter a title for the frame in the Name area.

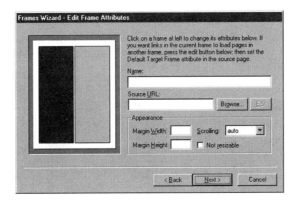

Figure B.9

Defining the left frame

12. Setting a margin width places some space between this frame and the other frames. Entering "2" in the Margin <u>W</u>idth area keeps your frames from running into each other.

13. Leaving the Not <u>r</u>esizable check box unchecked allows your visitors to change the size of frame windows as they view your site. It's the nice thing to do. The contents of your left frame should all be defined.

14. Don't click the Next button yet, because you still need to define the other frame on your page.

15. Click the right frame in the Frames Wizard, Edit Frame Attributes dialog box.

TIP The right side of the page mock-up is dark so that you can now define it.

16. Click the Br<u>o</u>wse button in the Source <u>U</u>RL area and double-click the page that is to appear on the right side of the frame page.

17. Enter a title for the right frame in the N<u>a</u>me area.

18. Setting a margin width places some space between this frame and the other frames. Here, again, entering "2" in the Margin <u>W</u>idth area creates some space between your frames.

19. You can again let visitors resize your frames by leaving the Not resizable check box unchecked. The contents of your right frame should be defined, as in the example in Figure B.10.

Figure B.10

Right frame—defined

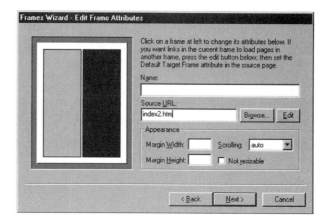

20. *Don't click Next yet!* You still have more to do. You can now define the size of the frames by clicking and dragging the line between the frames, as shown in Figure B.11.

Figure B.11

Sizing frames

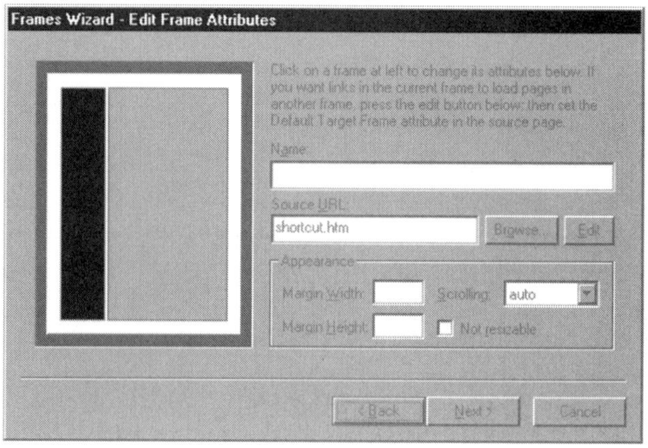

21. Take your best guess at a good layout for the frames. You can readjust it later.

22. Now you can click the Next button in the Frames Wizard, Edit Frame Attributes dialog box.

23. In the Frames Wizard, Choose Alternate Content dialog box, click the Browse button and double-click the backup, alternate home page you created (see Figure B.12).

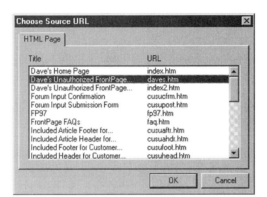

Figure B.12

Assigning an alternate page

TIP The alternate home page shows up in the Alternate Page URL area. You cannot enter a page here; you must select one using the Browse button.

24. When you have defined an alternate page URL, click the Next button.

25. Enter a title for your page in the Title area of the Frames Wizard, Save Page dialog box.

26. If you want the framed page to be the home page that visitors see when they go to your site, enter **Index.htm** in the URL area, as shown in Figure B.13.

27. If you remember that you missed something, you can change earlier dialog boxes in the Frames Wizard by clicking the Back button.

28. When you've defined your page to your satisfaction, click the Finish button in the Frames Wizard, Save Page dialog box.

Be sure that all open pages are saved.

Figure B.13

Making the framed
page the home page

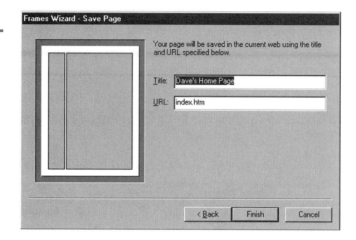

Viewing Your Frame Page

When you visit your frame page using a Web browser, one of two things will happen. You will either see your frame page with frames, or you will see the alternate Web page—it depends on whether your browser supports frames. To visit a site with frames:

1. Launch your Web browser.

2. In the URL address line in your Web browser, enter the site address exactly as it appears in the FrontPage Explorer title bar.

NOTE

If you created your frame page somewhere besides the index page, navigate to that page in your browser.

If your browser does not support frames, you'll see the alternate page. If you have not designated an alternate page, visitors without frame-friendly browsers will see an unpleasant message, as shown in Figure B.14. If your browser does support frames, you'll see the frame page in Figure B.15.

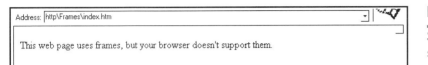

Figure B.14

Some browsers don't support frames

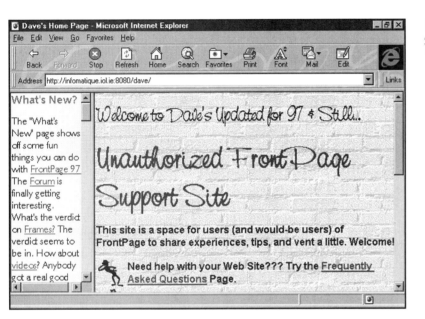

Figure B.15

Viewing frames

 TIP It's a good idea to test your frame page with a browser that supports frames as well as one that does not.

 TIP Try navigating around both frames in the frame page.

Editing Frame Configuration

As you may have noticed, you cannot edit your frame page in WYSIWYG editing in FrontPage Editor. You can, of course, edit the component pages that make up the frame page. Those pages can be opened, edited, and re-saved. If you want to edit the relative sizes of the frames, you need to go back into the Frames Wizard.

After you have created a frame page, you can launch the Frames Wizard from FrontPage Explorer to edit your existing frames. Try that. To edit frames:

1. Double-click the frame page you wish to edit in FrontPage Explorer.

 TIP

Double-clicking a frame page in FrontPage Explorer launches the Frames Wizard.

2. You can edit any of the dialog boxes in the Frames Wizard. You'll likely pay a few visits to the Frames Wizard while you fine-tune the size of the frames, as shown in Figure B.16.

Figure B.16

Editing frames

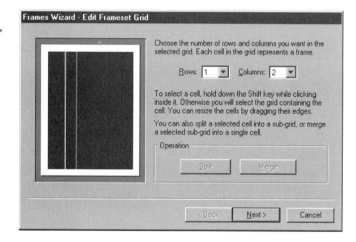

3. Click the Next button in the Wizard dialog boxes until you are prompted to finish editing your frames.

4. After you click the Finish button, you'll be prompted to replace your old frame's URL. Do that, and using a browser that supports frames, examine the changes in your Web.

5. Retest your Web site by scrolling around the frames and determining the right layout.

To Frame or Not to Frame?

As millions of browsers—including users of America Online and other Internet access providers—assist their users in downloading Internet Explorer 3.0, the critical mass will shift. More and more people will be surfing the Web with browsers that do interpret frames. Someday it will not be necessary to have an alternate page for those not using frames. For now, I would still advise it.

A nice, neat, two-frame page can pack twice as much information on a page and make users feel even more in control of what they are seeing. In short, used carefully, frames generally enhance a site. The choice, of course, is yours.

Appendix C
Creating a
Password-Protected Site

FrontPage enables you to assign password protection to your site so that only those individuals to whom you have assigned user names and passwords can enter.

You might want to restrict visitors to a page on your Web site for many reasons. Access can be restricted to paying clients, members of your organization, selected employees, or just people you like. *The New York Times*, for example, currently requires visitors to first contact the paper and get a password before they can read all the news that's fit to print via the Web. Even though *The New York Times* doesn't charge you to browse their pages on the Web, they do have an accurate count of how many people are registered, which they can present to advertisers when they sell space. When a visitor attempts to visit a password-protected site, an imposing dialog box appears, as in Figure C.1.

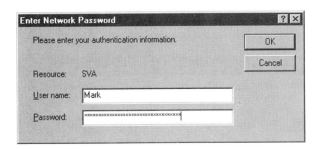

Figure C.1

Halt! Who goes there?

If an uninvited user enters an invalid password, they will not be able to get beyond the Enter Network Password dialog box. If they cancel the Password dialog box, they will end up at the dead end, as in Figure C.2.

Figure C.2

Oops! Wrong
password.

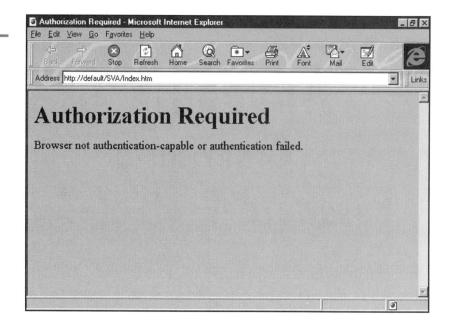

One limitation of the password protection in FrontPage is that it must be applied to an entire Web site. You cannot, for example, protect only one page in your site. The workaround is to arrange with your FrontPage-friendly Web site provider to use two different Web sites—one that is open to the public at large, and one that is restricted to registered visitors. You can discuss this when you shop for a site.

Not all Web site providers, even FrontPage-friendly ones, allow you to password-protect your site. The distinction is that they must assign you *administrator*, rather than *author*, rights to your Web. Check with your Web site provider before you rent space from them if password protection is going to be necessary for your site.

Defining Unique Permissions for Your Site

Although you cannot define different permission rules for various pages within your Web, you can assign password-protection rules to your entire Web site. Again, this is dependent on your Web site provider giving you administrator rights to your own site—something you need to check first. If you will need to assign password protection to your site, first ask a prospective site provider, "Do I have *administrator* or *author* rights to edit my site?" If the answer is, "author rights only," you will need to negotiate an arrangement for administrator rights or shop for a Web site provider that offers them. To assign unique permissions:

1. Open your Web site in FrontPage Explorer.

TIP   You can test this process using the Personal Web Server, but you will need to redo it when you have copied your site to a Web site provider, as discussed in Chapter 7, "Sunday Evening—Publishing Your Site on the World Wide Web." Copying a site from your default or local host site (using the Personal Web Server) to an Internet Web site provider will *not* copy password protection.

2. Select <u>T</u>ools, <u>P</u>ermissions from the FrontPage Explorer menu.

3. In the Settings tab, select the Use unique permissions for this web radio button, as shown in Figure C.3.

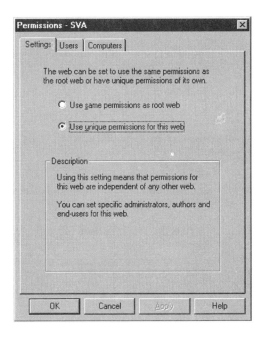

Figure C.3

Choosing unique permission for your Web site

TIP If you have your own server, you do not need to define unique settings, but if the Settings tab appears in your Web Permissions dialog box, you do.

4. Click OK in the Web Permissions dialog box.

Restricting Your Site to Registered Users Only

Restricting access to registered users is as simple as clicking a radio button. After you assign password protection, you need to define registered visitors and assign them passwords. First, though, you need to protect the site. To restrict access:

1. Open the site in FrontPage Explorer to which you are assigning password protection.

2. Select Tools, Permissions from the FrontPage Explorer menu. You should have previously defined unique permissions for this site in the Settings tab of the Web Permissions dialog box.

 TIP If you did select Unique permissions in the Settings dialog box but the radio buttons in the End Users tab are grayed out, you must contact your Web site provider to arrange for authorization to assign permissions.

3. Click the Users tab in the Web Permissions dialog box. Notice the current Permissions setting. The Everyone has browse access radio button should be selected, as shown in Figure C.4.

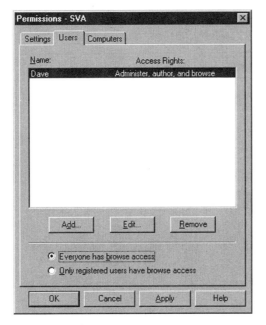

Figure C.4

Everyone has access.

4. In the Users tab of the Web Permissions dialog box, click the registered users only radio button. The Add and Remove buttons in the top half of the Web Permissions dialog box will become active, as shown in Figure C.5.

5. Click OK in the Web Permissions dialog box.

You can now test your site for access using your Web browser. Your own user name and password are the same as the name and password you use each time you open or edit the site in FrontPage Explorer.

Figure C.5

Dave has access.

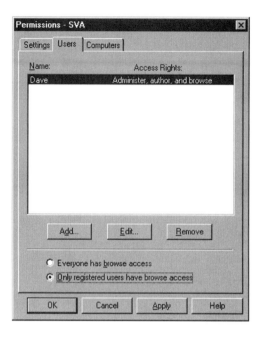

Creating Lists of Authorized Users in the Root Web

Access to a password-protected Web site is granted by creating a list of approved visitors and assigning them passwords. Normally, if you define password protection, you have a plan to select and inform registered users of their passwords. Of course, you will always be able to access the site because you are the administrator (or author). You can use the same password that you use to open and edit the site. To assign registered users:

1. Open the site in FrontPage Explorer to which you are assigning password protection.

2. Select Tools, Permissions from the FrontPage Explorer menu.

You must have previously defined unique permissions for this site in the Settings tab of the Web Permissions dialog box.

3. Click the Add button in the Web Permissions dialog box.

4. Enter the registered user's access name in the Name area of the Add Users dialog box. No spaces are allowed. Make sure you tell the visitor exactly how their access name is spelled, including uppercase and lowercase characters.

5. Enter the registered user's password in the Password area of the Add Users dialog box.

6. Re-enter the registered user's password in the Confirm Password area of the Add Users dialog box, as shown in Figure C.6.

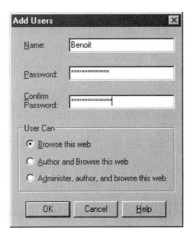

Figure C.6

Assigning a password to Benoit

TIP   Carefully note the user's password, including uppercase or lowercase notation.

7. Click OK in the Add Users dialog box.

8. Repeat the process as necessary to enter more registered users. Make sure you carefully inform registered users of their user name and password.

9. When you have entered all the registered users and their passwords, click OK in the Web Permissions dialog box.

You can assign more registered user passwords later by repeating these steps.

Password-Protection Issues

You may see more flexible password protection in future versions of FrontPage. The current requirement that an entire site must be protected does not make it easy to let visitors enter your site, register, and get a password before being allowed access to other pages.

As emphasized earlier, not many Web site providers are set up to let you take advantage of even this feature. If password protection is important to you, shop carefully and make sure that you can test the site before committing yourself to a long-term contract.

Finally, there's nothing magic about password protection. I'm no expert on cracking codes, but I wouldn't put your personal diary on a Web site and rely on a password to keep out unwanted visitors. With these limitations, FrontPage does let you restrict a site to registered users in a straightforward way.

Appendix D
Video! Sound!

FrontPage enables you to place video or sound files on Web pages. Background sounds can be attached to any page in your Web site. You have the option of playing your sound file once, many times, or endlessly.

When to Use Sound and Video

Like all good things, sounds can be abused, overdone, or done badly. In this way, sounds are analogous to page backgrounds. If they're too noisy, they distract you from the Web site. I personally find those insanely loud, disco beats that run endlessly on some sites a little distracting. Maybe that ambiance works at the BeeGees' retro site, but not when I'm shopping for a scanner on the Web. Using the right sounds can add a whole new dimension to your site.

Videos can be placed in your FrontPage 97 Web pages as easily as placing a graphic image. FrontPage lets you display a video player on the page so that visitors can play videos when they drop by.

Legal Disclaimer: Sounds and videos can be protected by copyrights. Violating those copyrights is easy if you're not careful. If you copy a sound or video from a disk or a Web site, make sure that there are no publisher or creator rights to them. Just because they're on the Web doesn't mean that they are freely available to use. I can't show you a picture of background sounds, but a video player looks like the one in Figure D.1.

Figure D.1

Video at your Web site

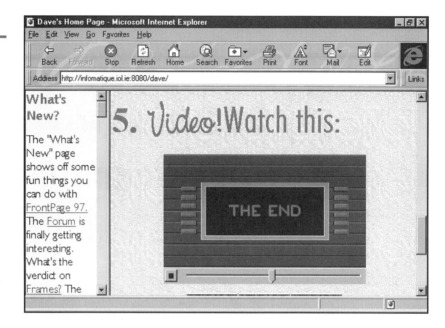

Will My Visitors Hear the Noise? See the Light?

Before you enter the nuts and bolts of placing audio and video files in your Web site, let's talk accessibility. Microsoft Internet Explorer versions 3.0 and higher introduced the first Web browser that can interpret sound and video files without any additional software. Additional software packages, called "plug-ins," are necessary to watch videos and hear attached sound files using Netscape Navigator 3.0. Therefore, Netscape visitors probably won't be able to hear or see your sound or video.

Of course, visitors who don't hear your background sound won't know what they're missing. Unless you place a big message on your screen saying, "If you can't hear this, you're missing out."

Your video player, however, takes up a nice chunk of the page, and visitors who can't watch will definitely know they're missing something. One option is to provide an alternate graphic image for them.

TIP You can also put a message on your Web site suggesting that your visitors download Internet Explorer, so that next time they can hear and see everything you have to offer.

Assigning Background Sounds

You need a couple of things in order to attach a sound file to your Web page: a Web page and a sound file. If you just came back from the computer store with a CD entitled, "1 Billion Noises," you've got many choices. Just find files in the *.**wav** file format and get set to plug them into your Web site.

If you aren't the owner of a large collection of background sound files, I will bet you can find a few on your hard drive. You'll just use one that came with other programs you installed.

You can use Windows Explorer (not FrontPage Explorer) to locate *.**wav** files on your hard drive. To find sound files on your hard drive:

1. Right-click the Start button, or use your favorite method to open the Windows Explorer.

2. Select Tools, Find, Files, or Folders from the Windows Explorer menu.

3. In the Find Files dialog box, enter *.**wav** in the Named field and navigate to the folder with Windows in the Look in: box.

4. Click the Include Subfolders check box and click OK in the Find Files… dialog box.

5. In a minute or two, you'll see a list of files you can use as background sounds in your FrontPage Web, as shown in Figure D.2.

Figure D.2

You've got sounds.

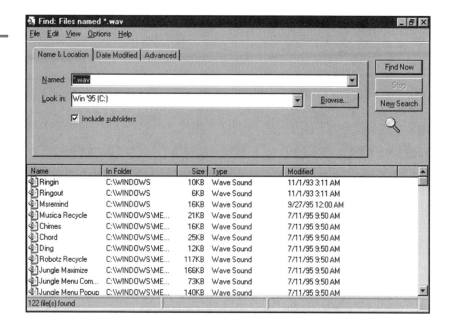

6. Leave this Find File window open because you'll refer to it later when you add a sound file to your site.

This part is almost too easy. It's just like adding a background image to your site, only easier. To add sound files to a page:

1. Open the Web page to which you will assign a background sound.

2. Right-click the page and select Page Properties from the shortcut menu.

3. Select the General tab.

4. In the Background Sound area of the Page Properties dialog box, click the Browse button.

TIP Now is the time to switch back to your Find Files ... window and note the name and location of an interesting-looking sound file.

5. Click the Other Location tab in the Background Sound dialog box and click the From File radio button.

6. Use the Browse button to navigate to the sound file you located using the Find File... window, as shown in Figure D.3.

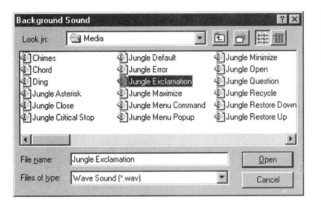

Figure D.3

Navigating to a sound file

7. Click OK in the Background Sound dialog box.

8. You can click OK in the Page Properties dialog box now or make some decisions about how many times to repeat your sound. If you want to do that, read on.

The choices are: Play it once, play it many times, or play it forever. Once is nice. More? Depends on the message. A pleasant tune might work well over and over. A loud chainsaw noise is best as a one-time attention grabber. To loop your sound:

1. Right-click your page and select Page Properties from the shortcut menu if the Page Properties dialog box is not open.

2. You want to be in the General tab.

3. In the Loop spin box, choose the number of times to repeat your sound. If you want the sound to run endlessly, click the Forever check box. In Figure D.4, you're playing your song four times.

Figure D.4

Repeating your sound
four times

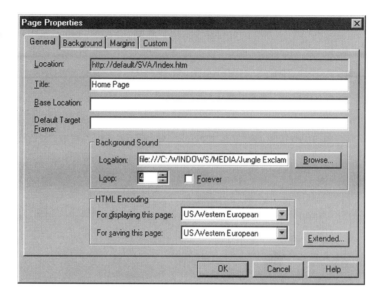

4. Click OK in the Page Properties dialog box.

5. Preview your page in your Web browser and decide if you want to change
the sound file or the number of times it repeats.

NOTE

> You'll note in the status bar that adding a sound file greatly increases
> your page-loading time. Visitors will still see your page while they wait
> for the sound file to load. You can decrease loading time by selecting a
> shorter sound file. A short sound file that repeats itself takes less time to
> load than a long sound file that plays once.

Taking Your Visitors to the Movies

To add video to your site, you need an *.avi file. Although I could almost promise
some sound files on your hard drive, I can't make that same commitment when it
comes to *.avi video files. Some may or may not be there.

One source for *.avi* video files on the Web is:

`http://tausq.resnet.cornell.edu/mmedia.htm`

This site has video files in other formats, but you want "Video for Windows," (**AVI**) files. Another source for *.avi* files is:

`http://www.tva-online.com/tva-avi.htm`

Checking Out Videos

If you see a video you like at these sites or another site, right-click the hyperlink to that video and select Save Target As from the shortcut menu. Refer back to the "Legal Disclaimer" at the beginning of this chapter, and make sure that you are not violating anyone's copyright when you copy the video file. Select a file folder and file-name, and click OK in the dialog box to save the *.avi* file to your hard drive, as shown in Figure D.5.

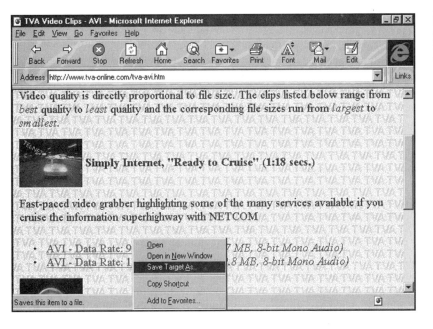

Figure D.5

Copying an AVI video file

TIP These files take awhile to download. They're big!

Inserting a Video in Your FrontPage Web

This part's easy. You need a Web page (you've got one if you've made it this far in the book). You need an *.**avi** format video file. If you don't have one, try one of my Web site sources that I previously listed, or search for **AVI video files** using your favorite search engine. Lots of them are out there.

Your main decision is whether you want to include a video viewer with your video. I think you do, because it makes it much easier for your visitors to watch your video as often as they like. To place a video on a page:

1. Open the page on which the video will be placed in FrontPage Editor.

2. You may want to enter some text to alert your visitors that it's showtime, as shown in Figure D.6.

Figure D.6

A title for your video

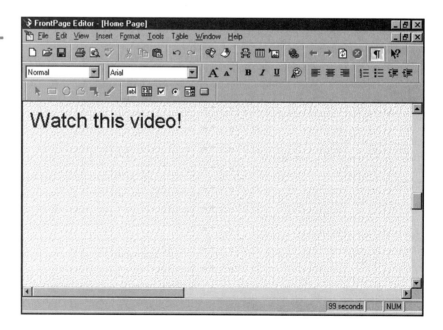

3. Select Insert, Video.

4. In the Video dialog box, navigate to a folder with a video and double-click the video, as shown in Figure D.7.

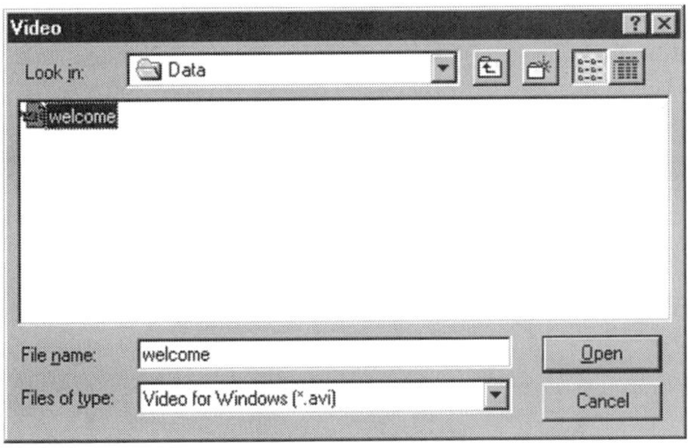

Figure D.7

Selecting an AVI video file for your Web page

The video inserts onto your Web page! To add controls to an online video:

1. Right-click the inserted video in FrontPage Editor.

2. Select Image Properties from the shortcut menu.

3. In the Image Properties box, the Video tab is selected because you opened this dialog box by right-clicking a video.

4. Click the Show Controls in Browser check box to give your visitors a little on-screen video player when they visit. This is highly recommended.

5. You can select from a variety of options for how to activate the video and how often it will run. If you chose to Show Controls in Browser, your visitors can make these decisions. If you want to decide for them, use the check box options.

6. Click the General tab and use the Text tab to enter alternate text, which displays for visitors who do not have Internet Explorer and cannot watch the video, as shown in Figure D.8.

Figure D.8

Alternate text—for those without Internet Explorer

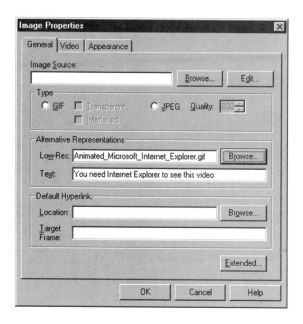

You can also assign an alternate GIF or JPEG image to display in browsers that cannot interpret the video.

 TIP

7. When you've defined how the video will present, click OK in the Image Properties dialog box, as shown in Figure D.9.

Figure D.9

Inserting a video—next comes showtime!

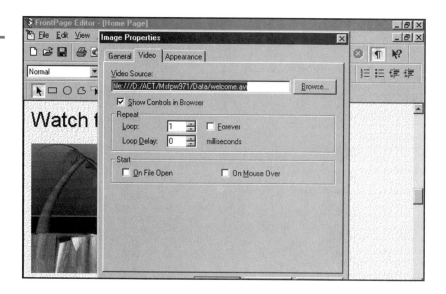

8. Save your page and use the Preview in Browser button to test out your video.

Appendix E
What's on the CD?

The CD that accompanies this book contains numerous tools and utilities to assist you in your Web publishing endeavors. There are animation tools, Web tools, HTML editors, Windows utilities, and more.

Running the CD

To make the CD more user-friendly and take up less of your disk space no installation is required. This means that the only files transferred to your hard drive are the ones you choose to copy or install.

Significant differences between the various Windows operating systems (Windows 3.1, Windows 95, and Windows NT) sometimes render files that work in one Windows environment inoperable in another. Prima has made every effort to insure that this problem is minimized. However, it is not possible to eliminate it entirely. Therefore you may find that some files or directories appear to be missing from the CD. Those files are, in reality, on the CD, but remain hidden from the operating system. To confirm this, view the CD using a different Windows operating system. Please note that this problem most often occurs while viewing the CD in Windows 3.1.

Windows 3.1

To run the CD:

1. Insert the CD in the CD-ROM Drive.

2. From File Manager, select File, Run to open the Run window.

3. In the Command Line text box type **D:\primacd.exe** (where D:\ is the CD-ROM drive).

4. Select OK.

Windows 95

Since there is no install routine, running the CD in Windows 95 is a breeze, especially if you have Autorun enabled. Simply insert the CD in the CD-ROM Drive, close the tray, and wait for the CD to load. If you have disabled Autorun place the CD in the drive and follow these steps:

1. From the Start menu, select Run.

2. Type **D:\primacd.exe** (where D:\ is the CD-ROM drive).

3. Select OK.

The Prima User Interface

Prima's user interface is designed to make viewing and using the CD contents quick and easy. It contains five category buttons, five options buttons, a title list, a description text box, a URL box, and Next and Previous buttons. Select a category button to display a list of available titles. Choose a title to see a description and the associated URL. At the title screen select an option button to perform the desired action.

Category Buttons

HTML Tools. An assortment of HTML and Java tools.

Internet Tools. Web tools and add-ons to help you create sophisticated Web pages.

Graphics Tools. Animation tools, graphics viewers, image converters, and drawing tools.

Utilities. File and system utilities to help manage your system and improve its performance.

Options Buttons

Explore. Left-clicking this option in Windows 95 and NT allows you to view the folder containing the program files, using Windows Explorer. Right-clicking in Windows 3.x, 95, or NT brings up the Windows File Manager from which you can easily explore the CD.

Run. If the selected title contains an executable file which runs without prior installation left-clicking the Run button launches the program. If the program requires installation, an appropriate message is displayed.

Install. If the selected title contains an install routine, selecting this option begins the installation process. If no installation is available, an appropriate message is displayed.

NOTE

You can install some of the shareware programs that do not have installation routines by copying the program files from the CD to your hard drive and running the executable (*.exe) file.

Information. Left-click to open the Readme file associated with the highlighted title. If no Readme file is present, the help file will be opened.

Exit. When you're finished and ready to move on, select exit.

Prev. Takes you to the previous screen. Please note that this is not the last screen you viewed, but the screen which actually precedes the current one.

Next. Takes you to the next screen.

The Software

This section gives you a brief description of some of the software you'll find on the CD. This is just a sampling. As you browse the CD, you will find much more.

Amazing JPEG Screen Saver for Win95/WinNT—A screen saver to display your corporate logos, family pictures, or any of your favorite JPEG images

AutoSpell 4.1—A spell-checker designed for use with online communications programs

Banner*Show (32-bit)—A JavaScript rotating banner creator

GifWeb—An easy-to-use shareware program that makes the background of your GIF images transparent

Guest*Star (32-bit)—A Windows application which allows you to create your own fully functional WWW guest book

Java Perk—A front end for creating Java applets to include in World Wide Web pages

WebPainter—An easy-to-use tool for creating eye-catching animated graphics for Web pages

WinZip—One of the leading file compression utilities for Windows 3.1, 95, and NT

Index

To Order Books

Please send me the following items:

Quantity	Title	Unit Price	Total
_____	_____	$_____	$_____
_____	_____	$_____	$_____
_____	_____	$_____	$_____
_____	_____	$_____	$_____
_____	_____	$_____	$_____

Shipping and Handling depend on Subtotal.

Subtotal	Shipping/Handling
$0.00–$14.99	$3.00
$15.00–$29.99	$4.00
$30.00–$49.99	$6.00
$50.00–$99.99	$10.00
$100.00–$199.99	$13.50
$200.00+	Call for Quote

Foreign and all Priority Request orders:
Call Order Entry department
for price quote at 916/632-4400

This chart represents the total retail price of books only (before applicable discouts are taken).

Subtotal $_____
Deduct 10% when ordering 3-5 books $_____
7.25% Sales Tax (CA only) $_____
8.25% Sales Tax (TN only) $_____
5.0% Sales Tax (MD and IN only) $_____
Shipping and Handling* $_____
Total Order $_____

By Telephone: With MC or VISA, call 800-632-8676 or 916-632-4400,
Mon - Fri, 8:30 - 4:30 P.S.T.

By E-mail: We're on the Web at http://www.primapublishing.com.
Send orders to: sales@primapub.com

By Mail: Just fill out the information below and send with your remittance to:

Prima Publishing
P.O. Box 1260BK
Rocklin, CA 95677

My name is _____

I live at _____

City _____ State _____ Zip _____

MC/VISA# _____ Exp _____

Check/Money Order enclosed for $_____ Payable to Prima Publishing

Daytime Telephone _____

Signature _____

Other Books from Prima Publishing, Computer Products Division

ISBN	Title	Price	Release Date
0-7615-0801-5	ActiveX	$40.00	Available Now
0-7615-0680-2	America Online Complete Handbook and Membership Kit	$24.99	Available Now
0-7615-0915-1	Building Intranets with Internet Information Server and FrontPage	$45.00	Available Now
0-7615-0417-6	CompuServe Complete Handbook and Membership Kit	$24.95	Available Now
0-7615-0849-X	Corporate Intranet Development	$45.00	Available Now
0-7615-0692-6	Create Your First Web Page in a Weekend	$29.99	Available Now
0-7615-0503-2	Discover What's Online!	$24.95	Available Now
0-7615-0693-4	Internet Information Server	$40.00	Available Now
0-7615-0815-5	Introduction to ABAP/4 Programming for SAP	$45.00	Available Now
0-7615-0678-0	Java Applet Powerpack	$30.00	Available Now
0-7615-0685-3	JavaScript	$35.00	Available Now
0-7615-0901-1	Leveraging Visual Basic with ActiveX Controls	$45.00	Available Now
0-7615-0755-8	Moving Worlds	$35.00	Available Now
0-7615-0690-X	Netscape Enterprise Server	$40.00	Available Now
0-7615-0691-8	Netscape FastTrack Server	$40.00	Available Now
0-7615-0852-X	Netscape Navigator 3 Complete Handbook	$24.99	Available Now
0-7615-0759-0	Professional Web Design	$40.00	Available Now
0-7615-0773-6	Programming Internet Controls	$45.00	Available Now
0-7615-0780-9	Programming Web Server Applications	$40.00	Available Now
0-7615-0063-4	Researching on the Internet	$29.95	Available Now
0-7615-0686-1	Researching on the World Wide Web	$24.99	Available Now
0-7615-0695-0	The Essential Photoshop Book	$35.00	Available Now
0-7615-0752-3	The Essential Windows NT Book	$27.99	Available Now
0-7615-0689-6	The Microsoft Exchange Productivity Guide	$24.99	Available Now
0-7615-0769-8	VBScript Master's Handbook	$45.00	Available Now
0-7615-0684-5	VBScript Web Page Interactivity	$40.00	Available Now
0-7615-0903-8	Visual FoxPro 5 Enterprise Development	$45.00	Available Now
0-7615-0814-7	Visual J++	$35.00	Available Now
0-7615-0383-8	Web Advertising and Marketing	$34.95	Available Now
0-7615-0726-4	Webmaster's Handbook	$40.00	Available Now
0-7615-0751-5	Windows NT Server 4 Administrator's Guide	$50.00	Available Now

License Agreement/Notice of Limited Warranty

By opening the sealed disk container in this book, you agree to the following terms and conditions. If, upon reading the following license agreement and notice of limited warranty, you cannot agree to the terms and conditions set forth, return the unused book with unopened disk to the place where you purchased it for a refund.

License:

The enclosed software is copyrighted by the copyright holder(s) indicated on the software disk. You are licensed to copy the software onto a single computer for use by a single concurrent user and to a back-up disk. You may not reproduce, make copies, or distribute copies or rent or lease the software in whole or in part, except with written permission of the copyright holder(s). You may transfer the enclosed disk only together with this license, and only if you destroy all other copies of the software and the transferee agrees to the terms of the license. You may not decompile, reverse assemble, or reverse engineer the software.

Notice of Limited Warranty:

The enclosed disk is warranted by Prima Publishing to be free of physical defects in materials and workmanship for a period of sixty (60) days from end user's purchase of the book/disk combination. During the sixty-day term of the limited warranty, Prima will provide a replacement disk upon the return of a defective disk.

Limited Liability:

THE SOLE REMEDY FOR BREACH OF THIS LIMITED WARRANTY SHALL CONSIST ENTIRELY OF REPLACEMENT OF THE DEFECTIVE DISK. IN NO EVENT SHALL PRIMA OR THE AUTHOR BE LIABLE FOR ANY OTHER DAMAGES, INCLUDING LOSS OR CORRUPTION OF DATA, CHANGES IN THE FUNCTIONAL CHARACTERISTICS OF THE HARDWARE OR OPERATING SYSTEM, DELETERIOUS INTERACTION WITH OTHER SOFTWARE, OR ANY OTHER SPECIAL, INCIDENTAL, OR CONSEQUENTIAL DAMAGES THAT MAY ARISE, EVEN IF PRIMA AND/OR THE AUTHOR HAVE PREVIOUSLY BEEN NOTIFIED THAT THE POSSIBILITY OF SUCH DAMAGES EXISTS.

Disclaimer of Warranties:

PRIMA AND THE AUTHOR SPECIFICALLY DISCLAIM ANY AND ALL OTHER WARRANTIES, EITHER EXPRESS OR IMPLIED, INCLUDING WARRANTIES OF MERCHANTABILITY, SUITABILITY TO A PARTICULAR TASK OR PURPOSE, OR FREEDOM FROM ERRORS. SOME STATES DO NOT ALLOW FOR EXCLUSION OF IMPLIED WARRANTIES OR LIMITATION OF INCIDENTAL OR CONSEQUENTIAL DAMAGES, SO THESE LIMITATIONS MAY NOT APPLY TO YOU.

Other:

This Agreement is governed by the laws of the State of California without regard to choice of law principles. The United Convention of Contracts for the International Sale of Goods is specifically disclaimed. This Agreement constitutes the entire agreement between you and Prima Publishing regarding use of the software.